Thomas Hobbes and the Political Philosophy of Glory

Gabriella Slomp
Lecturer in Political Theory
University of St Andrews
Scotland

First published in Great Britain 2000 by
MACMILLAN PRESS LTD
Houndmills, Basingstoke, Hampshire RG21 6XS and London
Companies and representatives throughout the world

A catalogue record for this book is available from the British Library.

ISBN 0–333–72642–1

 First published in the United States of America 2000 by
ST. MARTIN'S PRESS, INC.,
Scholarly and Reference Division,
175 Fifth Avenue, New York, N.Y. 10010

ISBN 0–312–23419–8

Library of Congress Cataloging-in-Publication Data
Slomp, Gabriella.
Thomas Hobbes and the political philosophy of glory / Gabriella Slomp.
p. cm.
Includes bibliographical references (p.) and index.
ISBN 0–312–23419–8 (cloth)
1. Hobbes, Thomas, 1588–1679—Contributions in political science. 2. Glory. I.
Title.
JC153.H66 S56 2000
320'.01—dc21
                                                                    00–023349

© Gabriella Slomp 2000

All rights reserved. No reproduction, copy or transmission of this publication may be made without written permission.

No paragraph of this publication may be reproduced, copied or transmitted save with written permission or in accordance with the provisions of the Copyright, Designs and Patents Act 1988, or under the terms of any licence permitting limited copying issued by the Copyright Licensing Agency, 90 Tottenham Court Road, London W1P 0LP.

Any person who does any unauthorised act in relation to this publication may be liable to criminal prosecution and civil claims for damages.

The author has asserted her right to be identified as the author of this work in accordance with the Copyright, Designs and Patents Act 1988.

This book is printed on paper suitable for recycling and made from fully managed and sustained forest sources.

10 9 8 7 6 5 4 3 2 1
09 08 07 06 05 04 03 02 01 00

Printed and bound in Great Britain by
Antony Rowe Ltd, Chippenham, Wiltshire

To the memory of my father, Domenico Slomp

Contents

ACKNOWLEDGEMENTS	x
ABBREVIATIONS TO HOBBES'S WORKS QUOTED IN THE TEXT	xi
INTRODUCTION. THE POLITICAL GEOMETRY OF GLORY	**1**
PART I. ELEMENTS OF POLITICAL GEOMETRY	**9**
CHAPTER 1. THE CO-ORDINATES OF MAN: TIME AND SPACE	**11**
INTRODUCTION	11
1.1 THE POLITICAL APPEAL OF MOTION	13
1.2 THE TIME DIMENSION OF THE MIND	17
1.3 TIME AND POLITICS	19
CHAPTER 2. FATAL EQUALITY	**22**
INTRODUCTION	22
2.1 EQUALITIES AND DIFFERENCES	23
2.2 HUMAN FRAGILITY	25
2.3 POLITICAL EQUALITY AND SOCIAL INEQUALITY	26
2.4 IS EQUAL DANGEROUSNESS SELF-EVIDENT?	28
CHAPTER 3. THE AXIOM OF GLORY	**31**
INTRODUCTION	31
3.1 DEFINITIONS OF GLORY	33
3.2 FORMS OF GLORY	34
3.3 VALUE-LOADED AND DESCRIPTIVE TERMS	36
3.4 GLORY AND HONOUR	38
3.5 GLORY AND SELF-PRESERVATION	40
3.6 GLORY AND FELICITY	43
CHAPTER 4. GLORY: PARALLELS AND INTERSECTIONS	**45**
INTRODUCTION	45
4.1 THE SOURCES OF HOBBESIAN GLORY	45
4.1.1 *Aristotle's honour*	46
4.1.2 *Biblical pride*	47
4.1.3 *Aristocratic honour*	48
4.1.4 *Glory and bourgeois greed*	49
4.1.5 *Bacon's* Essays	49
4.2 THUCYDIDES AND HOBBES ON GLORY: INFLUENCE OR COINCIDENCE?	51
4.2.1 *Glory, honour, and ambition*	52
4.2.2 *Accumulation of wealth and the pursuit of honour*	54
4.2.3 *The lessons of war*	55
4.2.4 *Thucydides' fate and Hobbes's faith in education*	56

Contents

CHAPTER 5. AMBITION: PARADOXES AND PUZZLES	58
INTRODUCTION	58
5.1 THE POLITICAL CONSEQUENCES OF AMBITION	59
5.1.1 Ambition in Anti-White	60
5.1.2 Ambition in Behemoth	60
5.1.3 Ambition in Elements of Law, De Cive, *and* Leviathan	61
5.2 CIVIL WAR IN THUCYDIDES AND HOBBES	63
5.3 THE IMPLICATIONS OF PRIVATE AND PUBLIC MONEY	65
5.4 THUCYDIDES' PARADOX OF AMBITION AND HOBBES'S SOLUTION	66
5.5 HOBBES'S PUZZLE	69
5.5.1 Beehives and behaviour	69
5.5.2 The three greatest things	71
5.5.3 Proximate and ultimate causes of conflict	72
CHAPTER 6. THE DILEMMA OF FEAR AND HOPE	74
INTRODUCTION	74
6.1 CHARACTERISATION OF FEAR	75
6.2 THE ROLE OF FEAR	78
6.3 THE EFFECTIVENESS OF FEAR	80
6.4 THUCYDIDES' DILEMMA OF FEAR	81
CHAPTER 7. THE TRAJECTORY OF GLORY	84
INTRODUCTION	84
7.1 THE GLORY-SEEKERS	85
7.1.1 Melancholy and madness	86
7.1.2 Riches, places of power, knowledge, and sensualities	86
7.1.3 Charity and laughter	87
7.2 THE MYSTERIOUS NON-GLORY-SEEKERS	88
7.3 THE FALL OF GLORY IN *LEVIATHAN* AND *DE HOMINE*	90
7.4 SHERLOCK HOLMES AND OTHER DETECTIVES	92
CHAPTER 8. GLORY AND THE EXCELLENT SEX	97
INTRODUCTION	97
8.1 HOBBES'S REJECTION OF NATURAL PATRIARCHALISM	99
8.2 HOBBES'S OPEN SOCIAL CONTRACT	102
8.3 HOBBES AND ARTIFICIAL PATRIARCHY	103
8.4 CUSTOM AND THE EXCELLENT SEX	105
CHAPTER 9. THE DETERMINANTS OF THE CITIZEN: NATURE AND NURTURE	108
INTRODUCTION	108
9.1 THE INTERDEPENDENCE OF THE HOBBESIAN GLORY-SEEKER	109
9.2 HOBBES ON EDUCATION	112
9.3 HOBBES ON NATURE AND NURTURE	114
9.4 FROM NATURAL AGENT TO EDUCATED CITIZEN	116

Contents

PART II: THEOREMS OF POLITICAL GEOMETRY   119

CHAPTER 10. THE RATIONAL ACTOR AT PLAY   121

INTRODUCTION   121
10.1 THE STATE OF NATURE AS A THOUGHT EXPERIMENT   122
10.2 ON THE APPLICABILITY OF GAME THEORY TO HOBBES   123
10.3 GAME-THEORY APPLICATIONS TO HOBBES'S THEORY   125
    10.3.1 *The Bees and Ants game*   126
    10.3.2 *Prisoner's Dilemmas*   126
    10.3.2.1 *Gauthier's* Logic of Leviathan *and assumption selection*   126
    10.3.2.2 *Kavka, Hampton, and the Repeated Prisoner's Dilemma*   128
    10.3.3 *Assurance games*   131
    10.3.4 *Neal's 'co-ordination' game*   133
    10.3.5 *Fowl games: Chickens, Hawks and Doves*   134
10.4 GAME THEORY Á LA CARTE   134
10.5 CHICKEN WITH SPICES: GLORY AND DEATH   135

CHAPTER 11. HOBBES'S IMPOSSIBILITY THEOREM   140

INTRODUCTION   140
11.1 THE REQUIREMENTS OF THE POLITICAL DEFINITION OF MAN   142
11.2 DEFINITIONS AND THEOREM   144
11.3 ESCAPE FROM THE IMPOSSIBILITY RESULT   148
11.4 GEOMETER, AGENT, AND READER   150
11.5 CORRESPONDENTS' RESPONSES TO THE THEOREM   152

CHAPTER 12. THE IDEOLOGY OF POLITICAL GEOMETRY   155

INTRODUCTION   155
12.1 HOBBES, IDEOLOGIES AND IDEAS   156
    12.1.1 *Conservatism, pessimism, and custom*   156
    12.1.2 *Fascism, Peace, and the State*   157
    12.1.3 *Christian morality, the beggar, and the apple tree*   158
    12.1.4 *The Utilitarian, the Happy, and the Poor*   161
    12.1.5 *Hobbes, the Oppressive Liberal?*   163
12.2 THE IDEOLOGY OF POLITICAL GEOMETRY   164
    12.2.1 *Hobbes, Orwell, and Room 101*   166
    12.2.2 *Hobbes, Camus, and* The Plague   167

NOTES   174

SELECTED BIBLIOGRAPHY   184

NAME INDEX   191

Acknowledgements

The story is told of the review editor who once asked a distinguished British economist to review a weighty tome of mathematical economics. Having taken the volume in her hands and skimmed through it, after a few seconds the economist turned down the request, claiming that she was not prepared to endure five hundred pages of right-wing twaddle. The review editor could not resist asking how she had reached her verdict (correct, as it turned out) on a highly technical work in such a short time. The economist replied that the author's acknowledgement of the 'help of a deeper sort' by his marvellous wife had given the game away.

This story plunges me into a serious moral dilemma. I am torn between, on the one hand, the duty of acknowledging the help of my life-long companion, Manfredi La Manna, in the production of many ideas in this book as well as the assistance of my son Camillo in the preparation of the index, and on the other hand, the duty of dispelling any illusion in the reader that I might entertain conservative leanings.

Unable to decide which of these duties should be over-riding, I proceed regardless and acknowledge my debt of gratitude to three academics, who, while not agreeing with many (if any) of my ideas, have always encouraged and supported my research on Hobbes, namely, Iain Hampsher-Monk, John Horton, and Preston King.

Also, I wish to thank those scholars who, over the years have accepted to comment on my ideas on Hobbes's theory. They include: Brian Barry, Martin Bertman, Keith Dowding, Murray Forsyth, Maurice Goldsmith, Kenneth Minogue, Robert Orr, Carole Pateman, Raia Prokhovnik, John Sanderson, and John Watkins.

Some of the ideas in this book have appeared previously in *Political Studies, History of Political Thought* and in two joint articles with Manfredi La Manna published in the *Canadian Journal of Political Science* and in *Constitutional Political Economy*.

Last and foremost, I wish to acknowledge my gratitude to Tim Farmiloe and Alison Howson of Macmillan Press for their help in bringing this project to fruition.

Gabriella Slomp
St Andrews

Abbreviations to Hobbes's works quoted in the text

For ease of reference, in the text I shall use the following abbreviations to Hobbes's works, followed by the relevant page number(s):

Leviathan = Thomas Hobbes, *Leviathan*, edited by Richard Tuck. London: Cambridge University Press, 1991.

De Civitate = Thomae Hobbes, *Opera Philosophica quae latine scripsit omnia,* In unum corpus primum collecta studio et labore Gulielmi Molesworth, vol. III, Londini: Apud Joannem Bohn, MDCCXLI. (Latin version of *Leviathan*).

Elements of Law = Thomas Hobbes, *The Elements of Law. Natural and Politic,* 2nd ed., edited by Ferdinand Tönnies. London: Frank Cass, 1969.

De Cive = Thomas Hobbes, *De Cive. The English version entitled in the first edition Philosophical Rudiments concerning Government and Society.* Volume III of the Clarendon Edition of the Philosophical Works of Thomas Hobbes, edited by Howard Warrender. Oxford: Clarendon Press, 1983.

Behemoth = Thomas Hobbes, *Behemoth, or the Long Parliament,* 2nd ed., edited by Ferdinand Tönnies. London: Frank Cass, 1969.

History, EW VIII = Thomas Hobbes, *The History of the Grecian War written by Thucydides*, vol. I, vol. VIII of *The English Works of Thomas Hobbes*, edited by William Molesworth. London: John Bohn, 1843.

History, EW IX = Thomas Hobbes, *The History of the Grecian War written by Thucydides*, vol. II, vol. IX of *The English Works of Thomas Hobbes*, edited by William Molesworth. London: John Bohn, 1843.

Rhetoric = Thomas Hobbes, *The Whole Art of Rhetoric*, (translation of Aristotle's *Rhetoric*), pp. 419-510, vol. VI of *The English Works of Thomas Hobbes*, edited by William Molesworth. London: John Bohn, 1840.

Anti-White = Thomas Hobbes, *Thomas White's* De Mundo *Examined*, translated from the Latin and edited by Harold Whitmore Jones. London: Bradford University Press,

Abbreviations

De Homine = Thomas Hobbes, *De Homine*, in *Man and Citizen*, edited by Bernard Gert. New York: Anchor Books, 1972, pp. 31-85. 1976.

De Corpore = Thomas Hobbes, *Elements of Philosophy*, vol. I of *The English Works of Thomas Hobbes*, edited by William Molesworth. London: John Bohn, 1839.

Dialogue = Thomas Hobbes, *A Dialogue between a Philosopher and a Student of the Common Laws of England*, pp. 3-160, vol. VI of *The English Works of Thomas Hobbes*, edited by William Molesworth. London: John Bohn, 1840.

Prose Life = Thomas Hobbes, 'The Prose Life', in Thomas Hobbes, *Human Nature and De Corpore Politico*, edited by J.C.A. Gaskin, pp. 245-253. Oxford: Oxford University Press, 1994.

Verse Life = Thomas Hobbes, 'The Verse Life', in Thomas Hobbes, *Human Nature and De Corpore Politico*, edited by J.C.A. Gaskin, pp. 254-264. Oxford: Oxford University Press, 1994.

Correspondence I = Thomas Hobbes, *The Correspondence*, vol. I: 1622-1659, edited by Noel Malcolm, volume VI of the Clarendon Edition of the Philosophical Works of Thomas Hobbes. Oxford: Clarendon Press, 1994.

Correspondence II = Thomas Hobbes, *The Correspondence*, vol. II: 1660-1679, edited by Noel Malcom, volume VII of the Clarendon Edition of the Philosophical Works of Thomas Hobbes. Oxford: Clarendon Press, 1994.

Three Discourses = Thomas Hobbes, *Three Discourses,* A critical modern edition of newly identified work by the young Hobbes, edited by N.B. Reynolds and A.W. Saxonhouse, Chicago: University of Chicago Press, 1995.

I shall also refer frequently to:

Brief Lives = John Aubrey, *Brief Lives*, edited by Richard Barber. Woodbridge: Boydell Press, 1982.

Introduction
The Political Geometry of Glory

Quentin Skinner's book on Hobbes[1] has been acclaimed by some as the masterpiece of the Cambridge Historical School. I do not know whether future generations will endorse this judgement, or indeed whether they will consider it a compliment. I suspect, though, that if Hobbes could talk from his grave he would show surprise at the method employed by Skinner to examine his work, astonishment at the results of the enquiry, and amusement at the implications of Skinner's interpretation.

First, Hobbes would be surprised. Contextualists such as Skinner like to remind us that in a passage of *Elements of Law*[2] Hobbes makes a general point about the difficulty of interpreting a book written in the past. What Skinner fails to mention is that Hobbes, referring to *his own opus*, unambiguously states that he expected posterity to appreciate his philosophy more than his contemporaries.[3] If Hobbes had thought that a necessary condition for understanding his works was the complete knowledge of his *curriculum studiorum* and an intimate acquaintance with all the libraries he ever visited, surely he would have given more chances to scholars living in his own times than to any academic, however talented, living three hundred years later. *Pace* Skinner, I believe that Hobbes wanted his theory to be analysed philosophically and logically, rather than historically.

Secondly, Hobbes would be astonished by Skinner's claim that he 'changed his mind' about rationality and rhetoric in the transition from *De Cive* to *Leviathan*. Indeed if Skinner's contention that between the two works there is 'a shift in outlook so profound and comprehensive'[4] were right, I am sure that Hobbes would have warned his friends about such a momentous change. Instead, he engaged in extensive discussion of his argument in *De Cive* with Leibniz and his French correspondents (du Verdus, Sorbière, Peleau) even *after* the English version of *Leviathan* had appeared.

In his dedicatory letter of *De Corpore*, dated 23 April 1655 and hence written when, according to Rogow, both *De Cive* and *Leviathan* were in circulation in London, Hobbes makes the following famous claim:

Natural Philosophy is therefore but young; but Civil Philosophy yet much younger, as being no older ... than my own book *De Cive* (*De Corpore*, ix).

Indeed, Skinner's major claim that Hobbes's unconditional commitment to science and the logical method was not life-long goes against all textual evidence, against Hobbes's prose autobiography and against repeated statements in the Correspondence. Hobbes writes about his *Leviathan*:

> He (Hobbes) wrote not merely to be read and heard by scholars, but in order that he might be understood by all thinking men of sound judgement, *in prose that was simple and direct, not in rhetoric* (*Prose Life*, 250).

Clearly, Skinner must doubt the sincerity of Hobbes in making the above claim and implies that on the role of rhetoric Hobbes wrote what he did not mean and meant what he did not write.

I do not contest the claim made by a number of interpreters, from McNeilly to Sorell, that there is a didactic element in *Leviathan* which is absent in *De Cive*. I myself argue this point in this work and advance a possible explanation based on a textual analysis of *De Homine*. However, Skinner's claim that in Hobbes's later works there is an 'ever-deepening scepticism in the power of reason'[5] and in the efficacy of rational arguments is unconvincing, and indeed unfounded.

Thirdly, I suspect that Hobbes would be slightly amused by the fact that the interpreter who queries his commitment to logic and scientific method is a man of the English establishment. Hobbes would probably take Skinner's criticism as fresh confirmation of his conspiracy theory, that dons of English universities and members of the Royal Society aim at distorting his views even now that he has been dead for over three hundred years.

Of course, I am not suggesting that Skinner mis-interpreted Hobbes deliberately. However, the fact remains that if his reading of Hobbes were correct, it would have serious implications for the location of Hobbes on the map of political thought. In fact, Skinner's argument deprives Hobbes completely of his intellectual radicalism. Hobbes, as described by Skinner, emerges as a sad, backward-looking pensioner who, after a juvenile flirtation with scientific ideals and concepts, becomes in *Leviathan* a voice of tradition and of the cultural establishment.

But whereas Skinner can detect in *Leviathan* mainly rhetoric, many

Introduction: The Political Geometry of Glory

generations of readers have been fascinated instead by the logic of Hobbes's thought, that goes relentlessly and uncompromisingly from assumptions to conclusions, from premises to implications, in a way that has been captured by the exquisite philosophical sensitivity of Michael Oakeshott:

> the inspiration of [Hobbes's] philosophy is the intention to be guided by reason and to reject all other guides: this is the thread, the hidden thought, that gives it coherence ... Civil philosophy, the subject of *Leviathan*, is precisely the application of this conception of philosophy to civil association.[6]

Is it possible, I wonder, that whereas history is an open book to Skinner, philosophy instead is an invisible one?

Whereas Skinner belongs to the camp that is elated by the discovery of traditional concepts in Hobbes's works, I belong to the larger crowd overwhelmed by Hobbes's originality, by the subversive way in which he uses customary concepts such as 'natural right', 'natural law', 'state of nature' and 'social contract', and "by the thoroughness with which he scrutinises and re-thinks his cultural inheritance".[7]

Two aspects of Hobbes's philosophy particularly fascinate me: his method and his theory of the individual. On the method used by Hobbes in his political writings, it can be argued that the works of John Watkins and Michael Oakeshott are still the most enlightening. On Hobbes's theory of the individual one can find penetrating analyses especially in the works by Leo Strauss, F.S. McNeilly, Maurice Goldsmith, Preston King, and Alan Ryan.

There is a long-standing debate as to whether there exists a valid link between Hobbes's method and his political philosophy. Although I am convinced by the claim made by Thomas Spragens that Hobbes's theory of motion is a unifying concept of the whole of his philosophy, for a long time, I had considered the study of method and the study of the passions of man as relatively independent enquiries. Eventually, however, I have changed my mind. I have come to think that the method that Hobbes deploys in his political works is neither independent nor autonomous from his theory of the individual. To substantiate this claim is one of the aims of this book.

Part I of the book (entitled 'Elements of Political Geometry') examines Hobbes's definitions of four characteristics of man – rationality, fear of death, desire for glory, and equality with other men. Among these, prominence is given to the meaning and role of the passion called Glory and to its relation with the other three concepts. The reason for singling out glory for special attention is three-fold. Firstly, whereas the Hobbesian concepts of self-preservation, equality, and rationality have been examined extensively and satisfactorily in the literature, glory is an undeservedly under-researched area. Secondly, what the Hobbesian scholarship, chiefly in the works of Strauss, McNeilly, and Macpherson, has to say on glory seems to me to be both incomplete and incorrect. Thirdly and most importantly, I hope to show in this book that the thorough analysis of Hobbesian glory can provide us with a new insight into Hobbes's political theory. This part of the book, even though it contains ideas that are, I hope, original, is chiefly an exercise in philosophical textual analysis, in so far as I have endeavoured not to stray from Hobbes's text, ensuring that all my claims are fully supported by textual evidence, or at least not contradicted by it.

Part II of the book (entitled 'Theorems of Political Geometry') develops an argument which, although firmly based on the concepts analysed in Part I, is speculative and as such leaves much more scope for debate and disagreement. Here I use concepts that were unavailable to Hobbes – such as 'impossibility theorem' and 'non-cooperative games', borrowed from rational-choice theory, thereby opening the door to criticisms by those who dislike (if not despise) this approach to Hobbes's theory. I hope that my suggested interpretation, although it takes some licence with the text, nevertheless respects the spirit of Hobbes's philosophy, and in particular fulfils Hobbes's stated ambition to become the new Euclid of political science.

The opening chapters of the book are devoted to explaining Hobbes's views on identity and equality. According to Hobbes, individuals are by nature more or less indistinguishable from one another, but have both the capability and the drive to develop a unique identity. This ability to self-differentiate remains almost inert in the state of nature, where people cannot make projects and plans, as they cannot form expectations on the behaviour of others. Here, the drive to become different leads individuals to self-destructive actions. The state of nature condemns them to complete anonymity.

Introduction: The Political Geometry of Glory

Later, I try to highlight the meaning of glory for Hobbes, and to show that it is substantially different from, but related to, the concepts of biblical pride, bourgeois greed, and honour, in its Aristotelian, aristocratic, and Baconian versions. In approaching the text, I follow McNeilly's advice that one should not make a 'splendid omelette' of Hobbes's 'broken eggs'. I do not confine my analysis to a selection of works, but I carry out a comparative analysis of *De Cive, Elements of Law, Leviathan, Anti-White, De Homine, A Dialogue between a Philosopher and a Student, Behemoth* and the Correspondence. Unlike McNeilly[8], I suggest that the meaning of glory is constant in all Hobbes's writings, as is its role in explaining the dynamics of conflict and war: in all Hobbes's writings, from *Anti-White* to *De Homine* and *Behemoth*, desire of prestige and ambition are for Hobbes crucial causes of conflict.

Although the *meaning* and *role* of glory in human conflict is constant in Hobbes's works, in Chapter 9 I highlight an interesting change in Hobbes's view of the passions, which, to my knowledge, has escaped attention. Whereas in early writings, (especially *Anti-White, Elements of Law,* and *De Cive*) glory is the *genus* of all passions, in later writings (*Leviathan, De Homine,* and *Behemoth*) glory becomes just a *species*, one instance of human passions, that affects only some people, and not all the time. No other single concept is given by Hobbes the central role played by glory in the earlier works.

I suggest two types of explanations for the fact that in *Leviathan,* unlike in *De Cive,* Hobbes no longer regards glory as the primary source of human behaviour. Of these, one is contextual, the other textual.

The contextual explanation – the effect of Scepticism on Hobbes – is mentioned but not explored in this book, as it has been widely examined in the literature, from Oakeshott to Tuck and Hampsher-Monk. As Oakeshott puts it, Scepticism was in the air when Hobbes was writing. The influence of Scepticism might explain why in *Leviathan* Hobbes was no longer confident that there was a single source for all human behaviour.

I concentrate instead on a textual explanation and refer to a source, *De Homine,* that according to Bernard Gert (and myself) has been wrongly overlooked. Here Hobbes makes a claim, without precedent in his earlier works, to the effect that human behaviour has a number (six, in fact) of sources, of which human nature is only one. In the state of nature, the remaining five sources (books, authorities, habits, etc.)

simply do not exist and therefore the cause of quarrel in the state of nature is entirely to be found in the nature of man. Not so in civil associations, however, where, according to Hobbes, it is the socially-determined sources of human behaviour and not human nature that are chiefly responsible for the actions of the citizens. In other words, if individuals within civil associations disobey the law, the principal causes are to be found in bad institutions, bad 'Universities', bad 'ecclesiastics', etc., rather than in human nature. In this perspective, I raise the question whether Hobbes in his later years considered the study of human nature as less important than the study of bad institutions. Moreover, it is suggested that the didactic element present in *Leviathan* and absent in *De Cive* may be explained as a result of Hobbes's growing conviction that it is society and not nature that provides five of the six sources of human behaviour.

Next, I turn my attention to the Hobbesian individual and, on the basis of my earlier analysis, I suggest that Hobbesian man, far from being 'given' and self-contained – as is often contended in the literature – is a thoroughly interdependent entity. I examine the Hobbesian individual at two analytical levels. First I consider the individual living in natural conditions, as described by Hobbes: the individual immersed in the present, troubled by the desire for glory and by the fear of violent death, wishing to avoid a state of war but uncertain as to the way to exit from such a state. This is the prototypical rational actor and I attempt to explain the reasons why the application of a game-theoretical approach to this part of Hobbes's argument is in my view quite justifiable. I offer a brief survey of the game-theoretical interpretations of the predicament of the Hobbesian individual in the state of nature, examining critically in particular the contributions by Gauthier, Kavka, Hampton, Neal, and Sugden.

On the constructive side, I put forward my own game-theoretical reading of Hobbes's state of nature, emphasising the glory-seeking nature of (some) Hobbesian men. I suggest that the strength of a game-theoretical approach to Hobbes is that it can demonstrate that, given Hobbes's assumptions, the state of nature is indeed a state of war. Conversely, no game-theoretical interpretation can offer the rational actor a way out of the state of nature. Against Hampton, however, I argue that this should not be read as evidence of the failure of Hobbes's project, but rather as a limit inherent in the rational-actor perspective.

My next step is to examine the 'other' individual who populates

Introduction: The Political Geometry of Glory 7

Hobbes's works – the individual he is talking to, the reader of his theory, the person to whom he is trying to explain his new geometry of politics. Unlike the agent in the state of nature, this individual is not overwhelmed by fear and by the desire of superiority, but instead is in a calm frame of mind, in a state of detachment, which is feasible only in the political state. Indeed, as Hobbes explains, philosophy requires leisure, and leisure requires safety, which in turn is possible only within political associations. It is to this individual, who is a detached observer of the imaginary drama rehearsed by rational actors in the state of nature, that Hobbes speaks as the new Euclid. Instead of defining line, point, and angle and deriving a theorem about triangles, Hobbes defines natural man and the state of nature and tries to derive a political theorem. I argue that from his assumptions about man and the state of nature Hobbes derives an *ante litteram* Impossibility Theorem. I suggest that Hobbes escapes from the Impossibility Theorem by the creation *ex machina* of the mighty Leviathan.

Unlike Hampton, I believe that Hobbes did not mean to offer the rational agent a way out of the state of nature, but rather to explain to his reader how to avoid the collapse of the political state into a state of civil war. Like Hume, Hobbes in 'A Review and Conclusion' to *Leviathan* shows himself to be fully aware that states are never born out of social contracts. Whereas for the Hobbesian agent, who is a victim of the state of chaos created by the assumptions of Hobbes's theorem (self-preservation, equality, rationality, glory, limited resources, unrestricted liberty) there is no salvation, to the detached observer, instead, Hobbes proposes a solution, which consists in relaxing one of the assumptions (unrestricted liberty) and in replacing it with unconditional obedience to the sovereign.

Of course, the agent in the state of nature and the detached observer addressed by Hobbes are not two different men, but two moments or two aspects of the same individual. I am not suggesting that the Hobbesian man has a split personality and that the agent is under the dominion of the passions, whereas the reader-observer is in charge of his rationality. On the contrary, both are for Hobbes rational, but individual rationality offers no salvation to natural man.

For Hobbes, the political man contains natural man. In other words, for Hobbes man always carries the state of nature inside his soul, as much as for Camus man always carries the plague inside his heart. Hobbes alerts man to the dangers of allowing the state of nature to take over his life. Were this to happen, man would lose his identity, his certainties, and would become an 'exile' in the sense of Camus, estranged from everybody and from everything.

I put forward the suggestion that when interpreters describe the Hobbesian individual, they tend to concentrate exclusively on the agent in the state of nature, overlooking completely the detached reader, the man to whom Hobbes is talking to in his works. The latter is mentioned rarely and then merely as a recipient of Hobbes's rhetoric.

The individual living in the state of nature is indeed a psychological simpleton, as implied by MacIntyre. But the individual to whom Hobbes is talking, the reader, has many of the characteristics that MacIntyre claims are lacking in the Hobbesian man: he has preferences about what he wants to be, plans about his future, and desires about what his desires should be. This man knows that anonymity is natural and that uniqueness is a social construction. He knows that identity, prestige, and inequality are products of social rules and conventions. He knows that in nature and by himself he is just a distressed animal capable of betraying any ideal, any person, any value, any belief. This, the Hobbesian man does not want. Or, at least, Hobbes trusts that he does not.

In the final chapter I suggest that the Hobbesian man that I describe in this book shares much less with the characterisations of human nature that we find in the 16th and 17th century (e.g., Machiavelli's and Locke's) man than with the individual who lives in the works of Camus and Orwell.

I am of course aware that my interpretation of Hobbes's method as leading to an Impossibility Theorem and my reading of the Hobbesian individual leave ample scope for debate. My consolation is that if someone of the standing of Quentin Skinner appears to have upset so few with his interpretation of Hobbes, then 'Harm I can do none, if I err no less than he'.

Part I

Elements of Political Geometry

Chapter 1

The Co-ordinates of Man: Time and Space

Introduction

Both Galileo Galilei and William Harvey were greatly admired by Hobbes,[1] who regarded the former as 'the greatest scientist of all time' (*Anti-White*, 123). According to Aubrey's account:

> when [Hobbes] was at Florence he contracted friendship with the famous Galileo Galilei, whom he extremely venerated and magnified and not only as he was a prodigious wit, but for his sweetness of nature and manners (*Brief Lives*, 161).

Harvey, described by Aubrey as 'an excellent anatomist', was believed by Hobbes to have been 'the only man, perhaps, that ever lived to see his own doctrine established in his life time' (*Brief Lives*, 133). Aubrey lists the pleasure of 'learned conversation' with William Harvey among the reasons why Hobbes decided to stay 'much in London till the restoration of his majesty' rather than 'stay in his lord's house in the country' (*Brief Lives*, 153).

Both Galileo and Harvey[2] had successfully applied the principle of *'motion'* to their relative fields of inquiry. The former had explained natural phenomena in terms of the laws of motion and the latter had discovered the circulation of the blood by using the same principle – motion. These discoveries impressed Hobbes greatly and convinced him that it was possible to extend the application of this explanatory concept –motion – from the natural sciences and physiology to the world of human motivations and actions.

In his *Verse Life* Hobbes highlights the importance of the notion of motion in his philosophy:

> Whether on Horse, in Coach, or Ship, still I
> Was most Intent on my Philosophy.
> One only thing in the World seem'd true to me,
> Tho' several ways that Falsified be.
> One only True Thing, the Basis of all
> Those Things whereby we any Thing do call [...]
> The internal parts only *Motion* contain:

> And he that studies Physicks first must know
> What *Motion* is, and what *Motion* can do.
> To Matter, *Motion*, I myself apply,
> And thus I spend my time in Italy.[...]
> Here [in Paris] with Marsennus I acquainted grew,
> Shew'd him of *Motion* what I ever knew.
> He both Praised and Approved it, and so, Sir,
> I was Reputed a Philosopher. [...]
> To various Matter various *Motion* brings
> Me, and the different Species of Things.
> Man's inward *Motions* and his Thoughts to know,
> The good of Government, and Justice too,
> These were my Studies then, and in these three
> Consists the whole Course of Philosophy:
> Man, Body, Citizen, for these I do
> Heap Matter up, designing three Books too. (*Verse Life*, 257-8; emphasis added).

In the Correspondence Hobbes suggests that everything can be explained in terms of motion: 'the variety of things is but variety of local motion' (*Correspondence I*, letter 19, 33). The concept of 'motion' permeates all his philosophical work, from *De Corpore* and *Anti-White* to *De Homine*, from the *Elements of Law* to *Leviathan*. It is clear that Hobbes's correspondents believed that he had succeeded in his attempt to develop the theory of motion and to apply it to the sphere of political life. For example, du Verdus (letter 75) referring to the 'the science of motion' says that Hobbes had 'developed [it] to the peak of perfection' (*Correspondence I*, 228). Leibniz himself shows great interest in Hobbes's ideas on motion 'a subject in which I greatly admire the foundations you have established' (*Correspondence II*, letter 189, 718).

Not only Hobbes considered himself successful in his application of the theory of motion to all fields of knowledge, but also almost all his contemporaries thought that he had succeeded in providing a whole body of philosophy grounded on the concept of motion.[3]

In this century many interpreters have lost interest in Hobbes's explanation of everything as matter-in-motion and the bearing of Hobbes's theory of motion on his political thought has been put in question by some critics.[4] Indeed it is difficult for today's readers of Hobbes to understand fully what Hobbes found appealing in the notion of motion as a means for explaining the very essence of political science.

This chapter puts forwards the thesis that Hobbes's emphasis on motion, far from being a mere tribute to mechanistic natural science, is the result of his profound philosophical conviction that motion alone can capture the identity of man. I shall corroborate my hypothesis by examining two main lines of argument, one pieced together from the analysis of motion in *De Corpore* and *Anti-White*, the other reconstructed by analysing afresh the description of the human mind carried out by Hobbes in the introductory chapters of the *Elements of Law* and *Leviathan*. As I will show in Chapters 2 and 3, Hobbes's conception of man as motion inspired also his views on some key blocks of his political theory, such as equality and self-preservation.

1.1 The Political Appeal of Motion

As a first step in the attempt to establish why Hobbes found the definition of man as motion politically appealing, we may start by examining the name 'man'.

For Hobbes, man is a 'universall name', which, as such, has no direct counterpart in the world (*Leviathan*, 26; *Elements of Law*, 20; *Anti-White*, 34, 52), but refers to an abstraction, or mental image. Since 'one Universall name is imposed on many things, for their similitude in some quality, or other accident' (*Leviathan*, 21) and 'a *man* denotes any one of a multitude of men ... by reason of their similitude' (*De Corpore*, 18), it follows that in Hobbes's view in order to define man we have to compare all individuals at the same time: whatever can be found in 'every particular of mankind' (*Elements of Law*, 19), that is man.

Therefore it is beyond doubt that Hobbes believed the *comparative analysis* of individuals to be a *necessary* exercise to arrive at the definition of man. What is more difficult to establish is whether in his opinion such an exercise would be also *sufficient*. Indeed, one can refer to a wealth of passages in Hobbes's works (especially in his analysis of universal and compound names, and in his explanation of the compositive nature of our mental processes) where he conveys the strong impression that the above-mentioned comparison across men at a given point in time is all that is needed to formulate the definition of man.

However, the view that a comparative criterion be sufficient to define man is unambiguously rejected in *De Corpore*[5] and in *Anti-*

White where Hobbes specifies an additional criterion that should be deployed in order to capture the identity of man. In both works Hobbes examines the long-standing problem of the principle of individuation. In *De Corpore* he addresses the question of whether the identity of man should be defined as either body, aggregate of accidents, or form. He rejects the identification of man with body, or unity of matter and observes that a man's body changes over time and so, if we were to identify Man and Body, we would be bound to conclude that young and old Socrates are not the same man. He writes:

> For it is one thing to ask concerning Socrates, whether he be the same man, and another to ask whether he be the same body; for his body, when he is old, cannot be the same it was when he was an infant, by reason of the difference of magnitude: for one body has always one and the same magnitude; yet, nevertheless, he may be the same man (*De Corpore*, 137).

Similarly in Chapter xii of *Anti-White*, Hobbes addresses the problem of whether

> 'Is a man, when old and young, the same being, *ens*, or matter, in number?' It is clear that, because of the continual casting of [existing] body-tissue and the acquisition of new, it is not the same material ... and hence it is not the same body; yet because of the unbroken nature of the flux by which matter decays and is replaced, he is always the same man (*Anti-White*, 141).

In *Anti-White* Hobbes compares the problem of the identity of man with the problem of identity of a commonwealth:

> The same must be said of the commonwealth. When any citizen dies, the material of the state is not the same ... Yet the uninterrupted degree [*ordo*] and motion of government that signalise a state ensure, while they remain as one, that the state is the same in number (*Anti-White*, 141).

In *De Corpore* Hobbes rejects the identification of man with 'aggregate of accidents', for, he argues, if we were to accept it we would be bound to say 'that a man standing would not the same he was sitting' (*De Corpore*, 137). In *Anti-White* Hobbes suggests that Thomas White's position on the problem of individuation implies such an absurd identification with man and accidents:

The Co-ordinates of Man: Time and Space

According to our author ... a man who sometimes blushes or sometimes goes pale; who sometimes ... does these things ... and at other times does something else, *will become*, in succession as many individuals as the different acts as he performs (*Anti-White*, 142).

In both works Hobbes alerts the reader to the disastrous *political* consequences of identifying man with either body or aggregate of accidents, and therefore of being unable to capture the continuity between young and old Socrates. In *De Corpore* we read:

he that sins, and he that is punished, should not be the same man, by reason of the perpetual flux and change of man's body ... *which were to confound all civil rights* (*De Corpore*, 136; italics added).

And in *Anti-White*

[If one endorses Thomas White's position, one] could say that, when someone has committed murder or theft, it is not the same man in number, but someone resembling him, who is punished – which is to violate all human laws and observances (*Anti-White*, 143).

Here Hobbes suggests that the inability to capture in the word 'man' the continuity between young and old Socrates would lead to political chaos.

Hence, according to Hobbes, a comparative analysis is not sufficient to arrive at a definition of man that would enable him to found (and not to confound) civil rights. Another necessary condition for such a definition is that it must capture the self-sameness of persons over time. Hence a comparative criterion has to be combined with what can be called a *time-series analysis* that pinpoints what is permanent in the same individual at different times.

Having thus ascertained the compound criterion necessary and sufficient to arrive at a politically relevant definition of man, we can interpret the early chapters of *Elements of Law* and *Leviathan* as an attempt to answer the following question: what is *common* to all men and *constant* in each of them over time?

As various interpreters have pointed out, Hobbes claim that people are different from one another not only in their appearances, tastes, and physical characteristics, but also in their desires, aversions, thoughts, judgements, and values. In *Elements of Law* he notices that:

while every man differeth from other in constitution, they differ also one from another concerning the common distinction of good and evil (*Elements of Law*, 29).

In *De Cive* he stresses the different desires and aversions of people and consequently their different values:

> such is the nature of man, that every one calls that *good* which he desires, and *evill*, which he eschewes; and therefore through the diversity of our affections, it happens that one counts that *good*, which another counts *evill* (*De Cive*, 177; see also 74-75).

In *Leviathan* Hobbes combines the notation that people are different in their perception of the external world with the observation that they differ in their evaluation of it:

> And divers men, differ not onely in their Judgement, on the senses of what is pleasant, and unpleasant to the tast, smell, hearing, touch, and sight; but also of what is conformable, or disagreeable to Reason, in the actions of common life (*Leviathan*, 110).

> for one man calleth *Wisdome*, what another calleth *feare*; and one *cruelty*, what another *justice*; one *prodigality*, what another *magnanimity*; and one *gravity*, what another *stupidity* (*Leviathan*, 31).

It is interesting to notice that Hobbes is as keen to stress that there are considerable variations across people as he is to point out that the same individual is different at different times, with different values, desires, thoughts.

In *Leviathan* we read:

> the same man, in divers times, differs from himselfe; and one time praiseth, that is calleth Good, what another time he dispraiseth, and calleth Evil (*Leviathan*, 110-11).

> all men [are] not alike affected with the same thing, nor the same man at all times (*Leviathan*, 31).

In *De Cive*:

> very often the same man at diverse times, *praises*, and *dispraises* the same thing (*De Cive*, 74).

and the same man what now he esteem'd for *good*, he immediately looks on as *evill* (*De Cive*, 177).

In *Anti-White*

the same things do not please or displease everyone, and ... they are not the same thing to the same person on every occasion (*Anti-White*, 378-9).

In *De Corpore*, after having rejected the identification of man with body or aggregate of accidents, Hobbes argues that the principle of identification of man is 'form' and remarks that 'man will be always the same, whose actions and thoughts proceed all from the same beginning of motion, namely, that which was in his generation' (*De Corpore*, 137). In the same spirit Hobbes in his political works argues that the permanent and common characteristic of man is the way of functioning of the body (vital motion) and of the mind (voluntary motion).

In conclusion, the concept of motion, when used to define man, had for Hobbes a strong 'political' appeal in so far as it satisfies both the comparative and the times-series criteria and thus allows him to found and not to 'confound all civil rights'. thus providing the appropriate starting point of his political theory.

1.2 The Time Dimension of the Mind

Although the concept of vital motion is omnipresent in Hobbes's argument as it forms a fundamental part of the 'self', or identity, that Hobbesian men want to preserve, Hobbes never gives an exhaustive account of it in his political writings. He felt that it is not 'the *course* of the *Bloud*, the *Pulse*, the *Breathing*, the *Concoction, nutrition*, &c' (*Leviathan*, 37-8) of people that have a bearing on politics, but rather those actions that proceed from their thoughts and passions. Thus Hobbes concentrates entirely on voluntary motion and describes moral and political philosophy as the study of that specific motion:

moral philosophy [studies] ... the motions of the mind, namely, *appetite, aversion*, ... what causes they have, and of what they be causes (*De Corpore*, 72).

the principles of the politics consist in the knowledge of the motions of the mind (*De Corpore*, 74).

The 'first beginning of all voluntary motion' is called by Hobbes 'imagination' and is described as the basis of all the operations of the mind. Imagination is the ability to 'retain an image of the thing seen ... after the object is removed'; 'memory' is the ability to recall that image; much memory or memory of many things is called 'experience' on the basis of which we found our 'presumption' or expectation of the future.

More than once in his writings Hobbes asks the reader to imagine what would happen if the world were to vanish. He claims that after the disappearance of the world, a person could nevertheless think in so far as 'the image of the things seen ... though more obscure' would still exist in the mind: '

> even if the whole world were destroyed except for one man, nothing would prevent this man from having an image of a world which he had once seen (*Anti-White*, 40).
>
> [because] the motions excited by objects remain, even when the object is removed (*Anti-White*, 365).

It may be interesting to perform the converse mental exercise, thereby highlighting the crucial importance of imagination and memory for Hobbes's conception of man. Let us suppose that the ability of the mind to store images of what we have perceived through our senses were to disappear. In other words, let us suppose that we had no imagination and thus when the object is removed, so is our consciousness of it. If we were conscious of external objects only at the very moment when they 'act upon us' (i.e., if we had no memory), then each moment would be spent (and wasted) in making ourselves conscious of the elementary objects around us. It is because what we have perceived has become knowledge that we can proceed and learn new things. Without memory, it would be as if we were reborn again at each moment. On the one hand the self at time t_1 would have very little in common (besides the body) with the self at time t_2. On the other hand, the 'self' and the 'other' at time t_1 would be very little different (except for the body) from one another. The very fact that the self is the same in its various experiences at time t_1, t_2, t_3, etc., is the condition for the diversification over time of the self with respect to the other.

Thus it is the continuity of the mind over time that allows the development of a particular identity and its diversification from other particular identities. It is the continuity of the mind that helps us capture the very notion of time, which in turn is motion: '"the image of motion" ... is what we call time' (*Anti-White*, 338-9). Hobbes's correspondents agree with this link between time and motion. Du Verdus, for example, writes (*Correspondence I*, letter 75, 225): 'I know that one cannot conceive of motion except by conceiving of the past and the future'.

In *Leviathan* Hobbes contrasts the time of the mind (past, present, and future) with the time of nature (present) (*Leviathan*, 22). 'Time' is the key word in the first chapters of *Leviathan*, mentioned repeatedly either directly or indirectly, through time-related words like Foresight, Prudence, Wisdom, Memory, etc. Not only in *Leviathan*, but also in *Anti-White* and in the *Elements of Law*, Hobbes, in his search for the definition of man, draws our attention to the time dimension of the mind, to its ability to remember the past and thereby to comprehend the present and conceive the future.

As the dimension of the body is space, so for Hobbes the dimension of the mind is time. As Space provides us with the basis on which we can distinguish between bodies, so Time, and its relation to the mind, provide the condition to distinguish between persons.

1.3 Time and Politics

Hobbes points to certain differences that exist between the voluntary motion in man and in animals. In these dissimilarities lies the distinctive identity of man. He suggests that there are two types of differences in human and animal voluntary motion, namely, differences in kind and differences of degree. Differences in *kind* refer to those characteristics that are present in man and absent in animals, like the ability to develop language (*Leviathan*, Chapter IV; *Elements of Law*, 18) and reason (*Leviathan*, chapter 5; *Elements of Law*, 19), the ability of thinking deductively (*Elements of Law*, 13-14) and a number of passions ranging from curiosity (*Elements of Law*, 45) to glory (*Elements of Law*, 156), from the desire to communicate to others one's wisdom, knowledge, and opinions (*Elements of Law*, 23) to the desire 'to innovate' the state (*Leviathan*, 119).

Differences of *degree* refer to those faculties − like imagination, memory, prudence, and inductive thought − that although shared by both men and animals, are nevertheless more developed in man (*Elements of Law*, Chapters 4 and 5; *Leviathan*, Chapter III). Hobbes's argument suggests that in the state of nature man can neither develop fully the abilities that he shares with animals (prudence, experience, memory) nor his specifically human abilities (language, knowledge, deductive thought). In the state of nature, man, like animals, becomes a victim of the present: 'it is impossible for beasts, lacking the aid of artifice, to compare past with present events' (*Anti-White*, 372).

In the Hobbesian state of nature, a person's identity is endangered in two ways: (i) in a crude and drastic sense: physical life is threatened; (ii) in a more sophisticated sense: the distinctive ability of the mind to detach itself from the present and to plan the future is wasted. For Hobbes the state of nature is a state of uncertainty, where one cannot trust anybody and least of all one's experience of the past. According to Hobbes, in the state of nature, out of the full range of passions one can experience only those related to the present, namely, sudden passions such as terror, weeping, anger, sensual pleasures, etc. The best pleasures of the mind, such as curiosity and knowledge, are denied. The only cathartic passion under these conditions is fear, which is described by Hobbes as been beneficial in so far as it is concerned with the future. In other words, in the state of nature people are victim of the present; *the time of the mind is forced to coincide with the time of nature,* which for Hobbes is the present.

According to Hobbes the sovereign power is created to guarantee the minimal condition necessary to be a person, namely, physical continuity. But in order to guarantee physical integrity, each individual's mental self-continuity has to be acknowledged in full so that rules can be enforced and punishment administered. Indeed, self-sameness is the necessary condition for personal responsibility. In the eyes of the State, Socrates acting today is responsible for what he did yesterday, for underneath both past and present Socrates there is the same self.

As self-continuity is the precondition for the establishment of the political state, so the political state, by developing a complex network of mutual expectations, creates the conditions which enable the mind to free itself from the concern with the immediate present and to focus on the future. The Hobbesian political state can even expand one's self-continuity beyond the limits of one's physical existence by enabling to bestow possessions, name, and titles on one's heirs.

Individuals who in the Hobbesian state of nature are almost indistinguishable from one another, their mind being completely absorbed in the present, find in the political state the conditions to differentiate from each other and to distance themselves from the animal world.

The Co-ordinates of Man: Time and Space

As in *De Corpore* Hobbes uses time to measure and compare motions in general, so in *Elements of Law* he applies the temporal dimension to distinguish between people and to explain the different attractions to pleasures like sensualities, riches, and knowledge. He argues that while some people look for easily obtainable pleasures and thus indulge in sensualities 'that please only for the present' (*Elements of Law*, 49), others aim at less fleeting pleasures and thus aspire at riches, authority, reputation, that 'have respect to the future' and the attainment of which requires long-term projects and effort. Finally, others aim at philosophy and knowledge, that are 'everlasting' pleasures which can be obtained only 'with great labours and time', and in comparison to which riches and places of authority 'are but sensuality ... a diversion of little pleasure' (*Elements of Law*, 46).

In all his writings, Hobbes is critical of people who do not resist the temptation of easy pleasures and remarks that 'the delight excited by things of the present is short lived' and he even defines happiness as 'the desire for good to come' (*Anti-White*, 463). In the Correspondence Hobbes shows himself concerned with the long-term pleasures of knowledge and philosophy (see especially *Correspondence I*, letter 21, 37-8).

To summarise, as Space is the dimension that helps distinguish between bodies, so Time is the dimension that helps distinguish between minds. As Geometry is the purest science of Space and the theory of motion is the purest science of time ('time is motion'), Political Geometry for Hobbes is the science of space and time, of bodies and minds.

Chapter 2

Fatal Equality

Introduction

Aubrey relates that Hobbes was 'but of plebeian descent': his father 'was one of the ignorant "Sir Johns" of Queen Elizabeth's time; could only read the prayers of the church and the homelies; and disesteemed learning' (*Brief Lives*, 148). His uncle, a rich glover '[h]aving no child ... contributed much to or rather maintained his nephew Thomas at Magdalen Hall in Oxford'(*ibid.*, 149).

This humble background must have had an impact on Thomas Hobbes at least as strong as that attributed by some scholars (e.g., Strauss) to the aristocracy for whom he worked first as a 'page' (*Brief Lives*, 151), and then as a tutor and companion for most of his life.

In *Anti-White* Hobbes shows some understanding of the predicament of people with 'poor parentage':

> some persons are born to riches and great place ... others are of poor parentage and obscure origins. Hence the latter must toil for the greatest part of their life to acquire possessions; and in the remainder of it, oppressed by the inconveniences of old age, they cannot use what they have secured (*Anti-White*, 481-2).

In *Anti-White* Hobbes lists poverty as one of the 'causes imparing happiness' (*Anti-White*, 481) and imputes this condition not to lack of merit or virtue, but to bad luck (*Anti-White*, 482). In *De Homine*, too, Hobbes imputes to fortune whether we have the advantage to be born in a rich or noble family.

In his daily frequentation of the aristocracy, Hobbes must have realised that their superiority was merely a human artefact. Indeed in his three main political works, Hobbes repeats almost *verbatim* the claim that equality is natural and that '[t]he inequallity that now is, has bin introduced by the Lawes civill' (*Leviathan*, 107).

As it is well known, Hobbes's main claim on natural equality is that despite the differences in intelligence and strength, individuals' chances of survival in the state of nature are the same in so far as even the weakest man has enough strength to kill the strongest.

Fatal Equality

The main aim of this chapter is to show that one can find two claims on natural equality in Hobbes's writings – a *strong* claim, put forward only on a few occasions, according to which the differences between individuals in natural powers like wisdom, wit, prudence, intelligence and strength are virtually unnoticeable; and a *weak* claim, held consistently, according to which men are different from each other, bar one fundamental respect, the exception being their equal ability to endanger each other's life.

In the rest of this chapter I shall address a central question on equality, the answer to which is critical for a proper understanding of Hobbes's entire political construct, i.e., why Hobbes maintains that, among all possible types of equality, the equality to kill is of fundamental importance.

2.1 Equalities and Differences

In Chapter 1 we have seen that the definition of man as 'motion' is for Hobbes necessary not 'to confound all civil rights'. This definition, however, by itself is not sufficient to found a theory of equal rights and duties. What individuals have in common, they may possess to a different degree, thereby providing a possible justification for the Aristotelian view of natural masters.[1] As for Hobbes motion generates power which, in turn, is the origin of new motion,[2] for him comparing the vital and voluntary motion of men involves comparing their power.

Hobbes's position on the equality of natural powers of individuals is not as clear and straightforward as one would have liked and there appear to be some variations not only from *Elements of Law* to *De Cive* and *Leviathan* but also within the same work.

For example, in places Hobbes suggests that the experience, prudence, and wisdom of people of the same age is little different:

> if we consider how little odds there is of strength or knowledge between men of mature age (*Elements of Law*, 70).

> the Experience of men equall in age, is not much unequall, as to the quantity (*Leviathan*, 52).

> Prudence, is but Experience; which equall time, equally bestows on all men, in those things they equally apply themselves unto (*Leviathan*, 87).

Whereas elsewhere he notices that some people are more prudent and wiser than others because their imagination is quicker and thus in the same amount of time they register more things (and consequently accumulate more experience, prudence, and wisdom):

> men of quick imagination, *cæteris paribus*, are more prudent than those whose imaginations are slow; for they observe more in less time (*Elements of Law*, 16).

On the one hand he notices not without irony that since all people are satisfied with their own share of wisdom and wit, it must follow that wisdom and wit are distributed equally:

> [men] will hardly believe there be many so wise as themselves: For they see their own wit at hand, and other mens at a distance. But this proveth rather that men are in that point equall, than unequall. For there is not ordinarily a greater signe of the equall distribution of any thing, than that every man is contented with his share (*Leviathan*, 87).

On the other hand, he points out that some people do not trust their own wit and that the wit of people is widely different in so far as it depends on which of their passions are dominant:

> The causes of this difference of Witts, are in the Passions: and the difference of Passions, proceedeth, partly from the different Constitution of the body, and partly from different Education (*Leviathan*, 53).

> The difference therefore of wit hath its original from the different passions, and from the ends to which their appetite leadeth them (*Elements of Law*, 49).

The list of apparently inconsistent statements made by Hobbes on equality could continue. This situation has prompted some interpreters to allege that Hobbes's entire argument on natural equality is 'conspicuously unsound' and to claim that the differences on the topic that exist between *Elements of Law*, *De Cive* and *Leviathan* 'contribute to the erosion of its credibility'.[3]

Other critics, instead, have attempted to organise different statements made by Hobbes on equality into a coherent discourse 'by making a rather generous interpretation of what is being said, or by augmenting it with hypotheses in the spirit of his philosophy'.[4]

However, the prevailing tendency among Hobbes's interpreters[5] has been to concentrate on a particular claim on equality that Hobbes made repeatedly and consistently in all his political works, namely, the equal ability of men to kill, and to ignore all his other statements on equality.

2.2 Human Fragility

In *De Cive* Hobbes puts forward the idea that the equal dangerousness of people is an essential form of equality:

> they are equalls who can doe equall things one against the other; but they who can do the greatest things, (namely kill), can doe equall things (*De Cive*, 45).

Examined out of context, Hobbes's claim of the paramount importance of men's equal ability to murder each other seems extravagant. Even if it were granted that people are equally dangerous, it might be contended that inequalities in other fields of comparison (e.g., wisdom) are more decisive. Hobbes's philosophical reply to this objection is that the source of all natural powers (such as wisdom, prudence, etc.) is one's vital and voluntary motion and thus the ability of preserving the vital and voluntary motion is necessarily one's most basic form of power. Hence killing is the 'greatest thing' that a person can perpetrate against another, not because it entails the greatest power in the murderer (on the contrary, as we shall see below, according to Hobbes killing takes very little effort indeed), but because it entails the annihilation of the most basic form of power in the victim, thus preventing the production of any other form of power (wisdom included).

We can accept Hobbes's contention that people's equality to kill is crucial even if we were to reject his identification of man with motion. Indeed, in so far as in the Hobbesian state of nature any dispute or disagreement that people may have about who is the 'better man' can be sorted out in 'battle', it follows that any other form of inequality becomes irrelevant *vis-à-vis* their equal dangerousness.

Throughout his writings Hobbes often concedes that strength is unevenly distributed among people, but stresses that even the strongest of persons is vulnerable to otherwise weaker individuals. He grounds his claim of natural equality on the observation of the *complete fragility of the human body*. For example, in *Elements of Law* he points out that

> the weaker in strength or in wit, or in both, may utterly destroy the power of the stronger, since there needeth but

little force to the taking away of a man's life (*Elements of Law*, 70).

Similarly, in *De Cive* Hobbes pointedly observes 'how brittle the frame of our humane body is' and makes the equality of people depend on it (*De Cive*, 45). The same view is repeated in Chapter XIII of *Leviathan*.

Hobbes's claim that individuals are equal in their physical fragility has two facets: on the one hand, it considers individuals as agents affecting the life of others and capable of endangering it (*positive equality*). On the other hand, it takes individuals as recipients of a particular treatment by others and vulnerable to physical attacks (*negative equality*). In Hobbes's theory negative equality is the exact mirror-image of positive equality.

We may see that Hobbes establishes the equality of individuals neither by considering them (like Locke) as children of God nor by considering their worth as members of the human race. Rather, Hobbes argues for the equality of men by comparing the success and failure of their actions in the state of nature.[6]

For Hobbes when the only thing at stake is self-preservation the abilities of people differ very little. It is only when other fields of endeavour – artificial fields, such as property, industry, arts upon words, science etc. – are opened up in political associations that people can differentiate themselves and grow unequal. Social inequality is an artificial creation and can materialise only *after* the social contract.

2.3 Political Equality and Social Inequality

If Hobbesian individuals were not equally dangerous – as postulated by Hobbes – the state of nature would be a state of peace, ruled by the most powerful. Stronger people would never agree to lay down their right to all things, hence there would be no social contract, no basis for equal rights, no Hobbes's theory. There are many passages in Hobbes's works in which he recognises openly that his theory of the social contract is predicated on the hypothesis of the equal dangerousness and vulnerability of men. Hobbes acknowledges that if some people were stronger than the rest there would be 'no cause' (i.e., no rational justification) for them to lay down their natural right to all things:

> Now if any man had so farre exceeded the rest in power, that all of them with joyned forces could not have resisted him,

there had been no cause why he should part with that right that Nature had given him (*De Cive*, 186).

In all three main political works, the first law of nature (from which all other laws of nature follow) rests entirely on the hypothesis of people's equal dangerousness. We read first in *Elements of Law*:

> But since it is supposed from the equality of strength and other natural faculties of men, that no man is of might sufficient, to assure himself for any long time, of preserving himself thereby, whilst he remaineth in the state of hostility and war; reason therefore dictateth to every man, for his own good, to seek after peace, as far forth as there is hope to attain the same (*Elements of Law*, 74).

then in *De Cive*:

> Yet cannot men expect any lasting preservation continuing thus in the state of nature *(i.e.)* of *War*, by reason of that equality of power, and other humane faculties they are endued withall. Wherefore to seek Peace ... is the dictate of right Reason (*De Cive*, 50).

and finally in *Leviathan*

> [in the state of nature] there can be no security to any man, (how strong or wise soever he be,) of living out of the time, which Nature ordinarily alloweth men to live. And consequently it is a precept, or generall rule of Reason, *That every man, ought to endeavour Peace, as farre as he has hope of obtaining it* (*Leviathan*, 91-2).

Hobbes anchors his theory of political equality of citizens inside political associations to the claim of the equality of people at the moment of the social contract. The acceptance by each and everyone of unconditional obedience to Leviathan is for Hobbes the only recipe for peace. Notice that no exception is made for the nobility.

In *Behemoth* one of the speakers remarks:

> we never shall have a lasting peace, till ... the nobility and gentry know that the liberty of a state is not an exemption from the laws of their own country, whether made by an assembly or by a monarch, but an exemption from the constraints and insolence of their neighbours (*Behemoth*, 59).

In the same work, to the speaker who talks of 'common people', the other retorts: 'What sort of people, as to this matter, are not of the common sort?' (*Behemoth*, 158).

In *Leviathan* Hobbes uses the image of stars and sun to explain the difference between political equality and social inequality: as different stars shine to different degrees when the sun is not present, so people in civil association occupy more or less prestigious positions and shine differently when the Leviathan is out of sight. However, as when the sun appears, the difference of brightness of the stars becomes imperceptible, so in front of the Leviathan, all citizens look the same:

> For in the Soveraignty is the fountain of Honour. The dignities of Lord, Earle, Duke, and Prince are his Creatures. As in the presence of the Master, the Servants are equall, and without any honour at all; So are the Subjects, in the presence of the Soveraign. And though they shine some more, some lesse, when they are out of his sight; yet in his presence, they shine no more than the Starres in presence of the Sun (*Leviathan*, 128).

2.4 Is Equal Dangerousness Self-Evident?

We have just seen that for Hobbes if some people were superior in their ability to kill it would not be rational for them either to lay down their right to all things or to enter the social contract. Such is the dependence of Hobbes's theory of equal rights on the hypothesis of equal dangerousness. The problem arises as to whether Hobbes considered equal dangerousness as self-evident.

Clearly at least one of his correspondents strongly opposed the claim that people are equal. For example, Peleau writes:

> invalids, madmen, fools, pigmies, and poltroons ... all these sorts of people prevent one from being able truthfully to assert that all men are equal ... not all men are equal in strength, experience, reason, or passion (*Correspondence I*, letter 90, 309).

Although Hobbes's reply has not survived, we know from du Verdus that it was a 'witty' one. Du Verdus says: 'I admired your punctiliousness in replying to all his arguments point by point' (*Correspondence I*, letter 94, 327).[7]

Among Hobbes's correspondents, Leibniz (*Correspondence II*,

Fatal Equality

letter 195, 734) has no problem in accepting 'the equality of people's forces (given that the strongest man can be killed by the weakest)'.

In recent times, all game-theoretical interpreters of Hobbes, from Gauthier to Hampton, from Kavka to Neal, seem to agree in suggesting that all Hobbesian agents are aware of this form of equality when operating in the state of nature. Whereas in places it is true that Hobbes suggests that this form of equality is uncontroversial, elsewhere he argues that such equality can be learnt only in the event of battle. He makes the important claim:

> in the condition of meer Nature, the inequality of Power is not discerned, but by the event of Battell (*Leviathan*, 99).

Here Hobbes suggests that many individuals are *not* aware of being as vulnerable as others until they actually engage in physical confrontation.

On equality to kill, Hobbes puts forwards two parallel views. As an *observer* of human nature, he advances the view that there is no doubt that in the long run people are all equally vulnerable. And this, according to Hobbes, is the view not only of all 'temperate men', but also of anyone who can afford to reflect calmly and dispassionately on human equality. However, Hobbes observes, many individuals do not admit that the equality that they see in others extends to themselves:

> For one [temperate] man according to that naturall equality which is among us, permits as much to others, as he assumes to himself ... another, supposing himselfe above others ... challenges Respect, and Honour ... [driven by] Vain glory (*De Cive*, 46).

According to Hobbes, agents in the state of nature believe to be smarter, wiser, or stronger and therefore more dangerous than the rest. For a vainglorious agent no form of equality is uncontroversial, not even the equal vulnerability of people.

The tension between each man's dispassionate assessment of his equality (as an impartial observer) and the tendency to over-estimate one's abilities in the heat of action (i.e. when directly involved as an agent) is supposed to be bridged by reason. It is reason that suggests to man, says Hobbes, to 'acknowledge' or at least to 'admit' mutual equality: 'equalitie must be admitted' (*Leviathan*, 107); 'men considered in mere nature, ought to admit amongst themselves equality' (*Elements of Law*, 70).

The passion that impairs the human mind in its ability to ascertain one's real abilities is (vain) *glory*. Thus, Hobbes's complex views on equality cannot be fully understood without a thorough examination of the fundamental concept of *glory*, to which the next chapters are devoted.

Chapter 3

The Axiom of Glory

Introduction

Aubrey's portrait of Hobbes is that of a person completely lacking in pomposity:

> [he had] whiskers yellowish-reddish, which naturally turned up – which is a sign of a brisk wit. Below he was shaved close, except a little tip under his lip. Not but that nature could have afforded a venerable beard, but being naturally of a cheerful and pleasant humour, he affected not at all austerity and gravity and to look severe. He desired not the reputation of his wisdom to be taken from the cut of his beard, but from his reason (*Brief Lives*, 156).

Aubrey remarks that Hobbes 'was well-beloved' by people who knew him: 'they loved his company for his pleasant facetiousness and good nature' (*ibid.*). The King himself liked his 'pleasant discourse' and was 'always much delighted in his wit and smart repartees.' Aubrey adds that

> The wits at court were wont to bait him, but he feared none of them, and would make his part good. The king would call him *the bear*; here come the bear to be baited (*Brief Lives*, 154).

According to Aubrey, Hobbes 'was marvellous happy and ready in his replies and that without rancour (except provoked).' (*ibid.*); however 'as he had many friends ... so he had many enemies (though undeserved; for he would not provoke, but if provoked he was sharp and bitter)'(*Brief Lives*, 161).

In the Correspondence we find many corroborations of Aubrey's characterisation. Here Hobbes comes across as witty

> I have a cold that makes me keepe my chamber, and a chamber ... that makes me keepe my Cold (*Correspondence I*, letter 24, 41).

epigrammatic:

they repeat the same words often when they talke with them that cannot heare (*Correspondence II*, letter 191, 726).

self-ironic, as when he warns du Verdus that he would have needed

> two teachers, a writing master to read [Hobbes's] letters, and an English master to understand [Hobbes's] French (*Correspondence I*, letter 84, 287).

From the *Correspondence* we learn that Hobbes had a very pleasant disposition. In letter 133 Sorbière regrets that '[we] shall not be able to avail ourselves of your subtle and penetrating mind, your lively humour' *Correspondence I*, 496); and elsewhere he thanks Hobbes for the 'sweetness of your wit in your friendly letters' (*Correspondence I*, letter 135, 500). In letter 166 Sorbière summarises what seems to have been the dominant feeling of most of Hobbes's correspondents:

> I admire ... your goodness, your courtesy, and all those fine qualities which make you a perfect gentlemen as well as a great philosopher. You fulfil all the duties of civil life, you are a good friend, a good courtier, and of the best temperament in the world (*Correspondence II*, 619).

In his private letters Hobbes uses a style devoid of sententiousness and affectation. He disliked flattery, even when motivated by true affection. In letter 94 du Verdus writes: 'you have forbidden me to write anything that savours of a compliment' (*Correspondence I*, 327). Critics of his mathematical attempts to square the circle did criticise strongly Hobbes's stubbornness and sometimes blamed his pride for his inability to listen to sound advice. However, in the Correspondence only Descartes attacks Hobbes's personality, and perhaps his vitriolic attacks tell us more about him than about Hobbes.

On the whole, from the surviving letters Hobbes emerges as a very fine man, with a balanced personality and no more than a healthy amount of self-esteem: bold and strong with his critics, generous, warm, and caring with his friends; not immune to professional pride, nor reluctant to engage in disputes; unwilling to compromise for the sake of academic harmony, yet tolerant of his friends' different religious inclinations; sometimes overwhelmed by fear of persecution.

This man with great nobility of character is the philosopher who offered one of the gloomiest pictures of human nature ever. This should be of no surprise for two reasons. First, decent people are inevitably the ones most shocked by human conduct and least willing

The Axiom of Glory

to proclaim their faith in the human race. Secondly and more importantly, in all his descriptions of human nature (unlike Descartes in the *Passions of the Soul*), Hobbes's interest in people is never from the standpoint of the physiologist or the psychologist, but rather from the perspective of the true political thinker. In other words, Hobbes's concern never was to give a complete account of the psychology of man. Rather, he wanted to isolate and emphasise those human characteristics that are politically relevant, i.e., that can help us understand the function and the aims of political associations. For this reason, Alasdair MacIntyre is unfair to Hobbes in attributing to him a description of human nature that is too reductive.[1] Love, generosity, loyalty, goodness do indeed exist in human relations, as Hobbes never denied. However, these captivating qualities do not explain why people need laws and punishment,[2] why there are conflicts and wars; why in human history peace has never lasted very long. In other words, these qualities are politically inconsequent.

Of all human passions Hobbes highlighted one that in his view was of paramount political importance – the human desire for 'glory', which in today's language translates not simply as the desire of prestige, but also the desire to acquire power over others.

The aim of this chapter is to give an account as accurate as possible of the *meaning* attached by Hobbes to 'glory' not only in the triad of *Elements of Law*, *De Cive* and *Leviathan* but also in *Anti-White*, *De Homine*, *Behemoth*, and in the Correspondence. This entails clarifying the distinction between glory, false glory, vain glory, establishing when glory is a pleasure and when an appetite, discussing beneficial and detrimental glory, distinguishing pride from just esteem; comparing glory and felicity; characterising glory *vis-à-vis* such concepts as honour and power; explaining the relation between glory, reason, and self-preservation. *Contra* McNeilly, it will emerge that Maurice Goldsmith's remark that *Elements of Law* 'is often plainer than *Leviathan*; occasionally it expresses a point that *Leviathan* compresses'[3] certainly applies to the definition of glory.

3.1 Definitions of Glory

In *Anti-White* Hobbes remarks that 'the mind's every happiness must consist in the recollection or ... vision ... of its own power or excellence.' He points out that power 'exists only by comparison, because if everyone's potential were the same it would not be potential, since if one ... acts upon another the potential [of the two] are mutually annulled'. In this work Hobbes claims that the

> [j]oy ... or the mind's delight, is nothing but a kind of triumph of the mind, or an internal pride, or boasting about its own potential and excellence in comparison with another [mind's] (*Anti-White*, 466).

In the *Elements of Law* the pleasure of observing one's power in attaining one's objectives is called by Hobbes 'glory'. As in *Anti-White*, so in the *Elements of Law* Hobbes maintains that the power of man to achieve his objectives is not absolute, but determined by the difference with the power of others (*Elements of Law*, 34). Thus, a more precise description of glory in the *Elements of Law* is the pleasure of superior power with respect to others (*Elements of Law*, 36-7).

In *De Cive*, too, Hobbes calls 'glory' the joy of superiority and describes it as man's dominant passion and ultimate end. The 'relational' status of glory and honour as concepts that 'consist in comparison and precellence' (*De Cive*, 44) is stated unambiguously.

The definition of glory given in *Leviathan* does not refer directly to other individuals.[4] This has prompted McNeilly to suggest that whereas glory is a relational concept in earlier works, it is no longer so in *Leviathan*. This claim is incorrect in so far as in *Leviathan*, too, Hobbes often uses glorying as synonymous with triumph of a man over another (*Leviathan*, 106), thereby retaining the essentially comparative feature of glory.

In *De Homine*, considered by some[5] as Hobbes's last word on human nature, glory is defined as 'elation of the mind' and the idea that others are essential for one's glorying is suggested again (*De Homine*, 58). Here Hobbes defines 'ambition' (that in previous works had been left unexplained) as the 'immoderate love' of a particular form of power, namely 'political power' (*De Homine*, 60).

3.2 Forms of Glory

In *Anti-White* Hobbes remarks that sometimes in dreams 'we assume as our very own ... the noble acts we have seen or heard of in heroes or others' (*Anti-White*, 367). This for Hobbes is an example of 'empty glory', i.e., an empty pleasure and 'in no way does it lead to happiness'. In addition to 'empty glory', in *Anti-White* Hobbes mentions the 'worthless glorification' inspired by flatterers. This type of glory induces to actions 'outcome [of which] will not be happy.' For Hobbes only 'if such pride springs from the assessing of future potential on the basis of previous deeds, the latter give ground for hope ... self-evaluation ... success ... and happiness' (*Anti-White*, 466).

As in *Anti-White*, so in the *Elements of Law* Hobbes examines three forms of glory, namely true, vain, and false glory. He provides us with two criteria for distinguishing between them.

The first of these criteria refers to whether these passions are based on either real or imaginary actions (*Elements of Law*, 37). If one's feeling of superiority is grounded on real achievements, Hobbes says, the deriving pleasure is 'glory'. If actions are not real and thus power is merely imagined either by the glory-seeker or by his adulators, then the resulting pleasure is fictitious and is either 'vain glory' (if it derives entirely from one's indulging in fanciful thoughts) or 'false glory' (if it stems from adulation by others).

The second criterion for differentiating between true, vain, and false glory refers to 'aspiring', i.e., to the urge to act and to augment one's power in the world. Hobbes observes that whereas true glory engenders 'aspiring', in so far as it spurs people to act so as to experience new glory, vain glory instead induces inaction, since no effort or achievement in the real world is required in order to indulge in this mental pleasure.

In *De Cive* the differences between true, vain, and false glory are not re-stated, but taken for granted, as can be seen, for example, from the fact that here Hobbes adheres to the practice established in the *Elements of Law* of always referring to vain glory in the context of the state of nature, and never to proper glory. This shows that he had not changed his view that true glory (i.e., based on true achievements) can never be attained under natural conditions.

In *Leviathan* vain glory subsumes false glory and as in the *Elements of Law* it is distinguished from glory in so far as it is grounded not on actions but on fancies, and it generates wishful thinking rather than purposeful action: 'the language of Vain-Glory [is] ... *Optative*' (*Leviathan*, 45). It is interesting to note that in *Leviathan* the term 'aspiring' used in *Elements of Law* as a criterion for distinguishing between vain glory and glory is replaced by 'attempt' (*Leviathan*, 42). As it will be argued in Chapter 7, this can be interpreted as a sign of the more general shift from the analysis of the inner thoughts of individuals typical of *Anti-White, Elements of Law,* and *De Cive* to the account of people's observable behaviour undertaken in *Leviathan*.

In *De Homine* Hobbes classifies 'excessive self-esteem' and 'excessive diffidence' as perturbations of the mind, whereas 'proper self-esteem ' is described as 'a state of mind that ought to be' (*De Homine*, 60-1). In this work, too, as in the *Elements of Law* and *Leviathan*, 'actions and deeds' are seen as the criterion for distinguishing between those 'who estimate their worth correctly' and 'those who estimate their worth too highly or who pretend to be what they are not or who believe flatterers' (*De Homine*, 61).

In the *Elements of Law* Hobbes refers to glory sometimes as a pleasure and sometimes as a desire. The two above-mentioned criteria can be used to clarify some of the ambiguities that this practice generates. In particular, according to the forward-looking criterion of 'aspiring' (or 'attempt') glory consists in desiring future victories over others and thus is an 'appetite'. The 'real action' criterion, instead, is backward-looking and describes glory as the feeling of admiration for our own past achievements, i.e., as a pleasure.

In *De Homine* the distinction between appetite and pleasure becomes blurred, in so far as desire and enjoyment are described as points of a continuum of motion:

> even the enjoyment of a desire, when we are enjoying it, is an appetite, namely the motion of the mind to enjoy by parts, the thing that it is enjoying. For life is perpetual motion that, when it cannot progress in a straight line, is converted into circular motion (*De Homine*, 54).

3.3 Value-Loaded and Descriptive Terms

In Chapter 9 of the *Elements of Law* Hobbes suggests that 'glory' is a descriptive and value-neutral word and that 'pride' and 'just esteem' are its value-loaded counterparts. Hobbes remarks that 'glory' is simply the name of a passion, whereas 'just esteem' and 'pride' disclose whether an observer approves or disapproves of someone else's glorying (*Elements of Law*, 37).

Keeping in mind the above distinction between glory, pride, and just esteem, we may notice that Hobbes often resorts to the value-free term (i.e., 'glory') and reserves the (negative) value-loaded version ('pride') only for special occasions, as in the description of the law of nature that forbids pride. This practice is adhered to in all three main political works (*Elements of Law*, 88; *De Cive*, 68; *Leviathan*, 107).

The Axiom of Glory

In his works, Hobbes at times condemns glory, at times he justifies it. In *Anti-White*, for example, Hobbes points out that

> the reason why authors [of philosophy] often fail to keep their promises' of delivering the truth 'is that, first seeking glory, and esteeming truth only afterwards, they are competing for renown and for the applause of their hearers (*Anti-White*, 27).

In the same work, though, Hobbes shows that sometimes the desire to be praised by others can lead to agreeable actions, like helping the poor. Although the motivation is 'vain glory' and the attempt to 'appear merciful or generous ...[is made] for reputation's sake' (*Anti-White*, 402-3), the resulting behaviour is nevertheless classified as 'pity'.

In the *Elements of Law*, too, it appears that Hobbes considers some forms of glory as detrimental for the human race, others as beneficial. In Chapters 4 and 10, for example, the desire of glory and honour is shown to spur people to perform to their best thereby developing those passions and faculties that are specific to man, ranging from curiosity to reason, from language to deductive thought. For Hobbes the pleasures of the senses are deleterious in so far as they distract the mind from the desire of honour and glory and thus hinder the development of man's cognitive powers, (*Elements of Law*, 49). Here is how Hobbes describes the mechanics whereby a man can be induced to better himself by the desire of honour:

> As when a man, from the thought of honour to which he has an appetite, cometh to the thought of wisdom, which is the next means thereto; and from thence to the thought of study, which is the next means to wisdom, etc (*Elements of Law*, 13-14).

In a similar vein in *De Cive* Hobbes remarks that if he had written this work 'out of desire of praise', this would have been no crime because 'very few doe things laudably, who are not affected with commendation' (*De Cive*, 36).

In *De Homine* Hobbes remarks that 'love of fame or renown, if it be excessive, needs be placed among the perturbations of the mind.' However he is keen to point out that 'moderation ... in the desire of fame ... is useful' (*De Homine*, 60).

In a revealing letter of his surviving correspondence (letter 28) Hobbes condemns glory-seeking behaviour as offensive and discourages Charles Cavendish from pursuing it. He advises the young Cavendish to 'avoyd all offensiue speech, not only openly reviling but also that Satyricall way of nipping that some use' (*Correspondence I*, 52). Hobbes remarks that a competitive, offensive, choleric, and derisory attitude is common among young people; for Hobbes 'this fault' is present in everybody until 'adversity or age' drives one away from it. Hobbes recommends moderation, but suggests that moderation is not natural, but must be taught. This view is consistent with his remark in *De Cive* that by nature man is neither political nor social, but must be changed by means of education.

Whereas in Letter 28 Hobbes is writing as a tutor to a pupil and condemns glory, elsewhere in the correspondence we can see that he himself was not immune to it. In Letter 30, addressed to Mersenne, Hobbes proclaims his own good faith in the quarrel with Descartes: 'It is not as if I had published anything which would make me feel bound to defend my errors stubbornly as a point of honour' (*Correspondence I*, 70), thereby suggesting that professional pride can at times interfere with the search of the truth. Elsewhere Hobbes shows that the elation of the mind called glory is a legitimate feeling, as long as it is well grounded. Offended by the way in which John Fell had maliciously amended the entry referring to Thomas Hobbes in 'The Antiquities of Oxford', Hobbes writes to Anthony Wood:

> Let them remove my name entirely, if they so wish from "The Antiquities of Oxford": I shall still be praised by most scholars of the present time, and by even more (I believe) of those of the future (*Correspondence II*, Letter 197, 747).

The type of glory that Hobbes consistently and unambiguously condemns in all his writings, from *Anti-White* to *Behemoth*, from *Elements of Law* to *Leviathan* is the presumption of those who without effort or labour think themselves wiser than the rest, and thus entitled to rule the life of others, to instruct them about what is right and wrong, to correct, change, and 'innovate' the government of a country. This form of ambition, Hobbes maintains, is the major source of all civil wars (see *infra* Chapter 5 on the role of glory).

3.4 Glory and Honour

The relationship between glory and honour is explained clearly by Hobbes in *De Homine*. Here Hobbes says that 'a certain joy that ariseth from the thought to be honoured is called glory' (*De Homine*, 58).

In Hobbes's works, whereas glory is one's joy to be superior to others, honour is the recognition of one's power by other individuals. Thus glory and honour are two types of reaction to an agent's power, respectively by the agent himself and by others:

> the acknowledgement of power is called HONOUR ... and to honour a man (inwardly in the mind) is to conceive or acknowledge, that that man hath the odds or excess of power above him that contendeth or compareth himself (*De Homine*, 34-5).

Glory and honour can be described as mirrors reflecting the power of a person; indeed, they are distorting mirrors, in so far as glory tends to enlarge the projection of one's power while honour tends to reduce it, because 'every man's passion weigheth heavy in his own scale, but not in the scale of his neighbour' (*Elements of Law*, 92). Hobbes does not suggest that either mirror is truer than the other, or that the true image of the power of a person lies in some sort of average of the two images. Instead he provides the reader with a criterion to explain different degrees of honour. The honour that we give to a man, he says in the *Elements of Law*, depends on his *value*, and his value in turn on the *use* that we can make of his natural or acquired powers ('strength', 'beauty of person', 'knowledge', 'riches', 'nobility', 'good fortune', 'authority', etc., *Elements of Law*, 35).

This suggests that the more useful certain natural characteristics or acquired skills are deemed by people, the higher is the value socially attributed to those individuals who possess them and the greater is their honour.

In his political works Hobbes does not discuss in any detail the validity of the above criterion grounding honour and value on use. However, he shows himself sceptical of man's ability to apply the above criterion correctly, namely to discern what is truly profitable and unprofitable He notices that people recognise little power and attach little honour to men of science and philosophy because they wrongly underestimate the importance of their activities.

For Hobbes the ingredient of glory and honour is power. In *Anti-White*, *Elements of Law*, and *De Cive* an agent's power is defined as the excess of power of an agent above another. Power is therefore an explicitly comparative concept. In *Leviathan* instead we read that 'The POWER *of a man* ... is his present means, to obtain some future apparent

Good' (*Leviathan*, 62). Such remarks have convinced McNeilly that in *Leviathan* power is no longer a relational concept (as it was in previous works), but on the contrary has become a human characteristic that can be defined in absolute terms. Interpreters, however, have pointed out a wealth of passages in *Leviathan* showing that Hobbes had not changed his view that power is never absolute, but depends on the power of others.[6] In *De Homine* too power is described as an inherently relational concept. In this respect, Hobbes remarks that 'if [power] be not extraordinary, it is useless; for what all have equally is nothing' (*De Homine*, 49).

In his works Hobbes suggests that it is not one's 'objective power' that matters, but the 'subjective opinion' of people about one's power. In *Anti-White* we are told that 'we honour people because of our opinion' of their power; in *De Cive*, too, honour is defined as the '*opinion* of anothers power' (*De Cive*, 188) or as 'the estimation of anothers power' (*De Cive*, 124) In *Leviathan* Hobbes says that 'Honour consisteth onely in the opinion of Power' (*Leviathan*, 66). He argues that to honour a man is to value him, pointing out that the worth that we give to a man is his *price*, namely what we are prepared to pay for the use of his abilities or powers, and that, as such, it 'is not absolute but a thing dependant on the need and judgement of another' (*Leviathan*, 63). As the needs and judgements of people vary with the circumstances, so do the value and honour of individuals.

In contrast with *Elements of Law*, in *De Cive* opinion acquires the novel role of generating power itself: 'by opinion of power, true power is acquired' (*De Cive*, 190). In *Leviathan*, too, Hobbes points out that power in human associations depends on people's 'opinion' and 'judgement' and remarks that 'Reputation of power, is Power' (*Leviathan*, 62).[7]

In *Behemoth* the link between power and opinion is put in even stronger terms: 'the power of the mighty hath no foundation but in the opinion and belief of the people' (*Behemoth*, 16).

3.5 Glory and Self-preservation

In Chapter xxxiii of *Anti-White* (408) Hobbes states that 'of the good things experienced by men ... none can outweigh the greatest of the evil ones, namely sudden death'. In all his political writings Hobbes repeats the above view which implies that self-preservation is more important than glory. In *De Homine* Hobbes reiterates the view that

The Axiom of Glory

'the greatest of good for each is his own preservation' (*De Homine*, 48).

In *Anti-White* Hobbes does not offer an argument to justify the claim that glory cannot compensate for death, nor does he specify whether people are driven away from lethal dangers by their passions, by reason, or by both. In *Elements of Law*, instead, Hobbes's stand on this point is clearer. He maintains that it is the whole 'nature' of a man (by which he means both passions and reason since 'reason is no less of the nature of man than passion', *Elements of Law*, 75) that usually drives him to avoid death:

> necessity of nature maketh men to will and desire *bonum sibi*, that which is good for themselves, and to avoid that which is hurtful; but most of all that terrible enemy of nature, death, from whom we expect both the loss of all power, and also the greatest bodily pains in the losing (*Elements of Law*, 71).

More precisely, even though passions can sometime lead man to reach a different conclusion, reason helps him understand that death is the greatest evil, self-preservation 'is that good and [its contrary] that evil, which not every man in passion calleth so, but all men by reason' (*Elements of Law*, 94). In the whole of *Elements of Law*, *De Cive*, and *Leviathan* one can find only a few examples given by Hobbes in which passions would lead a man to die rather than endure humiliation:

> inasmuch as life itself with the condition of enduring scorn, is not esteemed worth the enjoying, much less peace (*Elements of Law*, 86).

> For though it be not hard ... to make one's adversary displeased with his own fact; yet to make him acknowledge the same, is so difficult, that many a man had rather die than do it (*Elements of Law*, 39).

> most men would rather lose their lives... than suffer reproach (*De Cive*, 67; see also *Leviathan*, 107).

The above quotations provide instances of people willing to die in order to avoid dishonour, but Hobbes does not offer examples of men prepared to die in order to attain glory and honour. Although Hobbes never thinks that honour can compensate for loss of life, in an important passage of *Elements of Law* he suggests that the 'danger' or risk to one's self-preservation can be offset by 'honour, riches, and means whereby to delight the mind'. Referring to the sovereign power, he says:

> The inconvenience arising from government in general to him that governeth, consisteth ... partly in the danger of his person ... To balance this incommodity, the sovereignty, together with the necessity of this care and danger, comprehendeth so much honour, riches, and means whereby to delight the mind, as no private man's wealth can attain unto (*Elements of Law*, 138-139).

In *De Cive* we find the clearest and neatest presentation of the relationship between glory, self-preservation, and reason to be found in Hobbes's writings. On the one hand glory is described as the ultimate motivation of man: 'all the mindes pleasure is either Glory ... or referres to Glory in the end' (*De Cive*, 43).

On the other hand, reason is described as the method whereby each individual tries to attain his goal; more precisely, reasoning is said to consist in the 'seek[ing] out of the meanes to the end which he propounds to himselfe' (*De Cive*, 177). If we combine the description of dominion as the end of man with the definition of reason as the study of the means to an end, we arrive at the Hobbesian concept of self-preservation as a necessary precondition found out by reason for the attainment of glory. In fact a man cannot experience glory, namely the pleasure of dominion, unless he is alive. In the Epistle Dedicatory that opens *De Cive* Hobbes notices that whereas the desire to possess more than others is found by examining human psychology, the relevance of self-preservation is pointed out by reason (*De Cive*, 27).

However, it is not only reason that indicates to man the importance of self-preservation. In all his works Hobbes emphasizes strongly that fear of death is instinctive (*De Cive*, 47, 53).

Although in *Leviathan* glory is defined in some respect less precisely than in *Elements of Law*, Hobbes adds an important qualification on its meaning that was missing in his previous works. In *Leviathan* the desire of honour, glory, and power is distinguished from the desire of fame after death and from the desire of praise.[8] Whereas the 'desire of fame after death' may in principle be compatible with risking one's life, for glory-seekers, instead, death would nullify their chances of achieving their ultimate end, namely dominion over others.

In *De Homine* Hobbes states that

The Axiom of Glory

even though we think of fame after death as being neither unpleasing nor useless for others, we are nevertheless mistaken in looking at the future like the present, because we shall not experience it, nor can we mere mortals estimate its worth. For we would be making the same mistake as we would were we to be grieved because we had not been famous before we were born (*De Homine*, 60).

3.6 Glory and Felicity

The work in which Hobbes examines in greatest detail human happiness is *Anti-White*. Here Hobbes defines happiness as 'the desire for good that is to come' (*Anti-White*, 463) and remarks that 'the grounds of good and hence of happiness, consist in seeking' (*Anti-White*, 464) In this work Hobbes sets forth two beliefs that he will maintain throughout his life, namely the view that '[f]elicity therefore consists in the advance of the appetite from a good thing that has been obtained to another good thing that is to be obtained' (*Anti-White*, 464-5) and the conviction that 'he who has nothing to seek after enjoys no happiness' (*Anti-White*, 463).

In *Anti-White* Hobbes pinpoints some general characteristics common to those goals whose pursuit can give rise to happiness: on the one hand they must be *attainable*, since 'the yearning for things which there seems no means of attaining is not happiness: it is torment' (*Anti-White*, 464), on the other hand they must require *some effort* in order to be obtained

> the search for things easily obtained ... is not happiness;, if it were, then, ... someone would be happy who was ever itching and scratching himself in turn (*Anti-White*, 464).

Hobbes remarks that the ingredient of happiness is 'the acquisitive advance', 'the perpetual advance of appetite and hope' from a lesser to a greater power (*Anti-White*, 465). The individual's reaction to this advance is a special 'joy' or 'delight of the mind' for 'the mind's every happiness must consist in the recollection, ... or vision ... of its own potential or excellence' (*Anti-White*, 466).

In *Elements of Law*, too, the unambiguous objective of Hobbesian men is to try to obtain the pleasure of superior power; their life is compared by Hobbes to a race which has 'no other goal, nor other garland, but being foremost' (*Elements of Law*, 47). We find the image of the race also in *Anti-White* where we are told that 'whatever reason precludes a runner from performing well on a track, [this] same reason may prevent a person from achieving prosperity in this life' (*Anti-White*, 482). According to Hobbes once people have achieved excellence in one field they will turn to another 'as long as in any kind they think themselves behind any other' (*Elements of Law*, 30). In *Elements of Law* Hobbes gives the examples of Nero and Commodus, and in *Anti-White* Alexander, Augustus and Heliogatus are mentioned as examples of individuals who were spurred from one field to another by their desire of glory (*Anti-White*, 467).

There seems to be some interesting differences on happiness between *Anti-White* and all the other writings. Firstly, in *Anti-White* Hobbes treats happiness and glorying as virtually interchangeable concepts. Secondly, he maintains that 'happiness must consist in the *awareness* of a continued advance from a benefit already won to a benefit to be secured later' (*Anti-White*, 467; emphasis added).

Conversely, in Hobbes's other writings felicity and glory are two separate words that convey two different concepts. In *Elements of Law* the link between glory and happiness is explained by Hobbes in terms of the above-mentioned race: while 'glory' is 'to consider [others] behind', human 'felicity' consists in 'continually out-go[ing] the next before' (*Elements of Law*, 48). However, the distinction between glory and felicity captured in the analogy with a race should not be taken too literally, for in Hobbes's argument glory, too, derives from 'out-going the next before'.

In Hobbes's political writings, whereas glory is classified as a passion and described as the *conscious* aim of agents (in *Elements of Law* and *De Cive* of all agents, in *Leviathan* of some), felicity instead is never described as a conscious goal, but rather as an observer's description of an agent's way of life (*Leviathan*, 46; *Elements of Law*, 30).

In *De Homine* Hobbes says that 'the greatest good, or as it is called, felicity and the final end cannot be attained in the present life' (*De Homine*, 53). He explains that

> if the end be final, there would be nothing to long for, nothing to desire; whence it follows not only that nothing would itself be a good from that time on, but also that man would not even feel. [...] and not to feel is not to live (*De Homine*, 53-54).

Chapter 4

Glory: Parallels and Intersections

Introduction

Aubrey reports that Hobbes's 'contemplation was much more than his reading. He was wont to say that if he had read as much as other men, he should have known no more than other men.' (*Brief Lives*, 157). Although Skinner is probably correct in not taking Hobbes's boasting too seriously, nevertheless the fact remains that Hobbes attached importance not so much to his erudition, but rather to the independence of his thought. Whereas, for example, Bacon in the *Essays* openly relies on the wisdom of past masters to support his views, nowhere in his works Hobbes follows this practice. His interpretation of human psychology is presented as the result of first-hand observation and of independent reflection, unaffected by the received wisdom of mankind. This approach makes the search for the sources of Hobbesian glory extremely difficult and never conclusive.

Even so it is important to try to locate Hobbes's concept of glory defined in Chapter 2 on the map of the history of political thought with the aim to trace its origins and hence assess its originality. In this chapter I shall first review the most important sources of Hobbesian glory as highlighted in the literature, and secondly I shall concentrate on the text that in my view provides the deepest insight into Hobbes's concept of glory, namely Thucydides' *History*. My contention is that although in the works of Aristotle, Plato, Tacitus, Cicero, Augustine, Machiavelli, Castiglione, and Bacon (to name but a few), there are indeed some elements that find an echo in Hobbesian glory, it is only in Thucydides that we find in clear and unambiguous terms both a psychological analysis of human nature and an assessment of the political implications of ambition that mirror closely Hobbes's own argument.

4.1 The Sources of Hobbesian Glory

Hobbes's concept of glory is, of course, far from being completely original. It can be argued that there are some interesting similarities between Hobbes's glory and Aristotle's honour, aristocratic virtue, biblical pride, bourgeois greed, Bacon's vainglory, and Thucydides' ambition and honour. Most of the above ideas have been identified in the literature as possible sources of Hobbesian glory.

4.1.1 Aristotle's honour

In his biography Aubrey discloses that he heard Hobbes saying that 'Aristotle was the worst teacher that ever was, the worst politician and teacher of ethics ... but his rhetoric and discourse of animals was rare' (*Brief Lives*, 159). In the last sixty years, from Leo Strauss[1] to Quentin Skinner,[2] many interpreters have argued that Hobbes's discussion of the passions in the *Elements of Law* was greatly influenced by Aristotle's *Rhetoric*. The admiration for Aristotle's *Rhetoric* must have been the reason that prompted Hobbes to write a digest of that work – a digest which, as shown by Skinner, takes some liberties with the original text. On the one hand, I myself find an important similarity between Hobbes's digest of Aristotle's *Rhetoric* and his own account of the human passions not only in the *Elements of Law,* but also in *De Homine*. On the other hand, I believe that the similarities should not make us overlook the relevance of the differences between the two accounts. I shall give an example.

In Aristotle's *Rhetoric*, as rendered by Hobbes,[3] we read that '*honourable* are ... the works of virtue. And the signs of virtue ... And what we do for our country's good, neglecting our own' (p. 437). According to Strauss (p. 36) this view by Aristotle closely resembles the following remark made by Hobbes in the *Elements of Law* (35): 'HONOURABLE are those signs for which one man acknowledgeth power or excess above his concurrent in another'.

Contra Strauss, it seems to me that there exists a great contrast between these two views. In Aristotle's case the source of honour is virtue, in Hobbes's, power. Unlike Aristotelian honour, Hobbesian honour is devoid of morality. Whereas for Aristotle honour, virtue, and goodness are strictly related concepts, for Hobbes power and honour are independent of either classical or Christian morality. Hobbes suggests that a man is honourable whenever he is successful, even if he is not magnanimous, or virtuous or good in any moral sense.

The lack of a traditional moral content in Hobbes's concept of glory has induced writers like Macpherson to argue (wrongly in my view; see below) that the only morality of the Hobbesian glory-seeker is the morality of the bourgeoisie.

4.1.2 Biblical pride

Michael Oakeshott has highlighted a similarity between Hobbesian pride and Augustine's interpretation of the original sin,[4] an intuition later further developed by Tom Sorell.[5] This interpretation can certainly be underpinned with plentiful textual references. Indeed, there is a wealth of passages where Hobbes refers to the Bible in support of the view that pride has always been ruinous for man. In *De Cive*, for example, we read:

> the most ancient of all Gods commands is ... *Thou shalt not eat of the tree of knowledge of good and evill*; and the most ancient of all diabolicall tentations ... *Yee shall be as Gods, knowing good and evill* (*De Cive*, 147).

These references by Hobbes to Genesis show a connection between Adam's pride and the temptation for ambitious people in the political state to challenge the established authorities (*Elements of Law*, 112; *De Cive*, 95, 246; *Leviathan*, 201).

In my view, however, the similarity between biblical pride and Hobbesian glory is largely superficial.

First, Hobbesian glory is a wider concept than biblical pride in so far as the Hobbesian man is driven by a restlessness that is totally absent in Adam. The hunger for glory of the Hobbesian man does not suggest just one action, but an endless succession of choices, an entire life style, a permanent and incurable obsession, that is ended only by death.

Secondly, unlike Augustine, Hobbes nowhere in his description of man betrays an interest in the inner drama of Adam after the Fall from grace. For Hobbes, the only tragedy of the glory-seeker, and the reason for his occasional dejection or melancholy, is not Sin, but Failure. Revealingly, a state of grace is never included by Hobbes in his otherwise comprehensive lists of the delights of the mind, nor is loss of grace ever mentioned as a source of pain and sorrow. This indifference to the psychological implications of the original sin suggests to me that the biblical temptation of Adam did not inspire Hobbes's concept of glory, but was merely invoked to provide support to the view that his own interpretation of human nature was not unduly pessimistic but could be traced to the most widely accepted text of all – the Bible.

4.1.3 Aristocratic honour

Strauss argues that the account of glory and honour in Hobbes's early works owes much to the concept of aristocratic virtue.[6] For the aristocrat, unlike the bourgeois, honour is more important than profit. In the literature many have endorsed this claim. It has been argued that in Hobbes's writings 'glory is ... the passion of the aristocrat, who wields power on account of which he is feared and honoured.'[7] Oakeshott and Goldsmith have subscribed on the whole to this interpretation, with the qualification that in Hobbes's argument it is not the majority of glory-seekers but the minority of 'gallant' people who show some aristocratic traits (this minority will be examined in Chapter 7).

I have some reservations in endorsing this reading of Hobbes. In my view when in his political writings Hobbes speaks with a hint of admiration of 'a kind of gallantry' that some people show in their behaviour, he is not necessarily referring to the nobility nor to the codes of conduct as can be found, for instance, in *Il Cortegiano*.[8] In fact, admiration for 'Gallantry' is expressed by Hobbes not only (as claimed by Strauss) in his early writings, but also as late as in *Behemoth*, where Hobbes is very critical of the nobility.

In *Behemoth* the two speakers in the dialogue, wittily christened by Goldsmith 'Thomas' and 'Hobbes', express their respect for 'a kind of gallantry, that few are *brought up* to, and most think folly' (*Behemoth*, 38; italics added). In *Behemoth* Hobbes does not see much difference between the disposition and behaviour of the nobility and other people; he says that 'in their lives they [the gentry and nobility of Scotland] were as other men are, pursuers of their own interests and preferments' (*Behemoth*, 29), nor does he show much faith in the magnanimity of the nobility.

Hobbes not only does not believe that gallantry is not a hereditary trait, but even rejects the notion that it can be a natural disposition; rather, he regards it as an attitude that needs to be cultivated. For example, writing as a tutor to the young Cavendish, Hobbes recommends gallant behaviour (letter 28); both in this letter and in *Behemoth* Hobbes distinguishes true gallantry from the 'gallantry' of 'fine clothes, great feathers, [and] civility' connected to a particular class (*Behemoth*, 31). Hobbes suggests that only age, experience, custom, and especially education can help to control and correct the sort of ungallant behaviour inspired by youth.

4.1.4 Glory and bourgeois greed

Strauss has argued that, in *Leviathan,* unlike earlier works, Hobbes's examination of the passions reminds one of the bourgeois morality. Macpherson has gone farther along this path and has claimed that the Hobbesian glory-seeker is the new 'market man', the profit maximiser of the 'new market society',[9] which at Hobbes's times was beginning to replace feudal relations. In Macpherson's view, accumulation of possessions is an ineliminable feature of the Hobbesian man, as in a 'possessive market society' property is the chief source of power and recognition.

This reading of Hobbesian glory is misguided. Although 'riches' are indeed desired and pursued by Hobbesian glory-seekers, they are not the necessary source of honour. In *De Homine* Hobbes states that 'poverty without need is honourable' – hardly a manifesto of bourgeois morality. Moreover, Hobbes's warning to the sovereign power that dangers to the established order come from those people who are wealthiest and 'most at ease' distances him from the aims and ideals ascribed by Macpherson to the bourgeoisie of 17th century. In *Behemoth* Hobbes criticises the men of the Church for failing to condemn 'greed': 'they did never in their sermons, or but lightly, inveigh against the lucrative vices of men of trade or handicraft' (*Behemoth*, 25). Indeed in *Behemoth* Hobbes betrays a strong dislike for the rising bourgeoisie and makes a point about the wealthy 'merchants' that even a Marxist would have no trouble in endorsing:

> They [the merchants] are said of all callings the most beneficial to the commonwealth, by setting the poorer sort of people on work. That is to say, by making poor people sell their labour to them at their own prices (*Behemoth*, 126).

4.1.5 Bacon's Essays

Aubrey tells us that

> The Lord Chancellor Bacon loved to converse with him [Hobbes]. He assisted his lordship in translating several of his essays into Latin ... His lordship would often say that he better liked Mr Hobbes's taking his thoughts, than any of the others, because he understood what he wrote, which the others, not understanding, my lord would many times have a hard task to make sense of what they wrote (*Brief Lives*, 151).

The admiration that Hobbes had for Bacon is confirmed in the Correspondence. In Letter 68 for example du Verdus says to Hobbes that he knows 'how highly [Hobbes] regards 'Mr Bacon's writings' (*Correspondence I*, 196). In letter 168 du Verdus mentions Hobbes's role as 'a secretary to Chancellor Bacon in his studies' (*Correspondence II*, 628) and in letter 172 du Verdus reveals his intention to address to Hobbes the 'dedicatory epistle ... put at the beginning of [du Verdus'] translation of [Bacon's] *De sapientia veterum*' (*Correspondence II*, 672).

In my view, it cannot be denied that Hobbes's direct familiarity with Bacon's remarks on vainglory, honour, and reputation in the *Essays* is evident in Hobbes's own observations on glory. To refer to just one example, both Bacon and Hobbes choose to illustrate the meaning of vain glory by relating the same story (which Bacon erroneously attributes to Aesop) of the fly sitting upon the axle-tree of the chariot wheel and exclaiming 'what a dust do I raise!'.[10] Bacon, not unlike Hobbes, remarks that vain glory 'stands upon comparisons' and he, too, attaches important social implications to 'opinion'; for example, when he warns that sometimes the lies of the vainglorious 'are sufficient to breed opinion, and opinion brings on substance'[11]. For Bacon vanity is present in all aspects of life, from the private to the public sphere, from military to academic life. He quotes Cicero's remark that 'men who write books on the worthlessness of glory take care to put their names on the title-page'[12] – a comment echoed in Hobbes's own writings.

There are, however, two main differences between Bacon's and Hobbes's arguments on glory, vain glory, ambition, and honour; one stylistic, the other substantive. The first difference was alluded to in the introduction to this chapter and consists in the contrasting way used by Bacon and Hobbes to support their views: whereas the former relies much on his erudition to buttress the definitions in his *Essays,* Hobbes never does so. Thus, in the case of Bacon for example, we know for certain that in the essay entitled '*Of Seditions and Troubles*' he was inspired by Machiavelli's *Discorsi*, because he openly says so.[13] In Hobbes's case, instead, we never know for sure which writers inspired his thought. Thus we may only presume that, as Hobbes admired Bacon, who in turn admired Machiavelli, Hobbes may well have been influenced by Machiavelli's concept of *gloria*. Hobbes himself provides no direct evidence to support this hypothesis.

Apart from the contrasting way to support their similar definitions of vain glory, there is another crucial divergence between Bacon's and Hobbes's views of on glory: they disagree on the political implications of this passion. For Bacon, unlike for Hobbes, 'there is use for it [vain glory] in civil affairs';[14] unlike Hobbes, Bacon does not see in the desire of honour and reputation an inherently destabilising force of political associations. In order to find parallels on the political significance of glory, we should look not to Bacon, but to Thucydides.

4.2 Thucydides and Hobbes on Glory: Influence or Coincidence?

According to Strauss '[i]t would be difficult to find another classical work whose importance for Hobbes's political philosophy can be compared with that of the *Rhetoric*.'[15]

I have no difficulty in pointing to such a classical work: Thucydides' *History*.[16]

Clearly, Hobbes's detailed list and discussion of the passions in the *Elements of Law* and *De Homine* owes much to Aristotle's approach in his *Rhetoric* and nothing to Thucydides. However, in spite of the very different structure of the arguments in Hobbes's political works and in Thucydides' *History*, the two authors' view of human nature and understanding of politics are quite similar.

Although all the sources of glory examined in Section 4.1 (biblical pride, Aristotelian honour, aristocratic virtue, bourgeois greed, Bacon's vainglory) share some aspects of Hobbesian glory, none of them highlights the crucial destabilising role attributed to glory by Hobbes. Only Thucydides' 'ambition' does.[17]

Hobbes, who spent much time and effort to produce his brilliant translation of the *History*, must have found in the way of thinking of the 'most politic historiographer that ever writ' a powerful inspiration for his own thought, especially at a time – the 1620s – when his attention was turning to political philosophy.[18]

The similarity between Hobbes and Thucydides' views on power, glory, and honour ranges from shared fundamental beliefs to matters of detail. Here I shall attempt to highlight the concordance between the two authors in their *psychological analysis of human nature,* leaving to the next chapter a comparative analysis of the political implications of ambition.

4.2.1 Glory, honour, and ambition[19]

It has been often observed that the portrait of the Athenians depicted by the Corinthian ambassadors in the *History* served as a model for Hobbes's description of man:

> What they have, they have no leisure to enjoy, for continual getting of more: nor holiday esteem they any, but whereon they effect some matter profitable; nor think they ease with nothing to do, a less torment than laborious business. So that, in a word, to say they are men born neither to rest themselves, not suffer others, is to say the truth (*History (EW VIII)*, 75-76).

The compulsion to act, the restlessness, and the competitive spirit of the Athenians are not confined to their international relations, but extend to their own social intercourse, where 'they claimed every one, not to be equal, but to be by far the chief' (*History (EW IX)*, 414). Without doubt, the Hobbesian individual for whom 'to have no desires is to be dead' and whose felicity does not lie in resting but in 'continually proceeding' mirrors much more closely the behaviour ascribed by Thucydides to the Athenians, both as private individuals and as a people, than the attitude of the 'market man' as portrayed by Macpherson.

For Hobbes, as for Thucydides, ambition and pride characterise not only the behaviour of single individuals but also the actions of entire peoples and nations. In *Behemoth,* for example, we are told that 'the Scots ... always esteemed the glory of England for an abatement of their own (*Behemoth*, 32) and that '[i]t is indeed commonly seen that neighbour nations envy one another's honour ... but that hinders them not from agreeing in those things which their common ambition leads them to' (*ibid.*).

The similarity between Thucydides and Hobbes goes beyond the shared belief that most people have a restless ambition to rule the life of others. Both writers recognise the 'epidemic' effect of the desire for power and notice that even those that are naturally disinclined to strive for superiority are compelled to join the race after power for the sake of their own survival. In the *History*, an example of a whole city unwilling to wage war for the mere desire to dominate over the rest is provided by Sparta. Thucydides describes the Lacedaemonians as quiet by nature, with no wish to interfere in their neighbours' internal affairs.[20] Yet, as the Corinthians make them realise, they cannot afford their peaceful posture, but instead must take sides in the war, for the sake of their own self-preservation:

> neither do any harm to others, nor receive it ... is a thing you hardly could attain, though the states about you were of the same conditions (*History (EW VIII)*, 76).

In Chapter 7 we shall see that for Hobbes, too, there are individuals who are by nature 'temperate' and 'moderate'. Like Thucydides, also Hobbes stresses that in the state of nature these people are forced by their concern for self-preservation to disregard their peaceful nature and join the ambitious in their race for power.

To underline the affinity of thought between Hobbes and Thucydides on the subject of honour, it may be interesting to note that they make a number of surprisingly similar and specific observations on this topic. One detail that can be found in the works of both is the notation that people tend to honour and praise the dead for these, having passed away, are not deemed to be a threat to the glory of the living. As Pericles puts it in the funeral oration:

> For every man useth to praise the dead ... For men envy their competitors in glory, while they live; but to stand out of their way, is a thing honoured with an affection free from opposition (*History (EW VIII)*, 200).

And Hobbes remarks in *Leviathan*:

> For men contend with the living, not with the dead; to these ascribing more than due, that they may obscure the glory of the other (*Leviathan*, 70).

A related point on which both Hobbes and Thucydides agree is the observation that people are as unwilling to admire the achievements of others as they are ready to discount them as false. Thus Pericles:

> For to hear another man praised finds patience so long only, as each man shall think he could himself have done somewhat of that he hears. And if one exceed in their praises, the hearer presently through envy thinks it false (*History (EW VIII)*, 189).

And Hobbes notices in *Elements of Law* (71): every man think[s] well of himself ... and hat[es] to see the same in others'.

As a final example of the extent to which Thucydides' views on honour overlap with Hobbes's own thoughts, one can point to their interpretation of friendship and enmity merely as signs of power. In the *History* the Athenians quite openly admit to the Melians that they are not going to treat them mercifully since to act friendly towards them would be construed by their other subjects as a sign of weakness: 'your friendship will be an argument of our weakness, and your hatred of our power, amongst those we have rule over' (*History (EW IX)*, 100-101).

In a very similar vein, Hobbes in chapter 10 of *Leviathan* lists friendship and enmity among the 'signs of power', whereby an individual makes others aware of his 'actual power'.

4.2.2 Accumulation of wealth and the pursuit of honour

In many places of the *History* the desire of riches is ranked very clearly below the desire or honour in people's preferences. Thus Pericles in the funeral oration:

> For the love of honour never groweth old: nor doth that unprofitable part of our life take delight (as some have said) in gathering of wealth, so much as it doth in being honoured (*History (EW VIII)*, 200).

Indeed in the *History* the Athenians' true objective is not the acquisition of riches, but dominion: they are said to 'think themselves worthy to have the command of others' (*History (EW VIII)*, 166) and feel 'how honourable a thing it would be for them ... to be inferior to none' (*History (EW IX)*, 82). They are ready to acknowledge their own 'desire to rule over others' and ascribe it to a 'natural inclination of man' (*ibid.*). Thucydides suggests that even individuals as venal as Alcibiades regard prestige and public recognition as their ultimate end.

This view is shared by Hobbes especially in the *Elements of Law* and *De Cive*. Therefore the fact that in his early works Hobbes subordinated desire of riches to desire of honour and glory cannot be taken as an unambiguous sign that then he had been influenced by the values of the aristocratic classes of his times, as suggested by Strauss. Alternatively, Hobbes could have been more directly influenced by Thucydides' *History*, where the desire of profit is often a weaker motivational force than the desire of honour.

In the *History* Pericles underlines the importance of money as a means for the attainment of one's ends and claims that people like riches 'for opportunities of action' (*History (EW VIII)*, 194). Throughout the *History* wealth is often described as the safest means to achieve social prestige. So if Macpherson is right in claiming that the bourgeoisie of the 17th century inspired Hobbes's views on the value of money, one is left wondering who might have inspired Thucydides' similar views.

In some passages of the *History,* though, accumulation of wealth and pursuit of honour appear to be separate objectives, pertaining to different people. For example, in his account of Athens' resolution to undertake the war in Sicily, Thucydides singles out the desire of glory and dominion as the drive of 'the old men' among the Athenians as opposed to the desire of gain, seen as the spur of 'the common sort of soldiers' (*History (EW IX),* 139). Similarly, when explaining the response by the Sicilians to the Athenians' aggression, Thucydides points to desire of glory as the main motivation of the Syracusans and to desire of gain as the chief drive of their confederates (*History (EW IX),* 283-284). This view, that desire of glory and desire of wealth pertain to different people, is theorised by Hobbes in *Leviathan* (see *infra* chapter 7) and explored in the account of the civil war offered in *Behemoth.*

4.2.3 The lessons of war

In the letter to the readers which precedes his translation of Thucydides Hobbes subscribes to the view, that in his times was widespread,[21] that Thucydides was 'the most politic historiographer that ever writ' (*History (EW VIII),* viii). In *Leviathan* he explains that a fundamental ingredient of a 'good History' is 'the Choyce of the actions that are more profitable to be known' (*Leviathan,* 51). A probable reason why Hobbes saw the *History* as a work of the highest political significance lies in the fact that in it Thucydides studies the dynamics of war between nations as well as of civil wars.

Throughout the *History* it is suggested that 'war is a most violent master' (*History (EW VIII),* 348). In his *Of the Life and History of Thucydides* Hobbes endorses wholeheartedly this idea and declares that 'men profit more by looking on adverse events, than on prosperity' (*History (EW VIII),* xxiv). Hobbes did not change his stand on this matter for the rest of his life – we find the very same conviction reiterated in the opening sentence of *Behemoth*:

> If in time, as in place, there were degrees of high and low, I verily believe that the highest time would be that which passed between the years of 1640 and 1660 (*Behemoth,* 1).

For Hobbes, from the height of 'the Devil's Mountain', i.e., from the perspective of civil war, one gains a better insight into the mechanics of politics than one would get from examining a nation at peace. The reason is that in times of war the passions of men can be observed at their most unrestrained and their effects derived most directly.

4.2.4 Thucydides' fate and Hobbes's faith in education

In his description of the civil war at Corcyra Thucydides suggests that the dramatic events that took place in that city are the outcome of the interplay of some key traits of human nature. For Thucydides the fate that befell Corcyra is a constant threat for every political association - a threat as permanent as human nature itself (*History (EW VIII)*, 348). He does not seem to believe that is possible to preserve future generations from disaster. Indeed, interpreters have highlighted numerous hints given by Thucydides in the *History* that history is bound to repeat itself and that no final salvation will ever be attainable.

In this respect, Hobbes's position, especially in his earlier works, is quite different from Thucydides'. In the *Epistle Dedicatory* that prefaces *De Cive*, Hobbes goes as far as suggesting to have found the formula for eternal peace:

> If the Morall Philosophers had discharged their duty ... [if] the nature of human Actions [were] distinctly knowne as the nature of *Quantity* in Geometricall Figures, the strength of *Avarice* and *Ambition* would presently faint and languish; And Mankinde should enjoy such an Immortall Peace, that ... there would hardly be left any pretence for war (*De Cive*, 25-26).

In *Leviathan* Hobbes points out that

> [t]hough nothing can be immortall, which mortals make; yet, if men had the use of reason they pretend to, their Common-wealths might be secured, at least, from perishing by internall diseases (*Leviathan*, 221).

In *A Dialogue between a Philosopher and a Student* (7-8), it is suggested that whereas one cannot expect 'constant peace' between nations, 'peace at home may be expected durable, when the common people shall be made to see the benefit they shall receive by their obedience'.

The difference between Hobbes and Thucydides is not that the latter has more faith than the former in people's natural ability and

Glory: Parallels and Intersections

willingness to learn from experience. On the contrary, in this respect Hobbes is very close to Thucydides. In *A Dialogue* we learn for example that 'there be very many ... whom ... the calamities of the civil wars have [not] thoroughly cured of their madness' (18). In the Dedication of *Behemoth* Hobbes suggests that the memory of people is very short and in the first dialogue asserts that

> people always have been, and always will be, ignorant of their duty to the public, as never meditating anything but their particular interest ... If you think the late miseries have made them wiser, that will quickly be forgot, and then we shall be no wiser than we were (*Behemoth*, 39).

The real difference between Hobbes and Thucydides is that Hobbes believes that people *can* be educated. In *Behemoth,* to one of the speakers who remarks that '[a]ll the states ... will be subject to these fits of rebellion, as long as the world lasteth', the other speaker tellingly replies: 'Like enough; and yet the fault ... may be easily mended, by mending the Universities' (71). What, of course, the Universities should teach, according to Hobbes, is his own theory of political obligation: '[t]he rules of *just* and *unjust* sufficiently demonstrated, and from principles evident to the meanest capacity, have not been wanting' (*ibid.,* 39).

To summarise the comparative analysis of the views of Thucydides and Hobbes on human nature, we can say that both agree
 (i) in singling out ambition as the strongest motivation of many individuals and nations;
 (ii) that outside the political state (i.e., in the Hobbesian state of nature and in Thucydides' account of international relations) the quest for power is contagious;
 (iii) that war affords a special insight into human affairs.

However, they disagree as to whether people can avoid future disasters, Thucydides' pessimistic view of fate contrasting sharply with Hobbes's optimistic faith in education.

The remarkable concordance between Hobbes's and Thucydides' thought is not limited to the psychological account of human nature examined in this chapter but extends, perhaps more importantly, to their analysis of the political effects of ambition – the subject-matter of the next chapter.

Chapter 5

Ambition: Paradoxes and Puzzles

Introduction

In his *Prose Life* Hobbes writes of his translation of Thucydides' *History*:

> Of all of the Greek historians, Thucydides was his source of particular delight. Gradually, in his own time, he translated the works of Thucydides into English. This work received considerable praise when it was published in 1628. In it the weaknesses and eventual failures of the Athenian democrats, together with those of their city state, were made clear (*Prose Life*, 246).

In his *Verse Life* Hobbes does not fail to mention his predilection for Thucydides' political vision:

> Homer and Virgil, Horace, Sophocles,
> Plautus, Euripides, Aristophanes,
> I understood, nay more; but of all these,
> There's none that pleas'd me like *Thucydides*.
> He says Democracy's a Foolish Thing,
> than a Republick Wiser is one King.
> This Author I taught *English*, that even he
> A Guide to Rhetoricians might be (*Verse Life*, 256).

In Chapter 4 I tried to show that in their *psychological analysis* of individual and collective motivation both Thucydides and Hobbes assign an equally prominent place to the desire of honour and dominion.

The present chapter has three main aims. Firstly, to show that Thucydides and Hobbes share also a very similar *political analysis* of the effects of ambition on civil associations. For both, uncontrolled ambition is a fundamental cause of civil war, which in turn is seen as spelling the end not just of a particular political order, but of society and civilisation itself.

Secondly, I shall trace a Thucydidean path that leads to the resolution of an apparent contradiction in the triad of *Elements of Law*, *De Cive*, and *Leviathan*. The final aim of the chapter is to highlight the substantial continuity that, in spite of some important differences to be examined in Chapter 7, runs through Hobbes's work in his analysis of the political implications of desire of power and glory. Not only in *Elements of Law, De Cive*, and *Leviathan*, but also in *Anti-White*, *Behemoth*, *Dialogue*, as well as occasionally in his Correspondence, Hobbes consistently and forcibly singled out ambition (tellingly defined in *De Homine* as desire of *political* power) as the ultimate motivation of individuals who pose a threat to the survival and stability of the political state.

5.1 The Political Consequences of Ambition

Thucydides identifies in ambition one of the origins of the sedition at Corcyra:

> The cause of all this [sedition] is *desire of rule*, out of *avarice* and *ambition*; and the zeal of contention from those two proceeding (*History (EW VIII)*, 350; emphasis in the original).

In the world described by Thucydides the universal consensus is that ambition and pride are the root causes of sedition. This view is voiced, for example, by people as different as the Syracusans and the Lacedæmonians. It also explains why the latter were prepared to shed their peace-loving and cautious nature and to resort to extremely brutal measures in order to defend their political institutions from the glory-seekers. Typical is the treatment that the Lacedæmonians meted out to the most ambitious among the Helotes (the underclass of quasi-slaves) so as to prevent them from destabilizing Sparta:

> [The Lacedæmonians] caused proclamation to be made, that as many of them [the Helotes], as claimed the estimation to have done the Lacedaemonians best service in their wars, should be made free; feeling them in this manner, and conceiving that, as they should every one out of pride deem himself worthy to be first made free, so they would soonest also rebel against them. And when they had thus preferred about two thousand, which also with crowns on their heads went in procession about the temples as to receive their

liberty, they not long after made them away: and no man knew how they perished (*History (EW VIII)*, 464-5).

Hobbes does not go as far as suggesting that troublesome glory-seekers ought to be 'disappeared', but warns the sovereign against the dangers created by ambitious people to the political order. When listing the internal causes that bring about the dissolution of governments (*De Cive*, Ch. XII; *Elements of Law*, 270; *Leviathan*, Ch. XXIX), Hobbes never fails to include ambition among the 'seditious attitudes of the mind'. This view is repeated throughout *Behemoth* and especially in the first dialogue on 'the seeds of the rebellion'.

Thucydides' diagnosis of the sedition of Corcyra is mirrored in Hobbes's analysis of the roots of civil war, in all his writings, from *Anti-White* to *Behemoth*, from *Elements of Law* and *De Cive* to *Leviathan*.

5.1.1 Ambition in Anti-White

In *Anti-White* Hobbes remarks that the reason why people 'wish for the governing of a country to be changed' is their 'envy of those placed above them in prudence and virtue' (*Anti-White*, 461). He points out that '[I]f not employed in the public service the ambitious are offended by reason of being passed over, as though insufficiently competent' and so they harbour seditious thoughts (*Anti-White*, 468); finally he claims that 'the sole cause of ... our land's present civil wars [is] that certain evil men who were not called to office thought that their own wisdom was less fairly valued than it deserved and advised the citizens to take up arms against the King' (*Anti-White,* 476).

5.1.2 Ambition in Behemoth

In *Behemoth* Hobbes laments that 'all this stubbornness and contumacy towards the King and his laws, is nothing but pride of heart and ambition, or else imposture' (*Behemoth*, 53). In the civil war 'the chief leaders were ambitious ministers and ambitious gentlemen' (23), while the common man was unaware of the 'ambitious plot ... to raise sedition against the state' (24). Few are spared the charge of being ambitious: the House of Commons (97), the bishops (95), orators (109), even the 'ancients' (94) are all castigated. Hobbes is vehement in condemning 'ambition which many times well natured men are subject to' (107). In the third and fourth Dialogues Hobbes again attacks 'those that by ambition were set upon the enterprise of changing the government' (115-6) and explains repeatedly in terms of

Ambition: Paradoxes and Puzzles 61

ambition not only Cromwell's behaviour (143, 179) but also that of other generals (198, 201). Regarding the Independents and the Presbyterians Hobbes notices that 'both the one and the other were resolved to destroy whatsoever should stand in the way to their ambition' (165). Hobbes's conclusion is that

> [F]rom the beginning of the rebellion, the method of ambition was constantly this: first to destroy, and then to consider what they should set up (*Anti-White*, 192).

5.1.3 Ambition in Elements of Law, De Cive, *and* Leviathan

In *De Cive* and *Leviathan* Hobbes suggests that it is not because of idealistic trust in popular wisdom, but because of their personal ambition that individuals tend to prefer democracy to monarchy (*Leviathan*, 172) in so far as they believe to have more chances to succeed and to have their views accepted and implemented. Hobbes argues that frustrated ambition and desire to excel one upon the other make this form of government more vulnerable and more prone to dissolution than monarchy:

> That men see not the reason to be alike in a Monarchy, and in a Popular Government, proceedeth from the ambition of some, that are kinder to the government of an Assembly, whereof they may hope to participate, than of Monarchy, which they despair to enjoy (*Leviathan*, 123).

Hobbes's view that a democratic government is likely to be preferred by the multitude because it provides greater opportunities for pursuing one's ambitions and his belief that for this very reason democracy is the most vulnerable form of government (*De Cive*, 143, 136, 188) are in line with the historical account provided by Thucydides.

Both in the *Elements of Law* and *De Cive* Hobbes links ambition to living 'at ease, without fear of want, or danger of violence' (*Elements of Law*, 169; *De Cive*, 153). In *Leviathan* Hobbes shows that whereas bees and ants 'are not offended by their fellowes' as long as they are at ease and their life is safe

> Man is then most troublesome, when he is most at ease: for then it is that he loves to shew his Wisdome, and controule the Actions of them that governe the Common-wealth (*Leviathan*, 120).

Very much unlike the mouthpiece of the bourgeoisie described by Macpherson, and following Aristotle instead, Hobbes is quite weary of very wealthy citizens.

Hobbes's observation that ambition can be found especially in men living in comfort and that 'in assemblies ... when they [the ambitious men] cannot have the honour to making good their own devices, they yet seek the honour to make the counsel of their adversaries to prove vain' (*Elements of Law*, 143) finds precise counterparts in the *History* especially in Alcibiades' political career.

For Hobbes the most dangerous 'doctrine' spread by the ambitious in order to attain political power is that the content of the civil laws can be put into question (*De Cive*, 146; 227, 230, 246; *Leviathan*, 223). He contends that this challenge to shared values and common laws can precipitate a political state into anarchy and he strongly warns the sovereign power against it. In the *History* we find an episode in Alcibiades' life which exemplifies the proneness of the ambitious to disregard common values. Thucydides reports that because of his ambition Alcibiades was deemed capable by his fellow citizens of the most disrespectful acts, such as the profanation of the 'Mercuries'. Tellingly, such behaviour, that disregarded common values and beliefs, was perceived as a challenge to the state itself:

> [the Athenians] took the fact [the disfigurement of the Mercuries] exceedingly to heart, as ominous to the expedition, and done withal conspiracy for *alteration of the state and dissolution of the democracy* (*History (EW* IX), 141, emphasis added).

In *De Cive* even more clearly than in *Elements of Law* Hobbes remarks that the sovereign can never remove ambition from human nature nor should he try to do so, as by steering men's actions in a socially beneficial direction 'by means of rewards and punishment' he can enjoy 'honour, riches and means whereby to delight the mind' and pursue its own glory *vis-à-vis* other states (*De Cive*,162-163).

The same task of directing human glory is given by Hobbes to the Leviathan, revealingly defined as 'the King of the Proud' (*Leviathan*, 221).

5.2 Civil War in Thucydides and Hobbes

As Thucydides and Hobbes agree that uncontrolled ambition can cause civil war, likewise they agree in maintaining that (in Hermocrates' words) 'nothing so much destroys a city as sedition'.

In his account of the *stasis* of Corcyra Thucydides shows that civil war does not just bring about the end of a specific form of political arrangement, but causes the disintegration of society as a whole. The list of institutions and customs that collapsed during the *stasis* in Corcyra includes the family ('the father slew his son', *History (EW VIII)*, 347), religion, piety (350), all social conventions and unwritten laws ('sincerity was laughed down', no oath was 'terrible enough' (351). Thucydides remarks that as an effect of civil war even 'the names and appellations of things' become matter of controversy. In his words, as translated by Hobbes

> The received value of names imposed for signification of things, was changed into arbitrary. For inconsiderate boldness, was counted true-hearted manliness: provident deliberation, a handsome fear: modesty, the cloak of cowardice: to be wise in every thing, to be lazy in every thing. A furious suddenness was reputed a point of valour (*History (EW VIII)*, 348).

It is interesting to note that this passage, and especially its opening sentence, are more in tune with Hobbes's own description of the arbitrariness in the field of language and signification in a state of anarchy than with Thucydides' original text.[1]

In *Behemoth*, Hobbes's own historical account of the civil war, he, too, registers the disagreement on the very meaning of words such as disobedience and patriotism: 'people were corrupted generally, and disobedient persons esteemed the best patriots' (*Behemoth*, 2).

In *A Dialogue between a Philosopher and a Student*, the speakers make the point that institutions like private property that do not exist in the state of nature, and hence owe their existence to the political state, are the first to collapse in a state of civil war: not only 'you cannot deny ... that law-makes were before that which you call *own*, or property of goods or land, distinguished by *meum, tuum, alienum*', but also 'when our laws were silenced by civil war, there was not a man that of any goods could say assuredly they were his own' (*Dialogue*, 29).

As in Corcyra during the sedition crimes of all sorts were

committed, so in the years between 1640 and 1660 'all crimes may be alleged as proceeding from ... the silence of the law occasioned by the civil war' (*Dialogue*, 146).

Thucydides suggests that all those aspects of social life that might appear to be independent of political arrangements (the signification of language, conventions, religion, family, etc.) in fact owe their existence to the latter. Civil war in this view is not merely a disease that society can cure and recover from – it spells the disintegration of society itself.

Many interpreters have claimed that Thucydides' account of the sedition in Corcyra, even more than his description of either ancient Greece or of the relationships between cities, provides the most striking similarities with the Hobbesian state of nature. I have some reservations in endorsing this view.

On the one hand, it is true indeed that like in Corcyra so in the Hobbesian state of nature there are no common values, no agreement 'of what is to be called right, what good, what virtue, what much, what little, what meum and tuum, what a pound, what a quart, &c.' (*Elements of Law*, 188, 23, 88; see also *De Cive*, 45, 48, 100-1, 246; *Leviathan*, 31).

On the other hand, in the case of civil war (as described by Thucydides in the *History* and by Hobbes in *Behemoth*) the collapse of all institutions and common values is a *consequence* of the collapse of the established political order. On the contrary, in the case of the state of nature, the disagreement on language and common measures and values is a *cause* of the conflict. This is hardly a minor difference. In my view, Thucydides' account of the events in Corcyra is closer to Hobbes's narration in *Behemoth* than to any of his descriptions of the state of nature in *Elements of Law, De Cive*, and *Leviathan*.

The obvious implication of Thucydides and Hobbes's shared view that civil war spells the disintegration of every aspect of civil associations is that there can be no civilized life outside the state. For Hobbes however bad any form of government may be, it is still preferable to no government at all, in so far as it implies some sort of society. Similarly, in the *History* we find the view that bad laws are better than anarchy. Speaking to his fellow citizens, Creon states very forcibly that 'a city with the worse laws, if immovable, is better than one with good laws, when they be not binding' (*History (EW VIII)*, 300). Although in general it is misguided to attribute any of any of Creon's views to Thucydides (who had strong personal reasons for

Ambition: Paradoxes and Puzzles

hating Creon) it seems to me that in this case, taking into account the overall analysis of the *stasis* of Corcyra, it is quite possible that Thucydides himself shared with Creon (and Hobbes) the belief that anarchy is worse than the worst government.

5.3 The Implications of Private and Public Money

In his diagnosis of the causes of sedition, quoted above, Thucydides mentions avarice $\pi\lambda\varepsilon o\nu\varepsilon\xi i\alpha$ as the human passion which, besides ambition, can cause *stasis*.

In his three descriptions of the state of nature in *Elements of Law, De Cive*, and *Leviathan* Hobbes, too, notices that one of the causes of conflict is desire of 'gain' and in *Behemoth* the common people are said to be motivated mainly by desire of gain:

> there were very few of the common people that cared much for either of the causes; but would have taken any side for pay or plunder (*Behemoth*, 2).

In his three political works, for the sake of peace, a part from stipulating a law of nature that forbids pride, Hobbes also recommends a law regarding distributive justice that explicitly forbids what 'the Greeks call $\pi\lambda\varepsilon o\nu\varepsilon\xi i\alpha$ which is commonly rendered covetousness.' (*Elements of Law*, 89; see also *Leviathan*, 142; *De Cive*, 69)

In the *History*, whereas excessive desire and possession of wealth by private individuals are described as destabilising factors for society, substantial public wealth is viewed on the contrary as a fundamental pillar of internal stability and as the precondition for success in international relations.

The belief that the honour of victory in wars usually goes to the richest contender is expressed in various key speeches and is supported by Thucydides' own account of the dynamics of the Peloponnesian war. In the introductory pages Thucydides explains that the Trojans initially succeeded in holding out against the Greeks 'not so much [for the latter's] want of men, as of wealth' (*History (EW VIII)*, 13). In the same spirit, Pericles reckons the Peloponnesians' depleted economic resources to be the foremost of their weaknesses (147) and remarks that 'the victory in war consist[s] wholly in counsel and store of money', (168). The idea that 'revenue' is the 'only strength against the enemy' is reiterated by Diodotus (313), while Hermocrates remarks that 'by the most gold and silver ... the wars and all things else are the best expedited' (*History (EW IX)*, 150). Archidamus epitomises aptly the view of all speakers in the *History* with his observation that 'war is not so much war of arms as war of money' (88).

The view in the *History* that excessive money in private hands is destabilizing for society, whereas public wealth is crucially important to internal stability and to successful foreign policies is echoed by Hobbes in *Behemoth*. In this work Hobbes repeatedly points out the crucial relevance of taxes, money, revenues (*Behemoth*, 28) for having a strong army and keeping peace at home or winning wars (32); A healthy treasure is according to Hobbes a necessary if not sufficient condition for a stable political order: 'when they [filling the coffers without much noise of the people and early severity] shall be jointly in one King they will easily cure the commonwealth ... but this without the former cannot be exercised (57). In the same spirit, in *A Dialogue between a Philosopher and a Student*, the Philosopher asks:

> How shall I be defended from the domineering of proud and insolent strangers ... that scorn us, that seek to make us slaves, or how shall I avoid the destruction that may arise from ... civil war ... unless the King has ready money, upon all occasions, to arm and pay as many soldiers, as for the present defence, or the peace of the people, shall be necessary? (*Dialogue*, 13).

5.4 Thucydides' Paradox of Ambition and Hobbes's Solution

The narration of the sedition of Corcyra suggests that *uncontrolled ambition* leads people to sedition, which in turn spells the end not only of a particular political order, but of society and civilization itself.

For Thucydides, however, ambition is the source not only of civil war. In the *History* the desire to excel is also the passion that led the Athenians to surpass all others and helped them reach the pinnacle of civilisation. In perfect analogy, in the *Elements of Law* the desire of glory and honour is also described by Hobbes as the spur that makes people perform to their maximum potential and induces them to develop those characteristics that are specifically human, from curiosity to speech and deductive thought (*Elements of Law*, 13-14; see *supra* Chapter 3).

Thucydides' argument that ambition on the one hand can cause *stasis* (as in Corcyra), but on the other can drive primitive people (like the forefathers of the Athenians) to 'grow civil' and to pass in a more tender kind of life (*History (EW VIII)*, 6), raises implicitly the following dilemma: under what conditions is ambition a beneficial passion that can foster civilisation and when does it become instead the very cause of political dissolution?

Hobbes's argument in the three main political works not only replicates this dilemma, but also offers a solution to it. Hobbes identifies in a strong political state the artificial instrument whereby individuals can channel and direct their natural ambition to the benefit of the 'commodious living' of all, by developing industry, navigation, arts, cultivation of land, science, technology, trade, etc.

In the political state, the establishment and credible enforcement of civil laws:
1. ensure the protection of every citizen's life, thereby excluding from the forms of competition the one field (endangering each other physical integrity) in which all individuals are equal; and
2. by defining common standards of *meum* and *tuum*, of right and wrong, of good and bad, etc., open up new fields of comparison between people, ranging from property to arts, from games to public morality (*Elements of Law*, 188-189; see also *De Cive*, 95, 102; *Leviathan*, 28-29, 41, 201).

Even though Hobbes does not dwell on the implications of the introduction of private property, it can be easily seen that property rights open up new field of competition for glory-seekers. On the one hand, private property poses a limit to competition in so far as appropriation via theft becomes an unacceptable mechanism for the transfer of wealth. On the other hand, unlike in the state of nature where something I make is mine only as long as I manage to keep it, property rights ensure that individuals can engage in *industry* and compete on producing things. Unlike competition on existing things, that is highly conflictual – so much so that it leads to competition for survival – competition through industry has a socially stabilising effect. Thanks to the production of goods, society becomes a non-zero-sum-game in the sense that gains by some do not necessarily imply corresponding losses by others, for the dimensions of wealth are no longer fixed but have become augmentable.

Moreover, the introduction of private property in the Hobbesian world has a freeing effect on people who attach little value to 'riches' (the minority to be examined in Chapter 7), in so far as the existence of exclusive property rights enables individuals to engage in field other than wealth accumulation. People interested in 'arts upon words', in science, in 'arts of public use' can follow their inclinations because their means of survival are no longer in danger. Whereas the unrestricted competition of the state of nature (which, because of its very lack of restrictions, collapses to competition on a single level, i.e., competition for survival) allows at most the emergence of individuals whose only relevant characteristic is to be alive, the regulated competition within the political state is multi-dimensional – it takes place at all levels and in all spheres (except survival) thus allowing the emergence of different and sophisticated personalities.

This beneficial effect of the introduction of private property in the Hobbesian world may seems to lend support to Macpherson's thesis that Hobbes, whether consciously or not, was voicing the views and the interests of the rising bourgeoisie. There is, however, one fundamental respect which crucially differentiates Hobbes from any bourgeois apologist: *for Hobbes citizens enjoy property rights against each other, but not against the state*. The citizens' private property is described as 'conditional', not as 'absolute'. It is explained that absolute property 'excludes the right of all others ... and in a kingdom, no man can have it but the king'; conditional property, instead 'excludes the right of all other subjects ... but not the right of the sovereign, when the common good of the people shall require the use thereof' (*Dialogue*, 154).

In view of this *crucial anti-liberal proviso* to the right to private property, that Hobbes repeats throughout his works, it is particularly unfortunate that many political economists have followed the lead by Brennan and Buchanan[2] and have (mis-) named a constitution that binds the government as the 'Leviathan model of government'.[3]

Indeed in *A Dialogue between a Philosopher and a Student*, to the student's enquiry whether 'you deny all property to the subjects', the Philosopher replies laconically but categorically: 'I do so' (148).

The argument deployed by Hobbes to deny citizens property rights against the state can be described as proceeding in four steps:
1. as in the state of nature individuals are unsuccessful in their attempt to safeguard their safety, they enter the social contract with the aim of having their safety protected by a stronger agency, namely the state;
2. in order to protect people's safety both at home and against external enemies, the state needs strong military and security forces, which in turn are provided for by 'healthy revenues';
3. to put limits to the state's power to tax means constraining its

ability to defend public safety; and limited power would imply that on some occasions the state might be inadequate in safeguarding its citizens;
4. the very possibility that the state might be unable to protect its subjects' lives would imply inevitably a return to the state of nature where at least individuals know that they can fight for their own survival unencumbered by any constraints.

In conclusion, for Hobbes either individuals bestow absolute power to the state – and therefore unlimited power of taxation – in order to have their lives protected or they should retain their right to all things. According to Hobbes, any other solution would not attach an overriding value to self-preservation and thus would be against reason.

5.5 Hobbes's Puzzle

To my mind one of the most striking and most puzzling similarities between the *Elements of Law*, *De Cive*, and *Leviathan* (in both the English and the Latin versions) is that in all these works Hobbes puts forward two apparently conflicting claims, namely:

Claim (i): glory *alone* is the origin of competition, sedition, and war; and

Claim (ii): concern for self-preservation, scarce resources, as well as glory, are *all* causes of conflict in the state of nature. Contrary to the implicit assumption in the literature that this apparent inconsistency is best ignored, here I shall put forward a possible solution to this puzzle, resorting once more to Thucydides' *History*.

5.5.1 Beehives and behaviour

The first claim, i.e., that glory is the unequivocal source of human discord is made in the concluding chapter of the first part of *Elements of Law*, repeated almost *verbatim* in Chapter 5 of *De Cive*, in the opening chapter of Book II of the English version of *Leviathan* and in Chapter XVII (*De Civitate*) of the Latin version of *Leviathan*.

Here Hobbes addresses the problem 'why concord remaineth in a multitude of some irrational creatures [like bees], and not of men' (*Elements of Law*, 102; *De Cive*, 87; *Leviathan*, 119; *Leviathan* (Latin version), 129-130).

In all four places glory is viewed unambiguously as the sole source of competition, sedition and war. In the passage in the *Elements of Law* all terms used by Hobbes (bar one) are glory-related: the difference between men and bees is put down to the fact that men seek 'precedence', 'honour', 'acknowledgement of one's another wisdom', 'dominion', 'superiority', and that they think 'to be wiser than the rest', and to know better than others what is 'right and wrong'.[4]

In the parallel passage in *De Cive*, Hobbes mentions again the desire of possessions as a cause of conflict, but derives this desire from the passion for glory and says that 'man scarce esteems any thing good which has not somewhat of eminence in the enjoiment, more than that which others doe possesse' (*De Cive*, 87). All the other items in the list given by Hobbes in *De Cive* to explain the difference in behaviour between bees and men, namely, 'honour', preferment', 'eminence' belief in one's own superior wisdom, contention for 'places of authority', are again glory-related.

In *Leviathan* even more forcibly than in earlier works, all causes of conflict listed by Hobbes are inspired by glory: 'honour and dignity', the joy of comparing oneself with others, the tendency to 'relish nothing but what is eminent', the opinion of being 'wiser', 'abler', 'better' than the rest, the strife 'to reform and innovate', the propensity to misuse language as to 'represent to others that which is good, in the likeness of evil; and evil in the likeness of good', man's 'love ... to shew his wisdom and control the actions of them that govern the commonwealth' (*Leviathan*, 119-20). Similarly, in the Latin version of *Leviathan* we are told that:

> homines inter se de honoribus et dignitate perpetuo contendunt ... Homini ... in bonis propriis nihil tam jucundum est, quam quod alienis sunt majora (*De Civitate*, 129-30).

In *Leviathan* the concept of private wealth mentioned in the *Elements of Law* as separate cause of conflict is dropped altogether. In these parallel passages of the *Elements of Law, De Cive and Leviathan* Hobbes does not mention either fear for one's self-preservation, or scarce resources as possible origins of competition and war. On the contrary, Hobbes goes as far as suggesting that if the sole concern of men were their survival they would cooperate like bees and live peacefully without the need for artificial covenants and bonds. In *De Cive* Hobbes shows himself to be well aware that his whole argument is conditional on resources *not* being insufficient to sustain the entire population. In the opening Epistle to the Reader he warns us that he can provide us with a recipe for

Immortal Peace ... unless it were for habitation, on supposition that the Earth should grow too narrow for her (*De Cive*, 25).

And when all the world is overcharged with inhabitants, then the last remedy of all is war; which provideth for every man, by victory, or death (*Leviathan*, 335).

5.5.2 The three greatest things

Whereas in the long passages of *Elements of Law*, *De Cive* and *Leviathan* cited above Hobbes claims that glory *alone* is the cause of human discord, in Chapter 14 of *Elements of Law*, Chapter I of *De Cive* and Chapter XIII of *Leviathan* war is explained as the *joint* outcome of fear of violent death and of concern for the scarcity of resources, as well as of desire of superiority:

> in the nature of man, we find three principall causes of quarrell. First, Competition; Secondly, Diffidence; Thirdly, Glory. The first, maketh men invade for Gain; the second, for Safety; and the third, for Reputation (*Leviathan*, 88).

I myself am among those Hobbes's readers[5] who have been impressed by the striking similarity between the three causes of quarrel mentioned by Hobbes in the above passage and the three greatest motivations listed by the Athenian ambassadors when, in the early stages of the Peloponnesian war, they justify their expansionistic policy in their oration to the Corinthians:

> we were forced to advance our dominion to what it is, out of the nature of the thing itself; as chiefly for fear, next for honour, and lastly for profit (*History (EW VIII)*, 81).

The Athenians attribute these three greatest motivations to all human beings:

> though overcome by three the greatest things, honour, fear, and profit, ... we have therein done nothing to be wondered at nor beside the manner of men (*History (EW VIII)*, 82).

Hobbes's concepts of gain, fear for safety, and reputation remind us respectively of Thucydides' ωφελία,[6] δεός and φοβός, and τιμή. The common practice among Hobbesian interpreters has been to take seriously Hobbes's remarks quoted in this section and to disregard altogether Hobbes's reflections on bees and ants examined in section

5.5.1. As a result, in the literature vain glory, fear, and scarce resources have been viewed as *concurrent* causes of conflict in the state of nature.

5.5.3 Proximate and ultimate causes of conflict

In my view it is inconceivable that in all versions of his political theory Hobbes failed to notice that he was putting forward apparently conflicting claims regarding the cause of competition and war.

In the Correspondence, du Verdus challenges Hobbes on the behaviour of ants and bees. In Letter 100 he writes to Hobbes:

> Who can be sure that ants and bees ... do not have ...honours and dignities? For who knows whether there are not some bees which in preference to others stand closer to the person of the king? ... Surely there are some parts of the hive which are more pleasant than others' (*Correspondence I*, 364).

Whereas elsewhere Hobbes accepted du Verdus' criticisms and included them in the Latin version of *Leviathan* of 1668, on this topic he did not revise his contention that desire of superiority is the ultimate reason why people cannot live naturally as peacefully as *apes et formicae*.

It is therefore important to reconstruct an argument that can accommodate consistently both the claim that glory *alone* is the cause of sedition (see *supra*, Claim (i), Section 5.5.1) and the claim that fear of death, scarce resources, and desire of superiority are *joint* causes of conflict in the state of nature (Claim (ii), see section 5.5.2). One such argument can be found by examining Thucydides' diagnosis of the Peloponnesian war. According to Thucydides it was 'the growth of the Athenian power; which putting the Lacedaemonian into fear necessitated the war' (*History (EW VIII)*, 27).

Here Thucydides is drawing a distinction between *proximate* (Lacedaemonian fear) and *ultimate* (Athenian ambition) causes of war. If the same distinction is applied to Hobbes's state of nature and thus diffidence, fear of death, and concern for the scarcity of resources are seen as the proximate causes of war under natural conditions, with glory remaining its ultimate cause, the apparent contradiction between the passages cited above disappears.

Admittedly, my tentative solution to the puzzle is speculative. However, in view of Hobbes's meditations on the *History*, and Thucydides' pervasive influence on Hobbes's thought,[7] it does not seem too far-fetched to suggest that Hobbes followed Thucydides in assigning a different status to glory and fear in the state of nature, with the latter being the proximate cause of conflict and the former its ultimate cause.

As we saw above, in *Behemoth* Hobbes mentions neither self-preservation nor scarce resources as causes of the Civil War. On the contrary he remarks that the people who brought about the war (the clergy, the lawyers, the people of the Universities) were motivated primarily by private ambition (see, for example, *Behemoth*, 90, 115-116) and sacrificed the common good for their personal or sectarian advancement, manipulating the ignorant minds of the common man to that end. Similarly in the Correspondence Hobbes points to 'disputes for precedence' as 'the causes of civil wars' (*Correspondence I*, 120).

To summarise, in this chapter I have tried to show, *contra* McNeilly, that the *role* of glory is the same in all Hobbes's works. The desire for glory and superiority is a fundamental cause of discord in the state of nature and the primary source of dissolution of political states, whether examined theoretically (*Elements of Law, De Cive, Leviathan*) or historically (*Behemoth, Dialogue, Correspondence*, and *Anti-White*). And this in spite of the fact that in the transition from earlier to later writings the status of glory in Hobbes's psychology of man undergoes a major change. It is the task of Chapter 7 to highlight this transformation, but first in the next chapter I shall examine an additional affinity between Hobbes's and Thucydides' thought, namely, the political implications of two 'further human dispositions', i.e., fear and hope.

Chapter 6

The Dilemma of Fear and Hope

Introduction

The portrait that can be pieced together from the Correspondence shows Hobbes as a man of remarkable intellectual courage, but quite timorous as far as physical danger is concerned.

Hobbes shows no hesitation in defending his proof of the squaring of the circle against the best mathematical minds of his times, even at the risk of endangering his reputation. On the other hand, when what was at stake was not his reputation, but his physical integrity, Hobbes was totally risk-averse. He not only went into exile 'fearing for his safety' (*Prose Life*, 247) when he perceived as dangerous his staying in England, but he cancelled and postponed many a trip abroad, whenever he felt that the passage was unsafe. The early letters of his surviving correspondence are peppered with remarks on the restrictions on his freedom of travel imposed by the wars and plagues of his times.

His greatest fear was physical violence. Whereas he shows despise for those who are afraid of debate, or disagreement, or disapproval, and defines them as weak, he shows respect for those who fear physical injury, seeing this as sign of rationality.

According to Hobbes, in fact, reason teaches abhorrence of pain and of violent death. This assumptions is not as innocuous as Hobbes thought – Leibniz, for example, recognised that Hobbes was asking much of his readers in saying that reason abhors death.

Hobbes was aware of his physical timidity and with self-irony in his *Verse Life* says that

> And hereupon it was my Mother Dear
> Did bring forth Twins at once, both Me, and Fear (*Verse Life*, 254).

As many Hobbesian scholars have pointed out, the passion of fear threads a constant theme in all Hobbes's political works and plays a fundamental part in his theory. The aim of this chapter is to try to outline the significance and relevance of fear and hope in Hobbes's

The Dilemma of Fear and Hope

works and to suggest that a fresh insight into this much-examined area can be gained by comparing Hobbes's views to Thucydides'.

As I have already pointed out in previous chapters, Hobbes has a special affinity with and respect for Thucydides,[1] whose extreme pessimism Hobbes might be expected to share. However, by analysing Thucydides' bleak views on the relationship between fear and hope (which Hobbes renders so vividly in his translation of the *History*), in this chapter I shall show that Hobbes did not endorse unreservedly such pessimism. The reason, I shall suggest, is not that Hobbes had more faith than Thucydides in human nature, but rather that he, as political theorist, had more trust than Thucydides, the historian, in the state's ability to circumscribe fear and ambition and channel them into beneficial pursuits.

In more detail, the aim of this chapter is to show that

(i) whereas there is a substantial convergence between Thucydides' and Hobbes's *characterisation* of fear and of its *role* in political associations,

(ii) Hobbes distances himself from Thucydides as to the *effectiveness* of fear to control the human hope to act as one pleases with impunity.

Hobbes shares with Thucydides the view that whilst fear is the binding element of political associations, ambition to rule is the dangerous solvent that may cause them to come apart and thus destroy civilisation.

6.1 Characterisation of Fear

Thucydides and Hobbes provide a remarkably similar characterisation of fear, both viewing it as deriving from *uncertainty*, resulting in *anticipation*, and affecting human judgement in a either *beneficial or detrimental* way depending on its time-horizon.

In Thucydides' *History* fear is not only one of the key concepts that explain the causes and the dynamics of the Peloponnesian war, but also the passion that permeated all ancient Greece before it grew 'civil'. In his description of ancient Greece Thucydides links fear to uncertainty. He writes:

> whilst traffic was not, nor mutual intercourse but with fear, neither by sea nor land; and every man so husbanded the ground as but barely to live upon it, without any stock of

riches, and planted nothing; (because it was uncertain when another should invade them and carry all away, especially not having the defence of walls); but made account to be masters, in any place, of such necessary sustenance as might serve them from day to day (*History (EW VIII)*, 2).

As argued by Klosko and Rice[2] both the main idea and the specific details of the above quotation remind one of a very well-known passage of *Leviathan*:

In such condition, there is no place for industry; because the fruit thereof is uncertain: and consequently no Culture of the Earth; no navigation, nor use of the commodities that may be imported by sea; no commodious building; ... and which is worst of all continual fear (*Leviathan*, 113).

Like Thucydides, Hobbes, too, establishes a clear connection between fear and uncertainty. Under conditions of complete uncertainty, each individual is deprived of his intrinsically human ability and need to plan his own future and is compelled instead to live in, and for, the present. Only when uncertainty is limited and thus fear is circumscribed, i.e., within the framework of social conventions created in the civil state, are the Athenians (first among all Greeks) able to progress to 'a more tender way of life' (*History (EW VIII)*, 6) and similarly are the Hobbesian people able to live a worthwhile life.

In Thucydides' narration the link between fear and uncertainty is not confined to the description of the people who lived in the murderous ancient world but applies to, and indeed explains, the relationships between cities after they have grown 'civil'. In describing the causes of the war Thucydides stresses the point that it had been fear generated by uncertainty about the intentions of a strong Athens what had driven weaker cities to unite against her and anticipate her attack. Thus Alcibiades:

when one is grown mightier than the rest, men use not only to defend themselves against him when he shall invade, but to anticipate him, that he invade not at all (*History (EW IX)*, 133-4).

Uncertainty about the intention of others, and fear that they may attack are in Thucydides' argument the foundations of his concept of anticipation and first strike. Thus in the *History* while uncertainty can be seen as the main cause of fear, anticipation is its most important outcome. On this point, too, Hobbes's argument is similar to

Thucydides'. In *Leviathan* he develops an argument in which anticipation is construed as the result of diffidence, which in turn is derived from fear and uncertainty. We read:

> And from this diffidence of one another, there is no way for any man to secure himself, so reasonable as anticipation (*Leviathan*, 111).
>
> fear of oppression disposeth a man to anticipate (*History, (EW IX)*, 88).

The logic of the argument that starts from fear and uncertainty and ends with anticipation and pre-emptive strike is essentially the same in both Hobbes and Thucydides.

In addition to their shared views on the connection between fear, uncertainty, and anticipation, Thucydides' and Hobbes's arguments contain another conspicuous affinity: they both ascribe to fear either a positive or a negative effect on human deliberation, depending on its time-dimension.

In Thucydides' *History*, the fear felt by the individual towards future enterprises is a positive passion, in the sense that it engenders beneficial effects – it alerts the mind to the problems ahead and drives people to deliberate prudently and wisely. Thus we find the generals of different cities urging their troops not to undervalue either the enemy or the circumstances, but to prepare themselves to face great dangers, since this is the only way to prepare rationally for victory.

Conversely, fear as a passion that dominates the individual in the present plays a negative and destructive role in Thucydides' narration. Indeed, as soon as the hostilities have commenced, soldiers are urged to attack without fear, since the key to victory lies in their courage. Fear in the present brings people to defeat, it makes them overestimate the difficulties and overvalue the enemy, it leads to rushed and irrational decision-making. Hermocrates speaks thus to the Syracusans:

> and every man to remember, that though to show contempt of the enemy be best in the heat of fight, yet those preparations are the surest, that are made with fear and opinion of danger (*History (EW IX)*, 152).

And Archidamus says to the Lacedaemonians:

> though the soldiers ought always to have bold hearts, yet for action they ought to make their preparations as if they were afraid (*History (EW VIII)*, 165).

Finley[3] numbers this dual aspect of fear among the unifying ideas of the whole *History*. In his 'Of the Life and History of Thucydides' that precedes his translation of the *History*, Hobbes echoes the view that fear has either a positive or negative effect depending on its temporal dimension and says that 'fear ... for the most part adviseth well, though it execute not so' (*History (EW VIII)*, xvi).

In his later political works Hobbes elaborates a fully developed conception of fear that encompasses the Thucydidean view on the ambiguous effects of that passion on human behaviour, depending on whether it inspires deliberations regarding the future or the present. In *Leviathan* fear in the present or 'sudden fear' is sometimes called by Hobbes 'terror' and is a negative passion. Conversely, fear of future dangers is the first passion mentioned by Hobbes as responsible for making people understand the necessity to escape from the state of nature and thus decide to create a political state (see *Leviathan*, 116).

6.2 The Role of Fear

So far I have shown that Hobbes and Thucydides' arguments on fear are in agreement in so far as they both (i) derive fear from uncertainty, (ii) point to anticipation and first strike as the natural outcome of fear, and (iii) establish a relationship between fear and deliberation. Both arguments share a further point, namely, (iv) they single out fear as the cornerstone of political order.

The role played by fear in Thucydides' *History* can be appreciated in all its implications by examining in some detail his account of the plague that had gripped Athens since the second year of the war. In a narration that has become deservedly a classic, Thucydides highlights the terrifying effects brought about by the generalised awareness of impending death. Such predicament frees totally individuals from any fear of either gods or men and precipitates a social organisation into a state of complete social chaos. When the natural restraint provided by fear is removed, the fundamental binding element of social order is lost and with it all laws, conventions, customs, and rules simply crumble away. In Thucydides' words, powerfully rendered by Hobbes:

> Neither the fear of the gods, nor laws of men, awed any man: not the former, because they concluded it was alike to worship or not worship, from seeing that alike they all perished: nor the latter, because no man expected that lives

would last till he received punishment of his crimes by judgment. But they thought, there was now over their heads some far greater judgment decreed against them; before which fell, they thought to enjoy some little part of their lives (*History (EW VIII)*, 208-9).

All supplications to the gods, and enquiries to oracles, and whatsoever other means they used of that kind, proved all unprofitable; insomuch as subdued with the greatness of the evil, they gave them all over (*History (EW VIII)*, 202).

By establishing the equation between lack of fear and social chaos Thucydides corroborates a remark made by Pericles in his funeral oration when he says: 'we do not break the laws especially because of fear'.

In a similar vain in his political writings Hobbes stresses the paramount importance of fear. In *De Cive* he points to fear not only as the origin of societies but also as the basis of 'lasting Societies' (*De Cive*, 44), the unrenounceable condition of social stability. In all his political works Hobbes stresses repeatedly the idea that 'there is in every man a certain high degree of fear' (*De Cive*, 58): his insistence that fear is a constituent part of our psychology is not to be taken as a merely incidental reference, but rather as underlying the fact that the assumption of fear is a fundamental proviso of his whole political construct.

Indeed it could be argued that not only Hobbes, but most political philosophers in the Western tradition would have no advice to offer that would be relevant to a world without fear, such as the limit-case of the plague of Athens. The difference is that Hobbes seems more aware than most writers both of the crucial function of fear in political associations and of the validity of his whole political theory being dependent on the assumption of fear-inspired behaviour.

In the *History* the Mytilenaians argue that 'equality of fear is the only band of faith in leagues' (*History (EW VIII)*, 278) and that pacts are kept 'more for fear than for love' (*ibid.*, 279). Hobbes puts forward a similar view and says that 'if all fear were removed men would much more greedily be carried by Nature to obtain Dominion, than to gain Society' (*De Cive*, 44); he is never tired to remark that 'mutuall fear', 'fear of mutual slaughter' (*De Cive*, 58; see also 50, 185), such as the fear between equals, is the basis of lasting societies.

6.3 The Effectiveness of Fear

In the *History* Pericles is reported to have said in his funeral oration that, apart from fear, 'inner shame' is also a valid deterrent from acting unjustly. This view, however, finds only partial support in Thucydides' account of the plague. Thucydides tells us that during the epidemic there were indeed individuals who 'out of shame ... would not spare themselves, but went in unto their friends' but stresses that they were only the minority of the 'honestest men' (*History, EW VIII*, 206).

In *Leviathan* Hobbes, too, mentions that there are two deterrents that prevent people from reneging on their contracts, namely 'fear' of the consequences of breaking their word and a sense of 'glory or pride' in keeping them. However, Hobbes shares Thucydides' pessimism in that he notices that 'this later is a generosity too rarely found to be presumed on' and concludes that 'the passion to be reckoned upon is fear' (*Leviathan*, 99). Hobbes points out that 'of all passions, that which inclineth men least to break the laws is fear' (*Leviathan*, 206). He remarks that fear 'is the onely thing, (when there is apparence of profit or pleasure by breaking the lawes,) that makes men keep them' (*ibid.*).

In Thucydides and Hobbes's characterisation of human nature people have in themselves not only the possibility to create a stable political order – by turning to their advantage their natural fear – but also the potential source of its destruction. As I argued in Chapter 5, for both Hobbes and Thucydides there are two human passions that, if allowed to over-ride fear, can undermine social and political associations: ambition to rule and covetousness. Hobbes's political construct can be interpreted as the theoretical underpinnings for Thucydides' powerful insight that whilst fear is the glue of political associations, ambition to rule is the dangerous heat that may cause it to melt and thus destroy civilisation.

On the *effectiveness* of fear to keep ambition and covetousness under control Hobbes distances himself from Thucydides. Here, in my view, is the limit of Hobbes's pessimism *vis-à-vis* Thucydides'.

In the *History* Thucydides suggests that men are guided in life more by hope of success than by fear of failure and that in this intrinsic optimism of human nature in disregarding difficulties sometimes leads men to ruin. In Book III of the *History*, for example, it is argued by Diodotus that capital punishment cannot work as a deterrent because the hope of people to achieve what they want without being caught is usually stronger than their fear to be apprehended, found guilty, and punished:

> death hath been in states ordained for a punishment of many offences ... yet encouraged by hope, men hazard themselves ... Men have gone over all degrees of punishment, augmenting them still ... but hope and desire ... this contriving the enterprise, that suggesting the success are the cause of most crimes that are committed (*History (EW VIII)*, 311-2).

Hobbes accepts the view that risky enterprises and crimes are inspired by hope of success. In *De Cive* in his analysis of the causes of the dissolution of political associations, Hobbes points to 'hope' of success as a passion 'to be numbered among seditious inclinations' (*De Cive*, 153). In *Leviathan*, too, he points to 'vainglory or ... hope of escaping punishment ... hope of not being observed' (*Leviathan*, 283) as the crucial disposition of mind that inclines to crime. In his description of the state of nature, 'equality of hope in the attaining of their end' (*Leviathan*, 87) is said to drive men to 'endeavour to destroy, or subdue one another', whereas fear of death is described as the main passion that inclines men to peace and to enter the social contract.

On the whole, Hobbes generally rejects the view (voiced in the *History* by Diodotus but arguably held also by Thucydides himself) that as a rule, hope of success prevails on fear of failure in determining behaviour. In Hobbes's view, fear is stronger in men than ungrounded hope of success which he calls sometimes vain glory (*Leviathan*, 311-2). In other words, although Hobbes accepts that 'the actions of men proceed from the will, and the will from hope and fear' (*De Cive*, 85), yet he maintains that fear is stronger than hope (*De Cive*, 44, 50, 185). For Hobbes, by means of effective policing and punishment, the sovereign power can ensure that individuals behaviour in the desired way: 'In vain is that law which may be broken without punishment' (*De Cive*, 173).

6.4 Thucydides' Dilemma of Fear

Thucydides' twin descriptions of ancient Greece and of the plague in Athens implicitly raise the following dilemma: given that a world where fear is the overwhelming passion (as in ancient Greece) is as undesirable and chaotic as a world without fear altogether (such as Athens during the plague), how is fear to be channelled so as to result in a stable social order?

In his political works Hobbes provides a solution to the dilemma of fear. He singles out in a strong political state the instrument whereby uncertainty can be controlled, thus removing a major source of fear. In fact, within a strong political state, people can form firm expectations on the behaviour of others, for fear of punishment channels people's actions into definite and stable patterns, thus rendering individuals' behaviour predictable. As a result, both anticipation and rushed deliberation are no longer inevitable. Through the artifice of the political state people are able to circumscribe (uncertainty-induced) fear by means of fear itself (in the form of fear of punishment). The political state envisaged by Hobbes can remove the uncertainty (and thus the fear) generated by the lack of conventions and rules (as in the state of nature) or caused by their unreliability (as under a weak political arrangement).

It can be safely assumed that Thucydides believed that neither his dilemma of ambition (examined above, see Chapter 5) nor his dilemma of fear could ever be solved. He doubted that the mere understanding of the function of fear and ambition in political associations were sufficient to preserve future generations from war and the dissolution of society. Indeed, in the *History* one can find numerous hints of his belief that history is bound to repeat itself and that no final salvation will ever be attainable. In this respect, Hobbes's position is diametrically opposed to Thucydides'. In fact, Hobbes's pessimism does not extend either to the ability of the political philosopher to decipher human interactions or to the ability of mankind to heed his message. In the Epistle Dedicatory that prefaces *De Cive*, Hobbes goes as far as suggesting to have found the formula for eternal peace:

> If the Morall Philosophers had discharged their duty [if] the nature of human actions [were] distinctly knowne the strength of Avarice and Ambition would presently faint and languish; And Mankinde should enjoy such an Immortall Peace, that there would hardly be left any pretence for war (*De Cive*, 25-6).[4]

Thus, despite the striking similarities in their diagnosis of the ultimate causes of the dissolution of society and of the necessary conditions for its stability, Hobbes shows more optimism than Thucydides in the philosophers' influence on human opinion and behaviour and in the effectiveness of the state to direct human action. Whereas in Thucydides' account fear, ambition, and gain are strong passions that keep the souls of the protagonists of the *History* in permanent turmoil and the reader is never allowed to believe that controlled fear will eventually prevail and order triumph, Hobbes's writings exude the confidence of the political philosopher that true understanding can alter human behaviour and that mankind will eventually realise that political salvation is feasible through the artifice of a powerful State that exploits the natural fear of people to restrain pride and greed, thus preventing the collapse into anarchy.

In his letter to the readers which precedes his translation of Thucydides' *History* Hobbes notices and endorses the view, that in his times was widespread,[5] that Thucydides was 'the most politic historiographer that ever writ' (*History (EW VIII)*, viii). In *Leviathan* he explains that a fundamental ingredient of a 'good History' is 'the choice of the actions that are more profitable to be known' (58). A possible and probable reason why Hobbes saw the *History* as a work of the highest political significance lies in the fact that in it Thucydides spells out both the necessary condition for a stable political order and the causes of civil wars.

It should be noted that Thucydides' deep observations on the effects of fear and glory on political association come from the analysis of two of the most dramatic events of the war, namely the plague of Athens and the sedition of Corcyra. This is so because according to Thucydides war and adversities teach more than times of peace: 'war ... is a most violent master' (*History (EW VIII)*, 348).

In his 'Of the Life and *History* of Thucydides', Hobbes endorses wholeheartedly this view and says that men profit more by looking at adverse events, than at prosperity (*History (EW VIII)*, xxiv). Hobbes did not change his stand on this matter for the rest of his life (we find the very same conviction re-iterated at the beginning of *Behemoth*) and maintained consistently that in order to understand the recipe of 'immortal peace' one ought to try to understand the dynamics of war; and that in order to explain the political state one should start from its negation, i.e. from the anarchy of the state of nature where the categories of fear and ambition can be observed at their most unrestrained and their effects derived most directly.

Chapter 7

The Trajectory of Glory

Introduction

In 1663 Sorbière wrote to Hobbes, referring to the meetings held at the Montmorian Academy by the arch-pompous physicists:

> I fear that what happens to our Montmorian Academy at Sourdis's house will come to confirm your political theories, and the less we achieve in the natural sciences, the more we prove, by actual practice, the complete truth of your most subtle Elements of political philosophy [*De Cive*]. For as du Prat used to say rather elegantly, laughing, while we were on our way to that Academy, at the dull behaviour of several of its members, 'Let us visit the physicists, so that they may teach us lessons in morals and politics without realizing it' (*Correspondence II*, letter 152, 553).

This letter by Sorbière is typical of the view, shared by Hobbes in the *Elements of Law* and *De Cive*, that people are full of vanity and self-importance. In these earlier writings Hobbes seems convinced that this attitude is universal; more precisely, he regards glory and superiority as the *chief* appetite of men, and violent and shameful death as their paramount aversion.

However, by the time Hobbes received Sorbière's letter, he had revised his previous understanding of human psychology. This chapter aims at showing that in the transition from *Anti-White*, *Elements of Law* and *De Cive* to *Leviathan* and *De Homine*, Hobbes becomes less confident in the very possibility of pinpointing any ultimate appetites common to all people.

I argued in Chapters 3 and 5 that the meaning and the political implications of glory are the same in all Hobbes's writings; Hobbes writes in *Leviathan* thus:

> hitherto I have set forth the nature of Man, (whose Pride and other Passions have compelled him to submit himselfe to Government;) (*Leviathan*, 220).

By contrast, the *status* of glory in relation to other passions does

The Trajectory of Glory

undergo a substantial change in the transition from early to later works. I shall argue that glory, described in *Elements of Law* and *De Cive* as the *genus* of all passions, in *Leviathan* and *De Homine* becomes just a *species*, or instance, of human emotions. This is not because some other concepts replace the crucial role previously played by glory, but rather because Hobbes, especially in *Leviathan*, focuses on men's quest for power and acknowledges that the motivations for this quest are various and varying, with the desire of glory being merely one amongst many.

Although to my knowledge no interpreter has gone so far as suggesting that *Leviathan* marks the change of the status of glory from *genus* to *species*, many have noticed the lesser emphasis on glory in *Leviathan*. In this Chapter I shall consider the main contextual explanations that have been given for this change of emphasis.

As a first step, I shall attempt to define the two sets of people examined by Hobbes in his writings, namely the 'glory-seekers' on the one hand, and the non-glory-seekers on the other. We shall see that in the *Elements of Law* and *De Cive* the set of glory-seekers contains virtually everyone, whereas the set of non-glory-seekers is almost empty. I shall argue that the very existence of this latter set (however sparsely populated) is difficult to accommodate within Hobbes's psychology of man as described in these earlier works. Conversely, in *Leviathan* and *De Homine* the set of glory-seekers shrinks dramatically, with the set of non-glory-seekers growing correspondingly.

7.1 The Glory-seekers

In *Anti-White* Hobbes offers a typically disconcerting portrait of individuals. The Hobbesian man in this work is 'stung by the preferment' of those whom he believes to be his equals; he is enormously pained by 'insults' (465), hurt by every 'difference of opinion' (466), pleased by 'honours friendships and riches ... only as a means to something further'; likes power 'only in relation to the gaining of delights not yet acquired' (467), and is inevitably envious of 'happiness in someone else' (478).

The description of human nature in *Anti-White* is largely unchanged in both the *Elements of Law* and *De Cive*. It is only in the *Elements of Law*, though, that Hobbes offers a detailed and comprehensive analysis of the psychology of man. Here Hobbes argues that *all* human passions derive from either the pleasure or displeasure that individuals obtain from either being honoured or dishonoured. In this work, as well as in *De Cive,* desire of glory is the criterion that explains all human actions. Without presuming to offer an exhaustive account of the whole range of individuals described in the *Elements of Law,* glory-seekers can be classified according to the following criteria:

(i) the *degree* of intensity of their inner glorying;
(ii) the *fields,* or activities, to which they are directed by the desire of honour;
(iii) the *behaviour* inspired by their superiority, once they have achieved it.

7.1.1 Melancholy and madness

A criterion for differentiating among Hobbesian individuals is provided by the varying degree of intensity of their glorying. Hobbes maintains that glorying is more intense in some people than in others and accounts for these differences on the basis of the more or less adequate working of their *vital* motion. At one extreme we find 'mad' men, characterised by an overactive vital motion and thus by an excessive degree of glorying. At the other extreme, there are 'melancholic' individuals whose defective vital motion produces an excessive degree of dejection. We may presume that between these two extremes lies the entire range of the human character (*Elements of Law*, 51-2).

7.1.2 Riches, places of power, knowledge, and sensualities

Another criterion for classifying Hobbesian persons refers to the different fields, or activities, to which they are directed by their desire for honour. In the *Elements of Law* three such fields are mentioned repeatedly, namely, riches, places of authority, and knowledge (*Elements of Law*, 14). As to 'sensualities', on the one hand Hobbes maintains that since these refer mainly to pleasures of the body, they distract the human mind from the desire for honour:

> Sensuality ... taketh away the inclination to observe such things as conduce to honour; and consequently maketh men less curious, and less ambitious, whereby they less consider the way either to knowledge or to other power; in which two

consisteth all the excellency of power cognitive (*Elements of Law*, 49).

On the other hand, in so far as sensualities involve also a pleasure of the mind, they too (like riches, places of authority, and knowledge) are explained by Hobbes in terms of glorying:[1]

> Lust ... is a sensual pleasure, but not only that; there is in it also a delight of the mind ... and the delight men take in delighting, is not sensual, but a pleasure or joy of the mind, consisting in the imagination of the power they have so much to please (*Elements of Law*, 43).

As to the problem why some people seek sensualities and others knowledge, Hobbes again seems inclined to ascribe these differences to the different working of the vital motion (*Elements of Law*, 50).[2]

7.1.3 Charity and laughter

Yet another criterion that can be used to distinguish between Hobbesian individuals is by considering the different way in which they express their feeling of superiority. In this respect Hobbes describes various types of behaviour on a spectrum ranging from scornful laughter at one extreme, to pity and charity at the other. In the *Elements of Law,* pity, magnanimity, and charity give rise to compassionate and generous behaviour towards those whom we overtake in the human race; in particular charity is explained as the strongest argument showing the superiority of a man above another. In Hobbes's words:

> there can be no greater argument to a man of his own power, than to find himself able, not only to accomplish his own desires, but also to assist other men in theirs: and this is that conception wherein consisteth charity (*Elements of Law*, 44).

At the other extreme of the range of possible attitudes of Hobbesian people when they feel superior to others we find 'laughter', described as a sudden reaction of joy 'to see another fall' (*Elements of Law*, 41-2):[3]

> the passion of laughter is nothing else but a sudden glory arising from sudden conception of some eminency in ourselves, by comparison with the infirmities of others, or with our own formerly (*Elements of Law*, 42).

In all Hobbes's writings, from *Elements of Law* and *De Cive* to *Leviathan*, from the Correspondence (see, for example, letter 28) to *De Homine* and *Behemoth*, laughter is seen as one of the greatest forms of provocation.

7.2 The Mysterious Non-Glory-seekers

In view of Hobbes's many references in the *Elements of Law* to the universality of glory, e.g., that life is a race to surpass others, that happiness consists in continually outgoing the one before, that honour is the basis for curiosity which in turn is the cause of human advancement, etc., one would expect that there could not exist individuals not motivated by glory. And yet in some passages of the *Elements of Law* Hobbes claims that the 'hope of precedency and superiority' affects 'the greatest part of men', but not all. He mentions people who would be content with their share of power, who do not seem interested in surpassing others and who would be happy with equality if only others did not try to subdue them (*Elements of Law*, 70-1). Hobbes does not dwell on this minority and simply describes it as being made up of 'moderate' men and shows some sympathy for them. One is left wondering as to their psychological and motivational make-up: as they do not seek superiority, what is the meaning of happiness for them? as they do not seem interested in excelling over others, what motivates their curiosity, what drives them to improve their cognitive power, to acquire wisdom and knowledge?

Hobbes leaves these questions unanswered. A possible, but speculative, explanation could be that this minority of 'moderates', although 'content with equality' in some fields of human endeavour (such as possessions) may still wish to excel in other fields of life that are not available in the state of nature.

As the *Elements of Law*, so *De Cive*, too, is permeated by the view that overwhelming ambition is a universal trait of man and yet the existence of non-glory-seekers is mentioned again (*De Cive*, 46) and their psychological characterisation left unexplained.

In *Leviathan* non-glory-seekers make their appearance again, and this time in much larger number than in earlier works. Hobbes again shows some sympathy for them, but does not offer any precise characterisation, and simply repeats his view that they are moderate and temperate.

The Trajectory of Glory

Interpreters have often tried to assist Hobbes on this point and have offered different explanations for the mysterious minority that exists in Hobbes's political writings. It is worth mentioning as examples the views of Oakeshott and Goldsmith.

In 1960 Oakeshott pointed out that the 'noble and generous creatures ... rare to be found' mentioned by Hobbes display aristocratic virtues; they, too, are proud, but – according to Oakeshott – their pride is not Satanic, but moral.

In 1966 Goldsmith, too, argued that the pattern of human behaviour attributed by Hobbes to a minority is aristocratic: 'The aristocratic man, or magnanimous man, disdains to owe his life or his contentment to underhand or shameful or fraudulent acts'.[4]

As I intimated in Chapter 4, the identification of the 'gallant minority' with the aristocracy is quite problematic. Firstly, Hobbes stresses that the main characteristic of this minority is to be 'content with equality' – hardly an aristocratic trait.

Secondly, in places of the Correspondence we can see that Hobbes himself expresses a genuine and strong interest in philosophy above fame and money, thus suggesting that he, too, belongs to the minority that is not obsessed with the pursuit of glory. In letter 21, written in 1636, he writes:

> the extreame pleasure I take in study ouercomes in me all other appetites ... I must not deny my selfe the content to study in ye way I haue begun (*Correspondence I*, 37).

Also, in his quarrel with Descartes, whereas the latter acts in the most immature and aggressive way and writing to Mersenne, says:

> I think it best if I have nothing to do with him ('the Englishman') ... I also beg you to communicate as little as possible to him of those of my opinions which you know, and which have not appeared in print. For ... he is aiming to make his reputation at my expense, and by devious means (*Correspondence I*, letter 33, 100).

Hobbes instead behaves with the self-respect and contained disappointment of the proud man, and confides to Mersenne:

> this quarrel was started by him [Descartes] ... I do not at all defend my errors ... Unless M. Descartes behaves in the same way, I shall certainly be his superior in moral conduct (*Correspondence I*, letter 34, 107, 112).

The fact that Hobbes, a man of humble origins, emerges from the Correspondence and from the account given by Aubrey as one of the minority of 'gallant people' proves the point that this behaviour is not related to a specific social class, but derives from an inner nobility that is rare and randomly found in society – an inner beauty that Hobbes not only admired in others and taught to his own pupils,[5] but also probably believed to possess himself.

In my view it should be acknowledged that in his writings Hobbes did not wish to give a detailed portrait of the minority of non-glory-seekers. He describes them by exclusion, by listing the features they lack (e.g., greed, arrogance, dishonesty, etc.), rather than by defining their specific characteristics. I would venture to suggest that the reason why Hobbes did not even attempt to provide a description of the minority of non-glory-seekers is that, because these individuals do not require the towering presence of Leviathan to behave in a non-aggressive manner, their very existence is as reassuring to the moral philosopher as is irrelevant to the political theorist.

7.3 The Fall of Glory in *Leviathan* and *De Homine*

In *Leviathan* Hobbes's set of human passions is larger than the set of passions described in the *Elements of Law*. The novelty, though, is not in the new additions, but rather in the changed definitions of some of the passions discussed in his previous work. In *Leviathan* Hobbes does not speculate, unlike in *Elements of Law*, on what *ultimate* motivation drives people to be magnanimous, covetous, ambitious, pusillanimous, etc. Consider, for example, the definition of charity and magnanimity: although in *Leviathan* Hobbes maintains, as in *Elements of Law,* that charity and magnanimity are honourable, he never states that people are magnanimous or charitable for the sake of honour. This shift of emphasis from the enquiry into the *inner* thoughts and ultimate motivations of people to the careful study of the *observable* behaviour inspired by each passion is a general and novel characteristic of *Leviathan*. When describing human passions in the *Elements of Law* Hobbes states that the 'nature' of all passions '[consisteth] in the pleasure men have, or displeasure from the signs of honour or dishonour done unto them' (*Elements of Law*, 36). It is highly significant that in *Leviathan*, instead, not one out of the forty passions described in chapter 6 is said to derive from the pleasure or displeasure that a man obtains from honouring. Nor does Hobbes suggest, as he had in *De Cive,* that 'all the minds pleasures refer to glory in the end'.

In *Leviathan* glory is no longer the *genus,* or ultimate source of all passions and desires, but becomes a *species,* or an instance of human passions. This different status given to glory marks a fundamental change in Hobbes's psychology of man.

The view held in *Leviathan* that (i) glory is just one of the passions, and (ii) it is not the common ultimate motivation of all people, is repeated by Hobbes in *De Homine.* Here Hobbes points out that 'there would be an almost infinite number of passions if we gave different names to all of them' (*De Homine*, 62). In his list of passions, he does mention glory (defined as 'elation of the mind' in observing one's superiority) as well as glory-related passions (such as ambition, envy, revengefulness, desire of praise, of contest, of competition, of victory). However, he also describes emotions completely unrelated to glory, such as admiration of novelty, compassion, and love. These are not minor exceptions, in so far as, for example 'love ... may be divided into almost as many passions as there are objects of love' (such as love of money, of power, of knowledge, etc., *De Homine*, 60).

In *De Homine,* as in *Leviathan,* Hobbes seems keener to show the link between passions and observable behaviour than to offer a universal psychological interpretation of man: one's pride can be detected in the fact that people blush when they make mistakes, or laugh at other people's shortcomings, or weep when humiliated or get angry when frustrated. In *De Homine* Hobbes offers a physiological account of all passions not unlike Descartes' in the *Passions of the Soul.* Excessive self-esteem is described as a swelling of the mind, whereas the shrinking of the mind is ascribed to depression and low-self-esteem.

Whereas glory loses its central place in the transition from *Elements of Law* and to *Leviathan,* 'power' does not. However, this should not be taken to imply that in *Leviathan* power replaces glory as the criterion underlying all human motivation. In *Leviathan* no concept is raised to the level previously occupied by glory. On the contrary, the motivation of desire for power is explicitly said to vary considerably across individuals. Power in *Leviathan,* unlike glory in *Elements of Law* and *De Cive,* is not the common drive, nor the greatest pleasure of the mind to which all the other pleasures refer in the end. Rather, the augmentation of power is the criterion that allows individuals to form expectations on the behaviour of others. Hobbes suggests that, even though the inner feelings or motivation of people can never be known, we can safely predict that individuals will always behave so as to increase their power. Whereas in *Elements of Law* and *De Cive* glory is invariably the motivation for the pursuit of power, in *Leviathan* it is so only occasionally.

In *De Homine* Hobbes completely abstains from explaining the passion that drives people to increase their power and confines himself to the observation that

> power if it be extraordinary is good because it is useful for protection; and protection provides security. If it be not extraordinary, it is useless (*De Homine*, 49).

Of course, there are some exceptions to my contention that in *Leviathan* glory is demoted from the *genus* to a *species* of human passion. Indeed, throughout *Leviathan* we can still find traces of the earlier position, especially in Book II, where Hobbes restates the view, typical of his previous writings, that 'men ... naturally love ... Dominion over others ...men are continually in competition for Honour and Dignity' and that 'man, whose Joy consisteth in comparing himselfe with other men, can relish nothing but what is eminent' (*Leviathan*, 117, 119). Moreover, laughter, weeping, shame, emulation, and envy are still defined in terms of glorying or dejection, (*Leviathan*, 46). In Chapter 8 of *Leviathan* the defect of the mind called by Hobbes 'madness' is once again put down, as in *Elements of Law*, to excessive vain glory or excessive dejection (*Leviathan*, 54).

In spite of these exceptions, on the whole Hobbes seems to be no longer convinced that glory is the fundamental universal motivation. Therefore the existence of non-glory-seekers is consistent with the general tenor of *Leviathan*, whereas their presence was inexplicable and contradictory in the context of the psychological theory of the *Elements of Law* and *De Cive*.

7.4 Sherlock Holmes and Other Detectives

> "... Now, my dear Watson, does anything remain for me to explain?"
> "Yes," said I. "You have not made it clear what was [the man's] motive' ...
> "Ah! my dear Watson, there we come into the realms of conjecture, where the most logical mind may be at fault. Each may form his own hypothesis ... and yours is as likely to be correct as mine."[6]

Perhaps it can be safely surmised that in his later years Hobbes may have agreed with Sherlock Holmes that, as far as establishing man's motives is concerned, even 'the most logical mind may be at fault'. In other words, perhaps Hobbes, under the influence of Scepticism, became uncertain about the possibility of finding a unitary theory of human motivation. In *Behemoth* he writes:

> ... we cannot safely judge of men's intentions (*Behemoth*, 72).
>
> It is a hard matter, or rather impossible, to know what other men mean (*Behemoth*, 37)
>
> I cannot enter into other men's thoughts, farther than I am led by the consideration of human nature in general (*Behemoth*, 29).

Also, it is quite possible that over the years Hobbes's friends and critics could have influenced him and made him realise that human nature is more complex than he had thought earlier. An example of a Hobbes's correspondent who expressed perplexity and some disagreement with Hobbes's views on glory and honour is Peleau, who in Letter 90 writes with reference to *De Cive*

> you define honour as the "estimation of another's power" ... this definition of honour is not valid: [it is not true] that we only honour those whom we think powerful, and whose power we esteem ... in fact ... we have respect for people from whom we neither hope nor fear anything. We honour virtue ... we honour people of great intellect, old people, and distinguished people whom we have never met ... we often honour people who are beautiful ... without being known to them (*Correspondence I*, 309-10).

Sorbière, too, indirectly criticises Hobbes's interpretation of human laughter as a perennial sign of derision and glory, when he points out that 'wise laughter ... is conducive to good health, both in body and in mind' (*Correspondence I*, letter 114, 435). Hobbes probably agreed with this, as he was in his private life a cheerful man, according both to Aubrey and to his *Prose Life*. The reason why Hobbes choose not to mention healthy laughter may have been the same that prompted him to ignore many other agreeable aspects of people, namely the fact that they are politically of no consequence.

Further, we may recall McNeilly's suggestion that Hobbes was concerned with the public's reception of *Leviathan* and hence diluted his 'public' pessimism for rhetorical reasons. Recently this line of reasoning has found the favour of many interpreters. It is not impossible that Hobbes, having realised that the strong assumption of glory as ultimate and universal motivation was unpalatable to his contemporaries, may have decided to replace it with the weaker, and thus more acceptable, version of limited glory-seeking behaviour *by some*.

The problem with this line of interpretation is that we have evidence that Hobbes was not afraid of polemic and controversy, as shown on matters of religion discussed at some length in *Leviathan*. In the correspondence Hobbes seems almost proud to have many enemies and critics.

To Sorbière he writes without showing any sign of distress that he is 'detested by almost all the ecclesiastics' and that when quarrelling with Wallis about the squaring of the circle he was 'dealing at the same time with all the ecclesiastics of England' (*Correspondence I*, letter 112, 429).

In another letter to Sorbière, Hobbes jokingly remarks that Sorbière

> will become a perpetual object of hatred to the doctors, just as I am (because of my political theory) to the theologians (*Correspondence I*, letter 118, 448).

In the letter to Cosimo de' Medici, Hobbes cannot help boasting that

> the two sweetest consolations of my old age [are]: the congratulations of my friends and the envy of my enemies (*Correspondence II*, letter 187, 711).

Hobbes's image, as emerges from these and other letters, is that of a strong and self-confident person who is not upset by criticisms but who almost finds delight in challenging common opinions. If this is a correct portrait of his character, it seems unlikely that he dropped the claim of universal glory-seeking behaviour just for fear to offend his readers.

Moreover, it has been argued that the weaker stress on glory in *Leviathan* should be ascribed to Descartes' influence. Unfortunately Descartes' 'objections' to Hobbes's political theory mentioned by Guisony in Letter 136 of the *Correspondence* have not survived. According to Pacchi, Hobbes in recasting his theory of the passions for *Leviathan* had in mind the model suggested by Descartes in his *Passions de l' âme*, which was published at the time the *Leviathan* was being written.[7]

Pacchi has argued that this interpretation is

> supported not only by his inclusion of jealousy and impudence [among the passions] ..., but by his use of the same system and pattern as Descartes, which derives the whole range of particular emotions from the small group of primitive passions.[8]

In my view a comparative analysis of the *Leviathan* and Descartes' *The Passions of the Soul* does not support but rather puts in serious doubt the hypothesis of a Cartesian influence on Hobbes's conception of the passions. For example, Descartes says that 'Scorn and Esteem ... are only species of Wonder'[9] and are thus connected to curiosity. On the contrary, in *Leviathan* Hobbes posits no connection between desire of novelty and 'scorn' or 'esteem', and even suggests that these passions often belong to very different people – desire of novelty spurring people to increase their understanding of the world and to develop the sciences, whereas 'scorn' is the hallmark of the glory-seeker.

Even on pride and vainglory Descartes' commentaries[10] show an altogether different approach from Hobbes's in so far as Descartes displays a total lack of interest in the political implications of the passions that instead play such crucial role in Hobbes's account.

On this point, I tend to think that the truth lies with the opinion of the majority of interpreters who, while accepting the influence of Descartes on Hobbes's natural philosophy, deny any Cartesian impact on his political theory.

Finally, one can wonder whether in his later years Hobbes may not have revised his views on psychology, much in the way he changed his position on rhetoric. As mentioned in the Introduction, according to Quentin Skinner, Hobbes when writing *Leviathan* became more pessimistic about people's ability to listen to reason and therefore abandoned his former unqualified rejection of rhetoric and found a new place for it at the service of political science.

The theory of a 'new pessimism in *Leviathan*', though, does not explain why Hobbes abandoned the idea that all men are glory-seekers in favour of the view that only some are, provided, of course, it is accepted that postulating a reduction in the number of ambitious and aggressive individuals is incompatible with holding a gloomier view of human nature.

I am no contextual detective, and therefore I should not know which, if any, of the above explanations of the lesser emphasis on glory in *Leviathan* and *De Homine* is the most probable. One could advance also some context-free explanations. One such can be deduced from the logic of Hobbes's own argument: as Hobbes loathed redundancy and whenever possible wielded Ockham's razor, it is quite likely that he dropped the assumption of universal glory-seeking behaviour for no other reason than logical neatness. In fact, for the Hobbesian state of nature to collapse into a state of perennial war, only a handful of glory-seekers are necessary, as Hobbes shows himself to be well aware when in *De Cive* he remarks that

> though the wicked are fewer than the righteus, yet because we cannot distinguish them, there is a necessity of suspecting anticipating, subjugating, selfdefending ever incident to the most honest (*De Cive*, 33).

In other words, the assumption of generalised glory-seeking behaviour held in earlier works was logically redundant to support Hobbes's argument and he knew it. It would have been entirely congruent with Hobbes's scientific enterprise to provide a neater presentation of his argument by jettisoning unnecessarily strong (as well as controversial) assumptions in favour of less demanding ones. Indeed, in Chapters 10 and 11, I shall argue that it is possible to verify that the main result of Hobbes's argument – that the state of nature turns rapidly into a state of war of everyone against everyone – is completely unaffected if it is assumed that there (may) exist only a handful of glory-seekers.

In Chapter 9 I shall advance another, possibly more insightful, philosophical explanation, based on an analysis of *De Homine*, of the reasons that may have induced Hobbes to drop the view that glory is a universal motivation.

Chapter 8

Glory and the Excellent Sex

Introduction

In letter 170 we learn that Hobbes had requested du Verdus to send him the full text of a poem of his about the love of two young lesbians. Their 'beautiful breasts clasping each other', their 'greedy devouring kisses', the 'delight ... in the sucking of lips of their two mouths joined together both kissing and kissed', their embracing each other's 'beautiful neck' suggests to me that this is no Platonic love.[1] Although it is likely that Hobbes made his request more out of courtesy than of love of poetry, nevertheless his interest in the subject-matter shows a healthy open-mindedness.

Aubrey informs us that in his private life Hobbes 'was, even in his youth, (generally) temperate, both as to wine and women' (*Brief Lives*, 157). Even so, at the age of ninety, in his love verses Hobbes shows, to borrow an expression of his, that 'a continent man has the passions he contains':

> Tho' I am past ninety, and too old
> T'expect preferment in the court of Cupid,
> and many winters made me ev'n so cold
> I am become almost all over stupid,
> Yet I can love and have a mistress too,
> as fair as can be and as wise as fair;
> And yet not proud, nor anything will do
> To make me of her favour to despair.
> To tell you who she is were very bold;
> But if I' th' character your self you find
> Think not the man a fool tho'he be old
> who loves in body fair a fairer mind.
> (quoted in Aubrey, *Brief Lives*, 160).

A (male) writer born in sixteenth-century England cannot be expected to be concerned about the status of women in society and so it comes as no surprise that Hobbes was not. Nevertheless, he made some important claims about women. For example, when du Verdus asked him:

Do you think that a woman who is the sovereign of a state is the head of its church and its religion? (on that point I am convinced that the answer is yes) (*Correspondence I*, letter 108, 416).

Hobbes replied affirmatively, and this view is confirmed by the fact (noticed by Malcolm (*Correspondence I*, 419)) that he included this point in the Latin text of *Leviathan*.

Hobbes's views on the status of women are at times ambiguous and this has given rise to opposite interpretations of the role of gender in his theory.

One position, expounded most forcibly by Preston King[2] in the 1960s, is that Hobbes's main concern is the destruction of patriarchal power. King interprets Hobbes's overall project as an attempt to formulate a uniform theory of authority, which did not simply happen to neglect gender, but which was specifically meant to exclude gender as a grounding principle. Whereas for Aristotle gender was a necessary feature of rule – maintains King – for Hobbes it becomes a mere accident.

The opposite position has been taken by Carole Pateman in the 1980s. She points out that modern patriarchy is conjugal and not paternal. She has challenged those writers who 'fail to explain why Hobbes's writings contain so many references to the rightful power of fathers – or why he endorses the subjection of wives to husbands'.[3]

In this chapter I hope to show that both interpretations contain some elements of truth. I shall argue that Hobbes makes two substantive claims.

Claim (i): nature denies the superiority of one sex over the other;

Claim (ii): nevertheless, the sovereign power can introduce rules of succession and inheritance that favour males over females.

It seems reasonable to speculate that if Hobbes had been concerned about the status of women, he would have not simply endorsed Claim (i) but also he would have opposed Claim (ii). In other words, he would have stated not simply the equality of the sexes in natural conditions, but also defended the status of women against patriarchal rules inside political states.

The likeliest reason why Hobbes maintained Claim (i) is that he was keen to reject *natural* patriarchalism, both because it could be used to set limits to the absolute power of the state and because it was one of the favourite weapons of the critics of the idea of the social contract. Conversely, Hobbes endorsed Claim (ii) i.e., patriarchal legislation created by the sovereign after the social contract, because the very notion of *artificial* patriarchalism reinforces his own argument of the limitless power of the state, in so far as the sovereign can introduce a form of inequality that otherwise would be denied by nature.

8.1 Hobbes's Rejection of Natural Patriarchalism

In Chapter 1 I tried to show that Hobbes does not identify human beings with what they do or want because, as the specific content of people's actions and the objects of their desires change over time and across individuals, this would render the underlying definition of person unsuitable for the foundation of civil rights. I argued that according to Hobbes a definition of 'man' adequate for the foundation of civil rights has to be arrived at by carrying out two complementary types of analyses: (i) a comparative analysis aimed at establishing what is common to all individuals. and (ii) a time-series analysis that singles out what is permanent in each person over time. In his political works Hobbes deploys both (i) and (ii) and arrives at a definition of 'man' as 'motion generating power'. From King to Pateman, most interpreters agree that this definition is gender-neutral.

The problem arises whether men generate more power than women or, in other words, whether in the Hobbesian state of nature women become subordinate to men.

Hobbes's views on the equality of the sexes are mixed. On the one hand, in places he suggests that there is no notable difference in either strength or prudence between men and women and rejects the view of the 'excellent sex' (*Leviathan*, 187). In *Behemoth* he suggests that there are as many people of weak judgements among men as there are among women (*Behemoth*, 16). In *A Dialogue between a Philosopher and a Student*, referring to the custom 'to burn the women but behead the men', the philosopher comments with the usual irony that this is 'so nice a distinction' (128).

On the other hand, Hobbes maintains elsewhere that 'generally men are endowed with greater parts of wisdom and courage ... than women' (*Elements of Law,* 136) and refers to women as the 'weaker sex' (*Behemoth,* 60).

From the discussion in Chapter 2 we concluded that the cornerstone of Hobbes's political theory is not some generic equality, but a very specific form of equality, namely the equal power of individuals to endanger each other's lives.

The question is therefore whether women are physically less dangerous than men. In fact, if it could be shown that Hobbes believed women to be inferior to men in this respect, then it could be argued that, after having offered a gender-free definition of 'man', Hobbes makes the theoretical move that deprives women of equal standing at the time of the social contract.

This seems to be the hypothesis favoured by Carol Pateman. She maintains that, although in principle Hobbesian women are as dangerous as men, pregnancy and child-caring make them very vulnerable, so much so that they are conquered by men in the state of nature, lose their status as free and equal individuals and thus lack the status to participate in the original contract.

Contrary to Pateman, it seems to me that for Hobbes not only men and women are equal 'by nature', but also they retain their equality as long as they live in natural conditions. Even the weakest woman, either alone or with the help of others, by deception or some other clever device can pose a lethal danger to the strongest man, because of the immense fragility of the 'human frame'. In the state of nature men and women remain independent. In *De Cive* Hobbes remarks:

> What some say ... that the Father by reason of the preeminence of sex and not the Mother becomes Lord [over the children] signifies nothing. For both reason shews the contrary, because the inequality of their naturall forces is not so great, that the man could get the Dominion over the woman without warre. And custome also contradicts not; for women, namely Amazons, have in former times waged war against their adversaries ... and at this day in divers places, women are invested with the principal authority (*De Cive*, 122).

In a similar vein we read in *Leviathan*:

> whereas some have attributed the Dominion to the Man onely, as being of the more excellent Sex; they misreckon in it For there is not always that difference of strength, or prudence between the man and the woman, as that the right can be determined without war (*Leviathan*, 139).

It is true that occasionally Hobbes suggests that in the state of nature some males may temporarily possess 'wives, children, and cattell' (*Leviathan*, 88), but this is insufficient evidence to support Pateman's claim that women are conclusively subjugated by men.

In spite of a few inconsistencies, however, in his political works Hobbes puts across the view that in natural conditions there is 'no dominion of persons', not even over fools and madmen (*Leviathan*, 150). He emphasises that 'in the conditions of mere nature there are no matrimonial laws' (*Leviathan*, 140), and therefore no patriarchal marriage. In *De Cive* Hobbes remarks that 'the word Lord is not in the definition of a Father' (*De Cive*, 121) and he points out that

> by the Right of nature, the Dominion over the infant first belongs to him who first hath him in his power; but it is manifest that he who is newly born is in the Mothers power before any others, in so much as she rightly, and at her own will, either breed him up, or adventure him to fortune ... Every woman that bears children, becomes both a Mother and a Lord (*De Cive*, 122)

In Hobbes's description of the state of nature, much as the temporary possession of land does not imply the existence of private property, so occasional possession of a 'wife' by some men does not imply the dominion by one sex over the other.

Whereas the *factual equality* of individuals is postulated by Hobbes in his account of natural conditions, *normative equality*[4] is recommended by the laws of nature which advocate the acknowledgement of the equal liberty of each and everyone and forbid pride.

It is also true that the 13th law of nature in *De Cive* seems to endorse the view that primogeniture is natural:

> Naturall is primogeniture (in Greek kleronomia, as it were given by lot) or first possession. Let this therefore stand for the thirteen law of nature (*De Cive*, 70; see also *Leviathan* 108).

Even Hobbes's contemporaries singled out the inconsistency of the above law within Hobbes's overall argument and pointed to the serious consequences that a concession to natural patriarchalism would entail for Hobbes's theory. Peleau, one of Hobbes's most inquisitive correspondents, writes thus:

> you say that primogeniture and first possession are natural ways of determining ownership by lot and that the seniority

of an elder child is a natural right to things (DC iii, 18); if that is so I think that there cannot be a right of every man to everything in the state of nature. I await your verdict (*Correspondence I*, letter 103, 382).

Unfortunately Hobbes's reply has been lost, but we can appreciate Peleau's point that to admit a natural right to primogeniture would imply rejecting one of the fundamental claims of Hobbes's theory, namely that in the state of nature individuals have a right to all things, which is what ultimately leads Hobbes to identify the state of nature with a war of all against all.

In spite of this inconsistency, in *De Cive* and *Leviathan* Hobbes stresses the crucial point that, whereas the power of mothers over children is natural, the power of fathers is not grounded in nature.

He points out that in natural conditions 'it cannot be known who is the father, unless it be declared by the mother' so that 'the right of dominion over the child dependeth on her will, and is consequently hers' (*Leviathan* 187, 201; *De Cive,* 123). With this simple yet brutally effective argument, Hobbes destroys the entire basis for natural patriarchy.

King quite rightly points out that Hobbes addresses his destructive argument exclusively against the natural *paternal* power of control, even if this leaves him exposed to the counter argument of the natural power *of the mother*. King explains Hobbes's oversight by recalling that nobody among Hobbes's audience would have raised such an objection.

8.2 Hobbes's Open Social Contract

We have seen above that the family is an accident and not a necessary feature of the Hobbesian state of nature. As King puts it,

> [for Hobbes] however natural birth may be, the family is not. It is a political arrangement ... not natural, but 'artificial'.[5]

When entering the social contract Hobbesian contractees know that they have to renounce all their natural rights (except the right to personal safety) and have to acknowledge the absolute power of the Leviathan. For the Hobbesian woman this means that she must give up her natural 'dominion' over her offspring. She is supposed to agree to this loss because according to Hobbes no civil arrangement implemented by the Leviathan can be worse than the permanent threat of violent death that characterises the state of nature.

At the time of the contract Hobbesian men and women do not know the content of civil laws and in particular they are innocent of any knowledge of whether patriarchal marriage and family will be introduced. It is worth noticing that in Hobbes's theory the subordination of women to men living in political associations is in no way a logical implication of the social contract, nor a necessary characteristic of political associations. As no specific system of government (monarchy, democracy, aristocracy) follows with logical necessity from the Hobbesian social contract, likewise no specific social arrangement, either patriarchal or matriarchal, is implied by it. Neither is excluded, for the only type of equality enshrined in the Hobbesian social contract is each person's equal right to physical integrity. Indeed the social contract by itself does not exclude the emergence of *inequalities* between citizens in virtually every other respect. On the contrary, Hobbes suggests that the political state is the origin of inequality:

> The question who is the better man, has no place in the condition of mere nature; where, as has been shewn before, all men are equal. The inequality that now is, has been introduced by the laws civil (*Leviathan*, 140).

The problem to be addressed here is why, after having argued that all people are equal by nature and remain so in natural conditions, Hobbes describes civil associations that are marked by inequalities and allows characteristics such as gender, that are irrelevant in the state of nature, to become a possible ground for unequal treatment inside the political state. I would suggest that the answer to this question is to be found, as is so often the case in Hobbes's theory, in his assumption that glory – or desire of superiority and prestige – is a fundamental human motivation.

8.3 Hobbes and Artificial Patriarchy

In his seminal essay on equality Bernard Williams remarks that the task of genuine political thought is to reconcile the conflicting claims deriving from the human desire of some sort of prestige and from the equality of all individuals as individuals.[6]

We have seen that in his works Hobbes raises the above dilemma in highly dramatic terms: on the one hand, he singles out 'glory', 'honour', and 'eminence' as the drives that distinguish the human race from bees and ants and points to the 'dejection' and even 'melancholy' with which the human mind reacts to failure and inferiority. On the other hand, he highlights the basic equality of all individuals, and lists among the laws of nature the recommendation that each individual is owed equal respect.

A fundamental feature of Hobbes's theory is that the clash of glory and equality is inevitable in the state of nature, but can be escaped in the political state. By introducing the civil laws the sovereign power enables otherwise equal individuals to decide 'who is the better man' and, we may add, which is the better sex.

In direct contrast with Williams' standpoint, for Hobbes it is not up to the reflecting agent or to the political philosopher to find a solution to the dilemma of equality and glory, but to the sovereign power.

In Hobbes's theory the *will* of the ruler(s) is acknowledged to be the *ultimate criterion* determining the rules of political associations. This *can* mean that the sovereign power introduces 'matrimonial laws' and other civil laws that favour males and give them a position of superiority over females, thereby making *gender* – that in the state of nature turned out to be irrelevant – an acceptable ground for unequal treatment.

It is true that according to Hobbes the sovereign power ought to graft the natural laws into the civil laws and for this s/he is responsible and accountable to God. However, the laws of nature are vague and in principle a ruler can interpret them as s/he thinks appropriate.

In *Behemoth* we are told that the fundamental law of nature

> binds us all to obey him, whatsover he be, whom lawfully and for our own safety, we have promised to obey; nor any other fundamental law to a king but Salus Populi, the safety and well-being of the people (*Behemoth*, 67-8).

The notion that the only binding law for the king is *Salus Populi* recurs both in *Behemoth* (67-8, 108) as well as in *A Dialogue between a Philosopher and a Student* (70).

In the name of *salus populi* the Hobbesian sovereign power can, and indeed does, introduce patriarchal legislation. Carole Pateman is amply justified in her claim that throughout his writings Hobbes associates often civil society with patriarchal marriage and with the legally-sanctioned subordination of women. In *Leviathan* we read:

> In commonwealth this controversie [between paternal and maternal power] is decided by the Civill Law: and for the most part, (but not always) the sentence is in favour of the Father (*Leviathan*, 140).

According to Hobbes, 'in a civill government if there be a contract of marriage between a man and a woman, the children are the Fathers' ... [and] the domesticall command belongs to the man' (*De Cive*, 124; *Leviathan*, Ch. XX; *Elements of Law,* Ch. 23).

Although he remarks that 'women may govern, and have in divers ages and places governed wisely' (*Elements of Law,* 136), thus suggesting that they are not in principle excluded from government, Hobbes shows a personal preference for legislation favouring male succession: 'women are not so apt [to govern] in general as men' (*Elements of Law,* 136). Hobbes explains male dominance inside civil associations mainly on the ground of 'not contradicted custome':

> ...the Males carry the predominance, in the beginning perhaps because for the most part (although not always) they are fitter for the administration of greater matteres, but especially of wars; but afterwards, when it was grown a custome, because that custome was not contradicted (*De Cive,* 128).

In other words, after having removed any natural justification for the superiority of men, Hobbes pointedly refuses to criticise marital power, as long as it is seen as a convention or a custom endorsed by the sovereign power.

8.4 Custom and the Excellent Sex

We have seen that Hobbes rejects the view that men are by nature the 'excellent sex' (*Leviathan,* 87). Section 8.1 has corroborated the claim advanced by King that Hobbes demolishes the alleged *natural* power of the *paterfamilias*. In section 8.2 I have shown that Hobbes describes a social contract which *per se* neither implies nor excludes the introduction of the patriarchal family. Section 8.3 supports Pateman's claim that marital power is endorsed by Hobbes inside political associations. For Hobbes, I have argued, patriarchal legislation is the product of *convention* and 'not contradicted custom' and not the result of *biological* characteristics. Gender, that in the state of nature is largely irrelevant, is seen by Hobbes as an admissible ground for different treatment of men and women living in political associations. Hobbes mentions that in history there have been exceptions to male predominance, as in the case of the Amazons (*Leviathan*, 140; *De Cive*, 122). Why then does he endorse the custom of patriarchal legislation? This cannot be explained as a sign of respect for custom as such. On the contrary, often in his works Hobbes is very critical of habits and traditions inside political associations. In *Behemoth* he points out that 'several men praise several customs' (45) and that customs and habits are to be judged as either good or evil depending on their effects on the commonwealth (46). In *A Dialogue between a Philosopher and a Student*, the Philosopher says:

> As to the authority that you ascribe to custom, I deny that any custom of its own nature can amount to the authority of a law. For if the custom be unreasonable, you must, with all other lawyers confess that is not law, but ought to be abolished; and if the custom be reasonable it is not the custom but the equity that makes it law (*Dialogue*, 62-3).

In the same work, we read: 'you know that unreasonable customs are not law but ought to be abolished' (*Dialogue*, 134).

It follows that Hobbes endorsed patriarchal rules inside political associations not out of respect of custom as such, but rather because he thought that this particular custom was beneficial to the commonwealth After all, Hobbes knew from history that patriarchal marriage can rely on women's customary acceptance of subordination and has the advantage of directing men's desire of dominion and superiority towards the private sphere (thus leaving the State unchallenged).

That Hobbes's endorsement of patriarchy is not a logical implication of his theory is also demonstrated by the fact that various arguments in his philosophy can be deployed precisely to undermine patriarchal legislation.

Firstly, one argument for opposing the custom of patriarchal rules could be derived from Hobbes's discussion of the dissolution of states. Hobbes argues that when people are dissatisfied with a particular social arrangement, either because they are dejected or because they expect a better deal, they desire political change, and act accordingly. He warns strongly the sovereign power against these dangers. Even though Hobbesian women have some psychological traits different from men,[7] they too are characterised by Hobbes as wanting power[8] and as capable of handling it well (*Elements of Law*, 138). Since they are described as able of defending their independence in the inhospitable state of nature, it could be argued that they would be dissatisfied with a position of inferiority *vis-à-vis* men inside civil associations. In so far as Hobbesian women are numerous and capable of leadership, they possess two of the 'four things requisite to the *hope of overcoming*' which Hobbes lists among 'seditious inclinations'. Theoretically there is nothing to prevent them from meeting the other two requirements for sparking off a rebellion, namely, 'mutual trust' and 'means' (*De Cive*, 153).

There is another argument that Hobbes could have used to exclude gender as a foundation for social superiority and male dominance. As I argued in Chapter 3, in *Elements of Law* (20-21) and *Leviathan* (45) Hobbes points out that the difference between *true*, *vain* and *false glory* is that only the first is grounded on real achievements and induces new 'aspiring', or endeavour to pursue new objectives. Vain and false glory, instead, are based on imaginary actions and do not induce any real 'attempt' to pursue excellence, for they can be reproduced effortlessly as mental states. For Hobbes, whereas the desire of true glory when duly channelled by the laws can be beneficial to mankind, vain and false glory lead people either to failure or to inaction, which are both detrimental. In so far as gender (unlike 'arts upon words', science, private property, etc.) is not the product of one's efforts and cannot be improved by people's activities, it can be argued that it can never provide the basis for the Hobbesian concept of true glory, but only for vain or false glory. As the latter are detrimental to mankind, gender ought to be excluded by the Hobbesian ruler as an admissible basis for social prestige.

The fact that Hobbes chose not to resort to any of the above arguments to oppose the introduction by the sovereign of patriarchal rules shows that the reason why he denied natural patriarchalism in the first place was not some concern for the status of women – a concern that would be anachronistic to expect of him. Rather, Hobbes was keen to demolish the natural foundations of patriarchalism because maintaining such power would have weakened his argument on the absolute and unconstrained power of the state. Conversely, Hobbes did not oppose *artificial* patriarchalism because it testifies to the unlimited power of the state, which can create an inequality between the sexes denied by nature.

Chapter 9

The Determinants of the Citizen: Nature and Nurture

Introduction

Aubrey's entry for the year 1665 in the life of Hobbes reads thus:

> This year he told me that he was willing to do some good to the town where he was born; that his majesty loved him well, and if I could find out something in our country [Wiltshire] that was in his gift, he did believe he could beg it of his majesty, and seeing he was bred a scholar, he thought it most proper to endow a free school there; which is wanting now ... After enquiry I found out a piece of land in Braydon forest (of about £25 per annum value) that was in his majesty's gift, which he hoped to have obtained of his majesty for a salary for a schoolmaster; but the queen's priests smelling out the design and being his enemies hindered this public and charitable intention (*Brief* Lives, 155).

Having been a tutor for much of his life, it is not surprising that Hobbes attached importance to education. But if human nature is fixed and invariable, what good can education do?

In Chapter 7 we have seen that when writing *Leviathan* and *De Homine* Hobbes seems to have abandoned the view held in previous works that glory is the source of all human passions at all times. Glory, instead, becomes just one instance of human motivations and no other principle is given by Hobbes the role played by glory in earlier works.

My aim in this Chapter is to suggest a possible explanation for Hobbes's change of mind. I hope to show that unlike in *Elements of Law* and *De Cive*, in *De Homine* and *Behemoth* Hobbes suggests that the influence of society on human behaviour is much more marked than the contribution of eternal and immutable human nature. In other words, in later works nurture rather than nature is singled out by Hobbes as the major source of human actions. Correspondingly

The Determinants of the Citizen: Nature and Nurture

Hobbes is less concerned with the definition of unchanging human characteristics and more interested in establishing the form of education that can benefit human behaviour.

This chapter is organised in two parts. Firstly, I examine the glory-seeker of early writings and I try to argue that he is far less independent and autonomous than it is usually contended in the secondary literature. Secondly, I argue that in *De Homine* and *Behemoth* Hobbes acknowledges to society a greater influence than ever before over the 'dispositions' and 'manners' of individuals and thus his views on the effectiveness of education change. Increased malleability is the novelty of the new Hobbesian man.

9.1 The Interdependence of the Hobbesian Glory-seeker

Imagine that there were countless Edens infinitely distant one from the other and that each Hobbesian man were given the chance to head to one of them, where he could enjoy a life of abundance and comfort in peaceful isolation. Would he take such an option? Although admittedly not many interpreters have raised this question, most have provided indirectly an answer. The Hobbesian individual has been often described as psychologically self-contained, autonomous, independent, self-sufficient. Preston King captured the feeling of many readers when he wrote:

> The pre-eminent characteristic of the individual is not physical isolation, but psychological self-containment. This belief, together with the doctrine of equality, constitute the central ground upon which Hobbes stands in his view of the individual.[1]

If the Hobbesian individual is self-contained, I believe that he should choose my dream journey to Eden. If fear of others and desire of commodious living are the only causes that drive him to enter a social contract, then my proposition would be a better deal than the mighty Leviathan.

But Hobbes says that 'Solitude is an enemy' to man (*De Cive*, 44). A plentiful Eden enjoyed in isolation is not what the Hobbesian glory-seeker wants. He desires dominion, success, prestige and control, not over animals but over human beings.

In the *Elements of Law* we are told that the desire of honour motivates people to study and to work; that the hope to surpass others induces in some the development of knowledge and in others the attainment of riches; that the yearn to show off their wisdom drives individuals to communicate their thoughts and to develop speech and deductive thought; that the longing for displaying their knowledge drives philosophers to write treatises:

> with what aim do philosophers write so many books if not to have as many witnesses as possible to their learning? (*Anti-White*, 478).

Without others, the glory-seeker would have no motivation to progress from achievement to achievement, he would have no desires, and a man without desires is dead, in Hobbes's view. Self-improvement in the *Elements of Law* is motivated by the aspiration of surpassing others. For Hobbes, without others, we would not develop many human capacities. In Eden we would probably compare ourselves and compete with animals and lose our drive to develop our human potential.

The glory-seeker needs to compare himself with others in order to know who he is. Without comparison, he cannot find himself. Hobbes suggests that the glory-seeker is constantly observing what is going on outside the self. The reason is that the conditions for becoming superior to others and being honoured by them are not fixed and immutable. For example, Hobbes points out that in times of war is more honourable to be the best 'conductor of soldiers' than the best judge; in times of peace the opposite is true. The hierarchy of prestigious positions changes in society, with the needs and wants of people. And so the Hobbesian glory-seeker must be not only a careful observer of other people's achievements, but also a careful assessor of their needs and wants; he must be flexible and adaptable; he must observe others and try to understand them.

I am not contesting that the reason why the Hobbesian glory-seeker is interested in others is because he is first of all interested in himself; but I find no textual reference to support the view held by so many interpreters that he is self-contained, self-sufficient and independent. Just the opposite, in fact.

As I argued in Chapter 3, glory is a comparative concept. I can find in Hobbes's discourse at least three distinct ways in which 'others' are important to one's glorying:

    (i) as passive *terms of comparison*;
    (ii) as *external observers* who decide whether our feeling of

The Determinants of the Citizen: Nature and Nurture

superiority is either well grounded (true glory, just esteem) or imaginary and unfounded (vain glory, false glory, pride);

(iii) finally, others play *an active role* in so far as their *opinion* of us can increase or decrease our own glorying. If they think highly of us, their judgement affects our self-esteem and also the responsibilities and powers we are granted. In other words, if others believe that one is gifted with a special ability or talent which is socially relevant, their opinion, whether well-founded or not, is the source of real power and true glory for one.

We can see now the difference between the Hobbesian glory-seeker and Macpherson's profit-maximiser. Imagine that the two of them were given the choice between taking up permanent residence in either Island Eden or Island Hell. Choosing Eden would mean to live in isolation, surrounded by an enormous amount and variety of goods, but with no communication with any other individual. Taking up residence in Hell, instead, would mean to lead a stressing existence in competition with other individuals. Whereas for the profit maximiser there may exist an allocation of goods that could compensate for the total isolation that characterises Eden, no such allocation can ever exist for the Hobbesian glory-seeker, who without others is, in a deep sense, dead.

Very often interpreters have highlighted the utilitarian aspects of Hobbes's thought that indeed exist throughout his writings, as I shall argue in Chapter 12. There is, however, a remarkable difference between a society populated by Benthamite Utilitarians and a society of Hobbesian glory-seekers. In the former, the maximisation of the utility of people is limited mainly by material constraints; in the society of glory-seekers, the maximisation of happiness is problematic, because to someone's glorying corresponds always someone else's dejection. Glory is intrinsically a very scarce resource. It is true that in political society there are many fields in which Hobbesian people can excel and therefore the total glory of their society is not necessarily a zero-sum game. However, as Bentham himself observed, desire of honour and power do create complications to the lawgiver wishing to maximise the overall happiness.

In conclusion, the Hobbesian glory-seeker is different from a profit maximiser, from a classical utilitarian, from a solipsist. He needs above all a relationship with others in order to understand who he is and in order to have desires and aims in his life.

9.2 Hobbes on Education

In the previous section, I have suggested that the Hobbesian glory-seeker is dead without competitors to surpass, without witnesses to impress and without others over whom to acquire power. The passion of glory cannot inspire any specific desire without the existence of others. The personality of the glory-seeker is like a box, full of desires when the human world surrounds it and empty when that world disappears.

In Hobbes's early writings, the individual is described as an example of a fixed and eternal human nature; according to Hobbes only to a very limited extent can society change people's natural disposition and transform individuals by means of education into more agreeable beings capable of living in peace with each other: 'Man is made fit for Society not by Nature, but by Education' (*De Cive*, 44). In *De Cive* Hobbes argues that education can correct most people only if applied when they are very young. He points out that some people are so proud that they can never be taught and are unable to accommodate themselves to others. They remain 'useless and troublesome' (*De Cive*, 67) and therefore they should be cast out of society.

Prima facie, on this topic there seems to be little difference between *Elements of Law*, *De Cive*, and *Leviathan*: as in previous works, in the first book of *Leviathan* Hobbes is very vague in his remark that people's dispositions and manners partly derive from nature and partly from education. He does not explain in any detail to what extent education can change attitudes. In *Leviathan*, too, Hobbes points out that some individuals may need to be excluded from society because their proud nature make them incapable of being taught: they are 'Stubborn, Insociable, Forward, Intractable' (*Leviathan*, 106).

However, many interpreters have pointed out that in *Leviathan* Hobbes expresses a greater faith in the effectiveness of education than in any other previous writing. It has been argued, for example by McNeilly, that unlike previous works *Leviathan* was meant for divulgation and education of the public. McNeilly's view can be supported with textual evidence from both *Leviathan*:

> Therefore I think it [the *Leviathan*] may be profitably printed, and more profitably taught in the Universities ... For seeing the Universities are the Fountains of Civill, and Morall Doctrine, from whence the Preachers, and the Gentry, drawing such water as they find, use to sprinkle the

same (both from the Pulpit, and in their Conversation) upon the People, there ought certainly to be great care taken, to have it pure, both from the Venime of Heathen Politicians, and from the Incantation of Deceiving Spirits. And by that means the most men, knowing their Duties, will be the less subject to serve the Ambition of a few discontented persons, in their purposes against the State (*Leviathan*, 491).

and his *Prose Life*:

> He [Hobbes] subsequently occupied his spare time in writing the book which is now most well known, not only in England, but also in neighbouring countries, called *Leviathan* ... In that work he described the rights of kings in both spiritual and temporal terms, using both reason and the authority of sacred scripture ... he hoped that this work might convince his countrymen ... of its truth (*Prose Life*, 248).

> Furthermore he wrote not merely to be read and heard by scholars, but in order that he might be understood by all thinking men of sound judgement, in prose that was simple and direct, not in rhetoric (*Prose Life*, 250).

In *Behemoth* Hobbes claims that most men that were active in the civil war were simply ignorant; and that their ignorance was manipulated in a way that was advantageous for the ambition of a small minority:

> the people in general were so ignorant of their duty as that not one perhaps in 10,000 knew what right any man had to command him, or what necessity there was of King or Commonwealth (*Behemoth*, 4; see also 39, 41).

For Hobbes a good education is a defence against manipulators:

> a man unacquainted with such art (eloquence) could never suspect any ambitious plot in them to raise sedition against the state (*Behemoth*, 24).

It could be argued that the rhetorical elements, that so many interpreters have highlighted in *Leviathan*, were used by Hobbes as means of persuading his readers to accept his theory and also as a means of acquainting them with the art of eloquence often abused by manipulators. In *Leviathan* Hobbes admires 'strength of reason' combined with 'gracefull Elocution', as he makes clear when he pays tribute to Sidney Godolphin (*Leviathan*, 484). Indeed, in the 'Review and Conclusion' to *Leviathan* Hobbes remarks that 'reason and eloquence ... may stand very well together' (*Leviathan*, 483-4). However, rhetoric (that he defines as the art of arguing for or against) for Hobbes is never a procedure to attain science, which is a prerogative that Hobbes ascribes exclusively to logic. Indeed, there is no evidence that Hobbes ever changed the following view expressed in *Anti-White*:

> He [Thomas White] might have stated that ...ethics and many other parts of philosophy *had not yet been treated* logically, but that they should not be so treated was the last thing he ought to have said (*Anti-White*, 27).

The evidence simply suggests that Hobbes in *Leviathan* speaks not just as a geometer (as in *De Cive*), who discovers a political theorem, but also as a teacher and educator, who tries to convince his readers of the validity of the theorem itself. The didactic element is the addition in *Leviathan* to the scientific demonstration given in *De Cive*.

9.3 Hobbes on Nature and Nurture

As it is well known, interpreters' views of *De Homine* vary enormously; at one end of the spectrum we find Gert according to whom Hobbes expresses in this work his most mature views on human nature; at the other end we find Pacchi according to whom in *De Homine* 'Hobbes showed the clearest signs of haste and fatigue'[2] and Martinich that suggests that 'Hobbes published *De Homine* mostly out of a sense of duty, to complete his trilogy'.[3]

On my part, I think that in *De Homine* Hobbes develops some of his earlier views and makes new reflections, that show that at the time of writing this work his mind had not retired.

In *De Homine* Hobbes shows a new interest in trying to ascertain the relative importance of nature and nurture in the behaviour of people. We read:

> men's dispositions ... arise from a sixfold source: namely constitution of the body, experience, habit, fortune, opinion one has of oneself and authorities ... When these things change dispositions change also. (*De Homine*, 63).

Never before had Hobbes been so accurate in assessing the sources of human behaviour. In *De Homine* Hobbes does not spell out if the six origins of human behaviour are equally important. In my view, the very fact that he does not suggest any hierarchy among the sources of human action suggests that none of them is more important than the others and all of them affect human behaviour. Of the six sources of dispositions listed in *De Homine*, it can be observed that only one (the constitution of the body) is given by nature and outside one's control. The other five sources (namely, experience, habit, fortune, one's opinion, authorities) take place in the interaction between the individual and the world in which he happens to live. Hobbes explains that by 'authorities' he means fathers, tutors, and especially books. As to the opinion that one has of oneself, for Hobbes it depends very much on how others value one, and therefore is not antecedent to human interaction.

If man's personality is influenced by the world that he experiences, by his background, by the people he meets and talks to, by the habits of the society in which he lives, by the books he reads, by his family, by his teachers, then man is not 'given' nor immutable.

Although there is scope for debate, I suggest that we may have found an indirect explanation for the fact discussed in Chapter 7, namely that Hobbes in *De Homine* seems to have lost interest in finding an ultimate appetite common to all people. Indeed, if the part of man that is unchangeable is just one of the many sources of his behaviour, it not crucially important to try to establish what it is; it is much more important to stress the malleability of man and the possibility to change and correct him.

In my opinion, in later life Hobbes did not change his view of how men behave in society. In *Leviathan*, *Behemoth*, and *De Homine* Hobbes is still adamant that ambition is the source of human troubles:

> men's Business, consisteth almost in nothing else but a perpetuall contention for Honour, Riches, and Authority (*Leviathan*, A Review and Conclusion, 483).

However, Hobbes seems to have changed his mind about the extent to which human behaviour can be moulded by society. In other words, since writing *Elements of Law* and *De Cive* Hobbes altered his view about the social influence in a person's behaviour so to write confidently in *De Homine* that there are multiple sources of human action, of which only one is natural. The other sources can be influenced to a large extent by the society in which one lives.

The only pessimism that I can detect in Hobbes's later writings is the view that experience (one of the six origins of human behaviour) on its own it is not enough to induce people to alter their behaviour in the long run. The problem, according to Hobbes, is that people forget the past. Hobbes is highly doubtful whether, for example, people will remember 'the late calamities' (*Behemoth*, 39); pessimistic about any useful lessons having being learned from the experience of war, and remarking dolefully that 'the Civill warres have not yet sufficiently taught men' their civic duties (*Leviathan*, 484). In other words, although experience does affect behaviour, by itself it is not enough to change people's attitude. Hobbes suggests that we should rely more on 'authorities' (books, teachers) to educate people than on experience.

Hobbes does not propose at all that we should exploit the fact that human beings are malleable to create by means of education model beings. Coherently with his early writings, Hobbes accepts the view that there are as many definitions of the good as there are people. What Hobbes insists on is that man has to be taught a particular definition of 'public good'. It consists, in *De Homine* as in all Hobbesian writings from *Anti-White* to *Behemoth*, in this:

> whatever the laws are, not to violate them (*De Homine*, 69).

> the virtue of a subject is comprehended wholly in obedience to the laws of the commonwealth (*Behemoth*, 44).

Thus, on the one hand Hobbes is very liberal and does not impose on us a particular definition of 'good' man nor suggests that the state should interfere and make model beings of its citizens. On the other hand, he is remarkably anti-liberal and maintains that the most important lesson that people have to be taught is that political disagreements, political dialogue and political participation have only ill effects.

9.4 From Natural Agent to Educated Citizen

From my analysis of *De Homine* and *Behemoth* it would appear that Hobbes did not change his judgement of how men tend to behave, but rather the extent to which man is natural as opposed to a product of society. Hobbes suggests in *De Homine and Behemoth* (not unlike Rousseau) that the proud citizen who thinks to be wiser of everybody else is more the product of a bad society, with bad Universities and bad

The Determinants of the Citizen: Nature and Nurture 117

ecclesiastics, than of immutable human nature.

Of the six sources of human behaviour listed in *De Homine*, five are silent in the state of nature and, as a result, in the state of nature the agent is a product of nature. Conversely, the citizen is more a product of nurture than nature, because his behaviour is affected above all by the books he reads, the sermons he listens to, the habits he observes, in a word, by his education in a wide sense.

In the next chapter we shall see that for the agent there is no escape from the state of nature: nature alone (which for Hobbes means both passions and reason) offers no salvation. In Chapter 11 we shall see, instead, that the citizen of the political state, thanks to education and exposure to the right books, such as Hobbes's own *De Cive* and *Leviathan*, can understand how not to fall victim of a state of civil war. Passions and reason combined with education deliver the Hobbesian citizen from evil.

Part II

Theorems of Political Geometry

Chapter 10

The Rational Actor at Play

Introduction

In Thucydides' *History*, as translated by Hobbes, we find what is quite possibly the earliest statement of the so-called prisoner's dilemma:

> Everyone supposeth, that his own neglect of the common estate can do little hurt, and that it will be the care of somebody else to look to that for his own good: not observing how by these thoughts of every one in several, the common business is jointly ruined (*History* (*EW VIII*), 147).

Mysteriously, game theorists never mention the above passage showing that although game theory was yet to be born, Hobbes had been exposed to some of its key constructs.

The publication of Gauthier's *The Logic of Leviathan* and of Watkins' 'Imperfect Rationality' marked the beginning of a whole literature that applies criteria and concepts drawn from the armoury of game theory to Hobbes's works in general and to the *Leviathan* in particular. Many Hobbesian readers have found the approach disagreeable and felt that they could get a better insight into Hobbes's theory through Oakeshott's kaleidoscope than by wearing the perfectly graded non-scratch lenses manufactured by game theorists. In a passionate attack against Gauthier, Taylor, McLean, Kavka, and Hampton, Patrick Neal voiced the opinion of many when he wrote that 'rational choice theory reaps a good less than Hobbes attempted to sow and serves to obscure more than to illuminate his teaching'.[1]

The aim of this chapter is to outline both the achievements and the limitations of the game-theoretic approach to Hobbes's political theory. On the positive side, rational-choice theorists can rightly claim to have shown conclusively that:

i) the Hobbesian state of nature can but be a state of war;

ii) there is no escape from Hobbes's state of anarchy (from a rational-actor perspective).

This is no small achievement. However, the rational-actor account does not explain how Hobbesian individuals can leave the state of nature and appoint the great Leviathan – surely a major aspect of Hobbes's enterprise. This result has been interpreted by some (e.g., by Hampton) as a failure of Hobbes's own model. In my own view, this failure, far from highlighting any logical problems in Hobbes's construct, merely shows the unsuitability of the rational-actor approach to offer a full account of Hobbes's theory of the social contract. As I shall argue in Chapter 11, in Hobbes's works one can find a different approach (what I call 'the geometer's approach') with as strong textual credentials as the rational-actor's and with superior heuristic power.

Readers well acquainted with game theory will find the discussion that follows irritatingly informal – I wish to refer them to my joint article with M. La Manna[2] for a treatment of the same material that they may find more congenial to their needs. As to the many who have an instinctive distaste for the often spurious precision of game-theoretic analyses of Hobbes's theory, I hope to offer some insight into the rational-actor approach, focusing on its substantive claims, often clouded by the formulas and the payoff matrices. More specifically, I shall trace the various games that have been offered as alternative explanations of Hobbes's state of nature back to their crucial feature, namely the different selection of the relevant assumptions.

10.1 The State of Nature as a Thought Experiment

The maintained common assumption to any game-theoretical explanation of the state of nature is, of course, that the state of nature can be analysed as a thought experiment. Critics of this approach have not failed to point out that throughout his works Hobbes suggests that the state of nature materialises in three different situations:

1. in primitive societies (Hobbes mentions 'the savage people in many places of America', *Leviathan*, 89);
2. under civil war; (see, for example *Behemoth*, 117);
3. in international relations unregulated by a common power.

These quasi-historical instances can be contrasted to the equally numerous passages where Hobbes suggests unambiguously that the state of nature is a thought experiment about abstract individuals living in abstract conditions:

> Let us return to the state of nature and imagine men as if but even now sprung out of the earth, and suddainly (like Mushrooms) come to full maturity, without all kind of engagement to each other (*De Cive*, 117).

In turn, critics of the interpretation of the state of nature as a thought experiment point out that it is no coincidence that the above quotation comes from *De Cive* rather than from *Leviathan* where Hobbes suggests that the state of nature is a historical stage.

I would counter this criticism by pointing out that in *Leviathan* Hobbes suggests not only that the state of nature is a hypothesis but also that the whole social-contract theory is a thought experiment. For example, in 'A review and Conclusion' to *Leviathan*, Hobbes makes the important remark that:

> there is scarce a Common-wealth in the world, whose beginning can in conscience be justified (*Leviathan*, 486).

If we take the above quotation seriously, we see that Hobbes's social-contract theory does not aim at explaining how historical states are born. The relevant question is therefore why Hobbes thought that the state of nature was the appropriate theoretical device to explain political obligation. In this respect it has to be remembered that traditionally the ideas of the state of nature and social contract had been invoked in order to impose limits on the power of kings. Hobbes, instead, uses them in a subversive way, i.e., to prove that the sovereign power ought to be absolute, indivisible, and irrevocable. He must have thought that the most effective way to challenge the opposition was to resort to their very armoury (the state of nature and the social contract), to combine it with his scientific method and thus prove beyond doubt that these elements together brought about the mighty Leviathan, i.e., precisely the opposite result from that desired by the proponents of the state-of-nature approach.

It is difficult not to share Pocock's puzzlement about the fact that

> Hobbes's transformation of the opposition ideology of rights and liberty into the basis of absolute authority is among the most remarkable but least noted of his accomplishments.[3]

10.2 On the Applicability of Game Theory to Hobbes

The fundamental assumptions made by Hobbes that allow the application of game theory to his argument without any major violation of the text are as follows:

IR: Instrumental Rationality. Hobbes states that 'every man by reasoning seeks out the meanes to the end which he propounds to himselfe' (*De Cive*, 167; see also *Leviathan*, Ch. V).

CK: Common Knowledge, in the sense that the description of the game is known to both players and each player knows that the other player knows, and so on.[4] Hobbes's reflections on the right of nature and the natural laws come very close to assuming common knowledge explicitly.[5]

B: Bipartition. Individual actions can be partitioned into two sets, namely actions that lead to conflict and the submission of others ('Fight') — attacking others, dispossessing them, provoking them 'by deeds or words' — and actions intended to avoid conflict ('Avoid'). It is not altogether surprising that in his description of the state of nature Hobbes gives an account of human behaviour in terms of this bipartition, as his aim is to assess whether the state of nature is a state of war or a state of peace.

These 'background' assumptions, while allowing us to interpret Hobbes's construct as a simple game-theoretic model, are obviously insufficient to capture the distinctiveness of his argument. All Hobbesian interpreters agree that the following statements by Hobbes are consistently maintained throughout his work to warrant the status of key assumptions of his model:

Equal Vulnerability and Dangerousness: all individuals inhabit a very 'fragile human frame' so that 'even the weakest has strength enough to kill the strongest' (*Leviathan*, 110; see also *Elements of Law*, 70, and *De Cive*, 45). I discussed this assumption in Chapter 2 and 8.

S: Self-preservation. Each individual seeks to avoid violent death at the hand of others. I examined this assumption in conjunction with glory in chapters 2 and 3.

Figure 10.1 below illustrates the condition of each agent in the Hobbesian state of nature: each person can choose either to Avoid fighting or to Fight; if both individuals fight, the result is War; if both avoid fighting, the result is Peaceful Independence; if one fights and the other avoids, the former obtains Dominion and the latter falls into a state of Subjection.

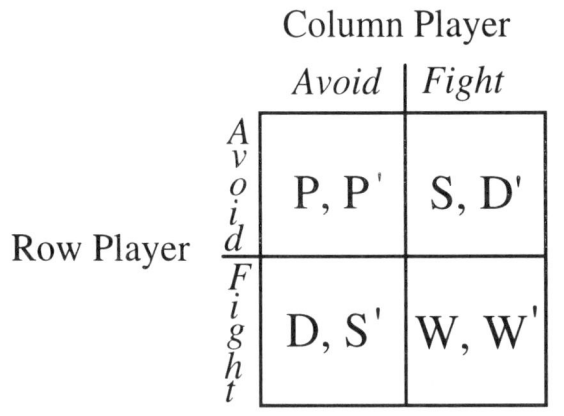

| | Column Player | |
	Avoid	Fight
Row Player Avoid	P, P'	S, D'
Row Player Fight	D, S'	W, W'

Figure 10.1: The generic bimatrix game

The outcome of the game depends on the preferences by each individual for the different states of affairs described respectively by Peaceful Independence, War, Dominion, and Subjection

On the one hand, game-theorists agree that for all Hobbesian individuals Peaceful Independence is preferable to a state of Subjection (mutual avoidance is preferable to unilateral avoidance) and that War is worse than Peaceful Independence (and hence that mutual fighting is worse than mutual avoidance).

On the other hand, there is widespread disagreement about the ranking suggested by Hobbes regarding all the other payoffs (namely, Peaceful Independence vs. Dominion, and Subjection vs. War). The reason for this bewildering disparity of views is that interpreters have selected different assumptions as crucial to Hobbes's argument. Hence the proliferation of game-theoretical interpretations, ranging from Prisoner's dilemmas to coordination games, from assurance games to dis-co-ordination games, as detailed below.

10.3 Game-Theory Applications to Hobbes's Theory

As mentioned above, Hobbes's text suggests consistently that Peaceful Independence is preferable to War ($P > W$) and preferable to Subjection ($P > S$) but is open to different interpretations as to the precise ranking of Peaceful Independence vs. Dominion, and

126 *Hobbes and the Political Philosophy of Glory*

Subjection vs. War. It can be noticed that eight rankings of the relevant payoffs are possible: $P < D$ and $S < W$; $P < D$ and $S = W$; $P > D$ and $S > D$; $P > D$ and $S = W$; $P > D$ and $S < W$; $P = D$ and $S < W$; $P < D$ and $S > W$; $P = D$ and $S > W$.

Interestingly enough *all of the above payoffs but one* have been traced back to Hobbes and buttressed with suitable quotations, giving rise to numerous game-theoretical interpretations of Hobbes's arguments.

10.3.1 The Bees and Ants game

Of the above eight payoff rankings only one has not been examined in the literature on Hobbes, namely the case in which Peaceful Independence is as good as Dominion; and Subjection is preferable to War *($P = D$ and $S > W$)* The reason for this omission is obvious. These payoffs, far from leading to the war that characterises the Hobbesian state of nature, produce the state of peace that according to Hobbes is enjoyed by bees and ants (for a detailed account of Hobbes's argument see above, chapter 5). The key equality ($P = D$) is the implication of *non-glory-seeking behaviour*: unlike human beings preoccupied with establishing their 'eminence' and superiority, bees and ants do not derive any benefit from fighting an opponent who refrains from fighting. On the other hand, as bees and ants are concerned with self-preservation, any state of affair is better than war.

10.3.2 Prisoner's Dilemmas

The payoff rankings ($D > P > W \geq S$) and ($D = P > W > S$) give rise to the prisoner's dilemma, that many interpreters have taken as the game that best describes the Hobbesian dilemma of the state of nature.[6]

As this is, perhaps, the most popular and well-known game-theoretical application to Hobbes, I have no desire to add to it. I shall confine myself to examining the crucial role of 'assumption selection' in Gauthier's classic treatment.

10.3.2.1 Gauthier's Logic of Leviathan *and assumption selection*

Gauthier's *Logic of Leviathan* is regarded as the classic example of the prisoner's dilemma approach to Hobbes. Indeed Gauthier used it to illustrate various aspects of the predicament in which the Hobbesian man finds himself in the state of nature.

Rather than analysing Gauthier's various games (which, while having been quite original at the time, now show their age and would be an unfair target for criticism), my interest here is to analyse and criticise the specific selection of assumptions that, in Gauthier's view, underpin Hobbes's model.

As mentioned in section 10.2, Gauthier, like all rational-actor interpreters, agrees that crucial premises in Hobbes's model are:

(i) 'an innate and original concern with self-maintenance'[7] – what I have termed assumption S;

(ii) 'the ability of one man to kill another'[8] – my assumption E; and

(iii) the fact that 'reason is taken by Hobbes to prescribe the means to man's ends, and chiefly man's chief end, preservation',[9] i.e., assumption IR.

From my perspective, Gauthier's key remark in this context is that 'if the state of nature were a state of plenty, then men might refrain from hostility'.[10] Thus, in Gauthier's view, scarcity of resources, and not natural competitiveness (as I claimed in Chapter 5), is an additional crucial assumption of Hobbes's model.[11]

As I argued in section 5.5, if by 'scarce resources' we mean that resources are insufficient for the survival of the entire population, in *Leviathan* Hobbes states unambiguously that no political alchemy (no social contract) can solve this problem: war is the only, inevitable outcome. Conversely, if resources are deemed to be scarce when their overall amount is so limited that some cannot enjoy the superfluous without others been deprived of what is necessary (and this is indeed Hobbes's view), then one has to explain why men do not behave like bees and ants, and pool their efforts to increase the common good. For Hobbes, desire of eminence is the reason why men fight; accumulation of resources is the way in which glory-seekers hope to achieve superiority. This strategy deprives others of their means of survival and fear leads them to conflict. In other words, in Hobbes's argument competition is not, as Gauthier claims, 'derivative', i.e., a product of fear. On the contrary, competitiveness is 'original', i.e., a natural characteristic of human nature, and fear is a consequence of the fact that we know that other agents (or at least some of them, that we cannot recognise in advance) are glory-seekers and therefore will try to deprive us of our means of survival in order to establish their power over us.

It is easy to see that the game chosen by Gauthier to illustrate the payoffs accruing to the prudent Hobbesian man from either keeping or breaking a covenant with others[12] falls in the prisoner's dilemma category. Gauthier illustrates the predicament of two 'rationally prudent agents', A and B, deciding whether or not to adhere to the covenant thus:

		Agent B	
		adheres	violates
Agent A	adheres	2 , 2	4 , 1
	violates	1 , 4	3 , 3

where the numerals 1 to 4 refer to the relevant agent's ranking of the outcome, 1 being the most and 4 the least advantageous, i.e., in my notation, $D > P > W > S$. From this Gauthier concludes that 'prudence will require each to violate the agreement'.[13]

It is worth emphasising that in all prisoner's dilemma versions of the state of nature individuals may understand in principle that a sovereign power would solve their problem, but they can never rationally give up their right to all things. The creation of the sovereign power can be introduced only *ex machina*, but is not an outcome of the rational action of prudent individuals.

10.3.2.2 Kavka, Hampton, and the Repeated Prisoner's Dilemma

Developing an insight originally due to Gauthier, Gregory Kavka[14] is among the interpreters who attach special importance to Hobbes's answer to the Foole (*Leviathan*, Ch. XV). Specifically, Kavka suggests that on the ground of what Hobbes says to the Foole, we should interpret the state of nature not as a single, but rather as a *repeated* prisoner's dilemma game. Whereas in a one-shot prisoner's dilemma rationality suggests non-cooperation, rational agents understand that 'the greater the number of iterations, the more potential gains there are to be reaped by mutual cooperation, and hence the more rational it is to try early cooperation' (Kavka, p. 135).

In all his models Kavka endorses the standard assumptions mentioned in section 10.2. In particular, he describes Hobbesian men as 'death-averse' (S), 'rational planners' (IR), 'roughly equal in natural endowments' (E), 'no special knowledge differentiates them one from another' (CK).

He adds to the list of assumptions certain psychological characteristics of the Hobbesian man, such as the 'concern for reputation' and self-interest, highlighting the distinction made by Hobbes between moderates and glory-seekers (whom Kavka calls 'dominators'). In Kavka's game-theoretical model a special status is reserved to the crucial assumption of 'forwardlookingness':

> Forwardlooking parties consider their long-run as well as short run desires and interests and give their desires and interests at different times equal weight in decision-making.[15]

Kavka suggests that Hobbesian individuals learn from past experiences and modify their strategies over time; he argues that 'cooperation in the state of nature is possible, but it is precarious' (p. 154). The main function of the assumption of forwardlookingness is that players will realise: (i) the prisoner's dilemma structure of their interactions in the state of nature (summarised in the payoff matrix below) and (ii) refrain from enjoying the short-term advantage derived from breaking the agreement and appreciate the long-term benefits of repeated cooperation.

		Party 2	
		keep	break
Party 1	keep	5 , 5	−1 , 6
	break	6 , −1	0 , 0

[Kavka, *Hobbesian Moral and Political Theory*, 154.]

Here I wish to examine two particular problems with Kavka's interpretation of the state of nature. First, whereas Kavka is right in saying that for Hobbes individuals are potentially forward looking, in my view he is wrong in believing that Hobbesian people can rely on this ability *in the state of nature*. As I argued in Chapters 1 and 6, in the state of nature uncertainty is supreme; individuals are victims of the present and cannot form firm expectations about the future. Their ability to plan is wasted; no agent is assured of anything; each can rely on nothing. The only forwardlooking passion is fear, which inspires diffidence and distrust, not cooperation. If we can rely on nothing learnt in the past, the potential for successful cooperation implicit in the Kavkian assumption of forwardlookingness never materialises in the state of nature – repeated games are pointless.

Secondly, and perhaps more importantly, as we can see from Kavka's payoff matrix, war and death (that result from mutual breaking) are not the worst possible outcomes. In other word, Kavka assumes that for Hobbesian individuals there is a state of affairs worse than war and death (unilateral keeping of the contract). There is overwhelming evidence that this is not Hobbes's view. The main criticism that can be levelled against Kavka's model (and many others in a similar vein) is that it does not take seriously Hobbes's view on the incommensurably bad outcome of war and the incommensurably negative value of death.

For Hobbesian individuals, the chance of learning and changing strategy is simply unavailable, because if their first move is wrong, then they die and have no opportunity to revise their strategy, whereas if they survive they have no incentive to change strategy and thus the next iteration of the game will be played precisely like the earlier one. In the long run, as well as in the short run, the only rational move is *not* to cooperate.

Like Kavka, Jean Hampton, too, argues that iterated prisoner's dilemma games can account for Hobbes's argument for cooperation in the answer to the Foole in Chapter 15 of *Leviathan*. At the same time, she argues that the one-shot prisoner's dilemma and its dominant strategy of fighting provide the theoretical framework to analyse Hobbes's account of war in the state of nature, as described in Chapter 13 of *Leviathan*. According to Hampton, the reasons why Hobbesian people in the state of nature tend not to cooperate (i.e., they tend to consider the prisoner's dilemma as a one-shot game rather than as an instance of many repetitions of the same game) are (i) shortsightedness, and (ii) fear of shortsightedness in other people. Hampton explains that

> The shortsightedness account of conflict ... explains conflict by reference not to disruptive passions but to fallacious reasoning, and this can be held to be extremely common among the inhabitants of the state of nature without in any way endangering Hobbes's psychological characterization of human beings.[16]

Hampton's interpretation is open to a number of criticisms. Firstly, although Hampton believes that

> there is enough textual evidence to indicate that Hobbes not only would welcome [the shortsightedness] account of conflict ... but may even been confusedly trying to present it himself in both *De Cive* and *Leviathan*.[17]

in fact her claim that the state of war is a result of 'shortsightedness' and 'fallacious reasoning' is flatly rejected by Hobbes thus

> It is a precept or generall rule of *Reason*, that every man when he cannot obtain [peace] he may seek and use all helps and advantages of Warre (*Leviathan*, 92).

Secondly, like Kavka, Hampton does not take war and death seriously enough. She admits that

> in high risk situation ... it would seem irrational to engage in a strategy of cooperating in order to teach one partner to do the same, because one would be unable to absorb the loss that might be involved in the teaching.[18]

In other words, she accepts that one cannot afford to play iterated prisoner's dilemmas in high-risk situations, but she does not seem to concede that the state of nature is exactly such a situation.

In conclusion, it can be argued that the very concept of a repeated game is not applicable to Hobbes's state of nature, because it contravenes Hobbes's view on the absolutely negative value of war, which is in turn brought about by the assumptions of the equal dangerousness of individuals and by the incommensurably negative value attached by Hobbes to violent death.

10.3.3 Assurance games

The payoff rankings $I > D, S < W$ give rise to *assurance games* that can be found, among others, in the works of Kavka,[19] Hampton,[20] and Taylor.[21]

Consider, as an example, Kavka's discussion of the choice of a sovereign in the state of nature, where he deploys an assurance game (he calls it an 'impure coordination problem'). He supplies the following payoff matrix:

		Player 2	
		A	B
Player 1	A	5 , 4	0 , 0
	B	0 , 0	4 , 5

[Kavka, *Hobbesian Moral and Political Theory*,184.]

The main obvious limit of Kavka's assurance game is that, in his own words

> we cannot tell what sort of solution rational parties in the state of nature would find for their impure coordination problems until we say more about these parties and the circumstances we suppose them to be in.[22]

When Kavka does tell us more about 'the parties and the circumstances' he introduces contextual assumptions and empirical considerations that distance him from Hobbes. To put it differently, his model cannot tell the rational actor anything specific as long as it remains recognisably Hobbes's and can suggest a course of action only when it becomes distinctly non-Hobbesian.

Like Kavka, Hampton, too, illustrates the 'leadership selection problem' faced by the inhabitants of Hobbes's state of nature with games with multiple equilibria[23] e.g., the following two-equilibria game (where the figures stand for preference rankings, e.g., 1 = most preferred, 4 = least preferred):

	A is sovereign	B is sovereign
A is sovereign	1 , 2	3 , 3
B is sovereign	3 , 3	2 , 1

[Hampton, *Hobbes and the Social Contract Tradition*, 152.]

She points out that the problem of selecting and empowering the sovereign

> is, in the main, a coordination problem, albeit one with considerable conflict of interest, that Hobbesian people are able to solve.[24]

Here, as in the rest of her argument Hampton plays down Hobbes's assumption of the desire of glory and superiority that characterises many Hobbesian people. More seriously, the very reason why Hampton suggests that people can address the leadership selection problem is that she thinks that people can detach themselves from the high-risk situation that is the state of nature. In her argument, the possibility of a state of war (with consequent death) acts simply as a pressing force (as a deadline) to reach a quick agreement. In Hobbes's argument, instead, the concern for self-preservation is overwhelming and no action can ever be suggested by reason that can distract the mind from the immediate problem of preserving life. As long as there is no enforced agreement, people are required by reason to fight for survival. It would be irrational to enter a truce and respect a deadline with the view to selecting a leader, while we are not sure that others will observe the same deadline.

In conclusion, Hampton has no hesitation in claiming that 'Hobbes's argument fails' (*Hobbes and the Social Contract Tradition*, 189-207), that 'it is badly wrong' (97) and that 'the geometric deduction of absolute sovereignty is flawed' (69). Most helpfully she develops 'on Hobbes's behalf' (91) all the arguments that apparently Hobbes himself was unable to provide, thereby 'salvaging' his philosophy.

Hampton provides perhaps the extreme example of over-confidence in the suitability of the game-theoretical approach for the assessment of the strengths and weaknesses in Hobbes's argument. At the other end of the spectrum, we could place Patrick Neal, to whose contribution I now turn.

10.3.4 Neal's 'co-ordination' game

An interesting critique of the whole game-theoretical approach to Hobbes's theory is offered by Patrick Neal.[25] He, too, shares with the literature the assumptions introduced in section 10.1 (some explicitly – instrumental rationality and common knowledge,[26] others implicitly), unlike the rational-actor brigade, he stresses the importance of the assumption of self-preservation in Hobbes's theory. Neal correctly points out that the interpretation of the state of nature as a prisoner's dilemma does not take into consideration 'the substantive payoffs available to human beings in the state of nature'.[27] He argues that all strategy combinations other than mutual cooperation lead to individual payoffs that make individuals as badly off as they can possibly be. More specifically he posits that $D = S = W$ = Death. In relation to our original matrix (see Figure 10.1), Neal suggests the payoff rankings $I > D$, $S = W$ as an alternative interpretation of Hobbes's state of nature.

Here is the graphic portrayal of Hobbes's state of nature, according to Neal:

		Column Player	
		Cooperation	Non-cooperation
Row Player	Cooperation	*Life*	*Death*
	Non-cooperation	*Death*	*Death*

Neil argues that the above situation is the one in which Hobbesian men find themselves in the state of nature, a 'situation which is not a prisoners' dilemma, but a 'coordination game' in which there is a stable and optimal collective outcome'.[28]

On the one hand, Neal makes a valuable contribution to the literature: (i) by considering the specific payoff of Death as crucial to an understanding of Hobbes's theory and (ii) by suggesting that if game theory does not offer a way out from Hobbes's state of nature this should not be interpreted as a flaw in Hobbes's arguments, but rather as a limitation of the rational-actor approach.

On the other hand, Neal's own model of Hobbes's state of nature does not take into account some critical preference patterns that are an integral part of Hobbes's model. Subjection, Dominion, and Independence are indeed three ways of being alive, but to Hobbesian men they are *not* equally desirable states of affairs. Neal seems to suggest that the inability of accounting for the subtleties of Hobbes's argument is an inherent limitation of the rational-choice approach. In this, Neal is perhaps guilty of underestimating the versatility of game theory, which, as I shall below, can account for the more complex pattern of preferences attributed by Hobbes to 'temperate' individuals and glory-seekers.

10.3.5 Fowl games: Chickens, Hawks and Doves

The payoff rankings $P < D$, $S > W$, typical of *dis-co-ordination* ('chicken') games, have been suggested (for example by Sugden[29]) as an interpretation of Hobbes's state of nature.

In my view these payoff rankings come closest to describing, within the confines of the rational-actor approach, Hobbes's own account of the state of nature, in so far as there is ample and incontrovertible textual evidence to support the view that in the state of nature Hobbesian individuals prefer dominion to peaceful independence and subjection to war.

10.4 Game Theory á la Carte

It could be argued that an accurate and helpful game-theoretical interpretation of Hobbes should try to put together the best insights of the models briefly surveyed in this chapter, namely

The Rational Actor at Play

(i) Gauthier's claim that Hobbes intended to give a rationality account of both conflict and cooperation;

(ii) Kavka's attempts to account for the variety of individuals described by Hobbes, ranging from 'moderates' to full-bloodied glory-seekers;

(iii) Hampton's argument that Hobbesian agents act under incomplete information, in the sense that they cannot distinguish 'the righteous from the wicked'.[30]

(iv) Neal's important insight that death for Hobbes is not just 'bad', but incommensurably bad, in the sense that no amount of goods can compensate for the loss of life.

(v) Sugden's suggestion that the Hobbesian individuals' prefer dominion to peaceful independence and subjection to war (i.e., $P < D$; $S > W$).

Conversely, a more adequate game-theoretical interpretation of Hobbes's state of nature should obviate some of the weaknesses in the models examined in this chapter, e.g.:

(i) the inability of Neal's model to capture the differences between being alive, subjugated, independent, or a dominator; (ii) the inadequacy of Kavka's models to capture the drama of death;

(iii) the failure of Hampton's interpretation to account for the dual claim by Hobbes that individuals are rational and yet the state of nature is 'the dominion of passion'.

The following section is an attempt to develop intuitively a 'composite' model encompassing the attractive features of the rational-actor approach to Hobbes's state of nature.[31]

10.5 Chicken with Spices: Glory and Death

Like the models analysed in the previous section, the present game – Chicken with Spices – assumes Instrumental rationality, Common Knowledge, Equal Vulnerability, and Bipartition of actions in 'Fighting' and 'Avoid' fighting. In addition, the following assumptions (that in different forms appear also in the models examined above) are explicitly made:

I I: Incomplete Information. Individuals 'cannot distinguish the wicked from the righteous' (*De Cive*, 33), the glory-seeker from the moderate.

S^∞: Self-preservation in a *strong* sense. 'Violent death at the hands of others' is *incommensurably* bad: 'of the good things experienced by men *none can outweigh* the greatest of the evil ones, namely sudden death' (*Anti-White*, 408, emphasis added).[32]

G: Glory. Some individuals seek glory, namely the pleasure of superiority and honour. Hobbesian glory-seekers aim specifically at the physical submission of their enemies: they 'use Violence, to make themselves Masters of other mens persons, wives, childrens, and cattell' *(Leviathan*, chap. XIII).

Assumption G implies that alongside glory-seekers there are 'moderate' individuals who, according to Hobbes, do not aim at superiority, but would be 'contented with equality' (*Elements of Law*, 70-1; see also *Leviathan*, 112).

From Gauthier to Hampton, all Hobbesian game theorists agree in considering G (namely the claim that *some* people are glory-seekers) as the prevalent view on glory put forward by Hobbes in Book I of *Leviathan*. The Chicken with Spices game would work *a fortiori* if *all* or *most* people were glory-seekers, as suggested in places of *Elements of Law* (47) and *De Cive* (43), and in Book II of *Leviathan* (156).

The argument is intuitively very simple. Imagine that:
1. all individuals attach an incommensurably negative value to the loss of life (assumption S^∞);
2. they are all equally able to endanger each other's life (assumption E);
3. they will use the most appropriate means for the attainment of their ends (assumption R);
4. that some attach a great value to becoming superior to others (assumption G), but
5. these glory-seekers are not detectable in advance (assumption II).

Suppose next that I am one of the glory-seekers, and thus my payoffs are: $P < D$, $S < W$. As a glory-seeker, if faced by an opponent disposed to refrain from fighting, I would prefer Fight to Avoid, for this would not only guarantee my self-preservation, but also yield the pleasure of glory in establishing my superiority over the retreating opponent. On the other hand, the over-riding concern for preserving my own life implies that, when faced by an opponent potentially inclined to fight, I would prefer to avoid fighting to the self-destruction of mutual fighting. Because of the assumption of Incomplete Information, I cannot know in advance the psychological make-up of any of my potential opponents.

The Rational Actor at Play

In determining my optimal strategy as a rational actor attempting to attain glory, I will reason as follows.

Firstly, since the outcome of opposed fight is death (as 'equal powers opposed destroy each other') and since death is incommensurably evil, it would seem to follow that my rational choice should invariably be to avoid fighting.

Secondly, as it would be invariably rational for me to avoid fighting, so it would be equally rational for any opponent of mine, who knows all that I know (this is the assumption CK, common knowledge), and therefore can arrive at the same conclusion that fighting is best avoided.

Thirdly, as I can work out that any opponent would be invariably disposed by reason to avoid fighting, it would be rational for a glory-seeker like myself to attack any such opponent, thereby attaining my goal of superiority and glory.

Fourthly, conversely, as I cannot ascertain in advance whether any potential opponent is a glory-seeker (II), but I know that any opponent knows what I know (CK), my line of reasoning is available to any potential glory-seeking opponent who can work out that I will avoid fighting and therefore will try to attack me.

If these are my rational thoughts, what will be my rational action?

It is easy to see that I am torn between the rationality of avoiding being killed by others and the rationality of fighting a retreating opponent, which would be a glory-yielding action.

The intuitive outcome of the game is that, in the circumstances envisaged in the rational-actor account of the Hobbesian state of nature, any glory-seeker is trapped in a viciously circular argument. As no individual in the state of nature can afford the luxury of inaction and reason offers no guidance as to the optimal course of action (in so far as it continually oscillates between attack and retreat), the source of inspiration for action can only come from each individual's *irrational* nature (what Hobbes calls the 'concupiscible part').

In other words, the game highlights the circularity of the dilemma that afflicts glory-seekers in the state of nature and thus the impossibility for glory-seekers of *individually* rational decision-making.

Whereas a standard 'chicken' game can be solved by rational players by tossing an appropriately weighted coin, the above is a special chicken game where the 'spices' that produce no solution and create the drama are the incommensurably negative value of death and the positive value of glory.

'Chicken with spices' makes sense of Hobbes's claim, unaccounted for and unexplained by any other rational-choice construct, that outside the political state there is a dominion of passions:

> Out of it [the political state], there is a Dominion of Passions .... In it, the dominion of reason (*De Cive*, 130).

'Chicken with spices' also provides an explanation for Hobbes's claim that in the state of nature war is 'perpetual in its own nature' (*De Cive*, 49). Any game-theoretic application to Hobbes's state of nature (whether of the prisoner's dilemma variety or a standard Chicken game) that yields war as the outcome of individually rational actions, implies that conflict would *not* be perennial, for the simple reason that 'equal powers opposed destroy each other' (*Elements of Law*, 34).

'Chicken with spices', instead, accounts for the impossibility of reaching a rational plan of action and the consequent reliance on the rule of passions that makes occasional battles possible and the *threat* of war a permanent menace in Hobbes's state of nature:

> war, consisteth not in battle only ... the nature of war, consisteth not in actual fighting; but in the known disposition thereto (*Leviathan*, 113).

In conclusion, a strong case can be made to say that 'chicken with spices' is more explanatory value than many other game-theoretical interpretations of Hobbes.

However, there is one fundamental feature that 'chicken with spices' shares with all other rational-choice accounts of Hobbes's state of nature, namely the property that rational agents are *unable to escape from anarchy*.

This result can be interpreted in three different ways:

i) as suggested by Hampton, it can be viewed as a failure in Hobbes's own model.

ii) as suggested by Kavka, it can be said that it was not Hobbes's intention to offer a way out of the state of nature because:

> the state of nature is used in Hobbesian theory, as a model of what would happen to us if central political authority were removed, and its purportive negative features serve as reason for us not to promote or allow such removal, for example, by provoking a civil war.[33]

This latter view is now endorsed by many Hobbesian critics, the most recent addition to its supporters being Hampsher-Monk's.[34] 'Chicken with spices' can be construed as lending support to this interpretation; however, endorsing this view does not exclude a more radical position, namely,

(iii) that the inability of all game-theoretical models to show a way out of the state of nature may be due to the simple fact that Hobbes *did not use* the rational-actor approach in his construct of the state of nature, but resorted instead to an altogether different analytical perspective. The task of substantiating this more radical claim is undertaken in the next chapter.

Chapter 11

Hobbes's Impossibility Theorem

Introduction

In the previous chapter I analysed Hobbes's state of nature taking a rational-agent approach – a perspective pioneered in the 1960s by Gauthier and Watkins and still favoured by many today. Accordingly, I imagined Hobbesian individuals in the state of nature, attributed to them some of the characteristics described by Hobbes (rationality, fear of death, desire of glory, liberty, equality), calculated the payoffs of their joint actions, and finally singled out the rational strategy for them to follow.

As I argued in Chapter 10 the rational-actor approach succeeds in demonstrating that the state of nature is, as claimed by Hobbes, a state of war. However, as many have pointed out (e.g., Brian Barry) the rational-actor approach is unable to explain how Hobbesian men reach an agreement and join the social contract.

It is no coincidence that only critics (such as McLean and Taylor) who assume the possibility of 'repeated games' in the Hobbesian state of nature can account for a way out from it. But in my view the very idea of a 'repeated game' violates Hobbes's claim that individuals in the state of nature take no chances about their self-preservation. It is easy to notice that an agent can engage rationally in a supergame strategy only if he is prepared to make mistakes, if he thinks that he can learn from those mistakes, and adjust his future behaviour accordingly. This option is not open to the Hobbesian man, because making a wrong judgement may cost him his life and therefore deprive him of the possibility of learning from the past and of revising his strategy. Unwilling to trade off personal safety for any amount of information about other people's attitudes, Hobbesian men can neither take risk nor deploy any supergame strategy.

However, the fact that the rational-actor approach cannot explain the social contract, does not entail, as claimed by Hampton, that Hobbes's argument fails. Rather, we should deduce that the rational-actor approach is inadequate to explain *the whole* of Hobbes's contractarian argument.

In this chapter I am going to consider an alternative approach to Hobbes's theory, an approach that, although suggested by Hobbes himself and followed by some of his correspondents (notably Leibniz), is unaccountably neglected in the literature: the viewpoint of the geometer of political philosophy.

As it is well known, Hobbes was fascinated by the method of geometry. The following passage from Aubrey's biography of Hobbes is rightly famous:

> He [Hobbes] was forty years old before he looked on geometry; which happened accidentally. Being in a gentleman's library Euclid's *Elements* lay open, and 'twas the forty-seventh proposition in the first book. He read the proposition. 'By G–,' said he, 'this is impossible!' So he reads the demonstration of it, which referred him back to such a proof; which referred him back to another, which he also read. And so forth, that at last he was demonstratively convinced of that truth. This made him in love with geometry (*Brief Lives*, 151-2).

Not only Hobbes saw his theory as an application of the geometrical method to politics, but also so did many of his correspondents (e.g. Sorbière, du Verdus, Leibniz).

In letter 195 (dated tentatively 1674 by Malcolm) Leibniz writes to Hobbes:

> you ... were the first person to place the correct method of argument and demonstration ... in the clear light of political philosophy ... I can see clearly enough that your demonstrations, like those of geometry, are universal and abstracted from the matter which they deal with (*Correspondence II*, 733-4).

It is important to focus on the differences between the political geometer's viewpoint and the rational actor's. Whereas the geometer chooses the assumptions that give rise to the human drama in the state of nature, the rational agent instead is at the mercy of the assumptions chosen by the geometer. Whereas the rational actor cannot but respond to the situation created by the assumptions of the model, the geometer, instead, is a detached observer and can, at will, intervene and change the assumptions of the model and thus the resulting state of affairs.

In what follows, I intend (i) to single out the criteria used by

Hobbes in choosing the assumptions of his model; (ii) to highlight the paradoxical nature of the theorem derived by Hobbes from these assumptions, and (iii) to examine the solution to the paradox proposed by Hobbes.

My contention is that whereas the differences between the rational-actor approach and the geometer approach are not significant in stages (i) and (ii), they become all-important in stage (iii).

In the course of the presentation of Hobbes's argument, I shall examine the reaction to the various steps of his demonstration by his correspondents, and in particular by Leibniz, who was both enthusiastic about Hobbes's model and perhaps the first to grasp the limitations of Hobbes's demonstration.

Finally, I shall argue that according to Hobbes the point of view of the geometer is not available only to himself and to an small elite of like-minded intellectuals, but on the contrary is accessible to *any* reader of his theory, to anyone in a calm state of mind living in the comfort of a peaceful political state – in a word to everybody *except* the rational actor in a state of anarchy, because the latter is necessarily completely absorbed in the struggle to keep himself alive and thus has no opportunity to detach himself from the battle for survival and to reflect on his predicament.

11.1 The Requirements of the Political Definition of Man

As Euclid begins with a number of definitions, so does Hobbes. It is important to reconstruct the criteria used (but not spelt out) by Hobbes to arrive at his political definition of man. In chapter 1, I identified two such criteria: the definition of man must capture something that is *permanent* in every man over time and *common* to all men. However, the resulting definition of man derived by Hobbes – man is motion – is very wide, too general as a building block of a political theorem. In fact, when Hobbes analyses the state of nature (*Elements of Law*, Ch. XIV, *De Cive*, Ch. I, *Leviathan*, Ch. XIII), he is far more parsimonious and uses only *some* of the defining elements of 'man as motion' described in the introductory pages of *Elements of Law* and *Leviathan*.

It is my contention that it is possible to identify two additional requirements implicitly deployed to Hobbes to simplify his initial definition of man as matter-in-motion and to select the assumptions on human nature relevant for his discussion of the state of nature.

Although for Hobbes political science can offer a form of

knowledge that is not absolute but only conditional (*Leviathan*, chapter IX), he thought that the political theorist must ensure that the presuppositions on which political science depends are not arbitrary, but acceptable to most people. In political science for Hobbes as much as

> in mathematical sciences wee come at last to a definition wch is the beginning or Principle, made true by pact and consent amongst our selues (*Correspondence I*, letter 31, 83).

So the definition of man to be chosen as the starting point of political geometry must according to Hobbes not contradict the common perception that we have of ourselves (through self-analysis: *redi te ipsum*) and of others (through observation). Indeed in his dispute with Descartes, Hobbes's main criticism is Descartes' disregard for individual experience

> his [Descartes'] hypothesis involved something *contrary to experience – not an insignificant objection* (*Correspondence I*, letter 30, 78; emphasis added).[1]

To sum up, Hobbes is aware that for his own demonstrations to be of any practical relevance his assumptions and definitions must be found acceptable by his readers.

This is not the only additional requirement for the political definition of man. In his correspondence Hobbes ridicules those writers who address pointless problems that cannot be of any relevance to the real world. He writes

> when it is demonstrated ... if it cannot also be practised tis worth nothinge, but like ye probleme How to make a bridge ouer the sea ... but such an arch cannot be made (*Correspondence I*, letter 16, 29).

In other words, if a demonstration is impracticable, it is pointless: hence for Hobbes the political definition of man must be able to explain the core problem of politics. In view of the perilous times he lived through, it is not surprising that Hobbes reckoned the essential problem of politics to be the occurrence of civil war.

It has been suggested[2] that any given author can be located on the map of history of political thought depending on whether his key interests refer to the antithesis of either order versus anarchy or freedom versus authority. In this taxonomy, Hobbes is definitely preoccupied with, indeed fascinated by, the former antithesis (whereas

Locke, for example, was attracted to the latter).

So the final requirement of the definition of man is that it should pass the test of political relevance, i.e., in Hobbes's view, it should account for the possible occurrence of civil war and internal conflict. It is on the basis of this criterion that Hobbes selects those aspects of human nature worthy of the attention of the political geometer, i.e., worthy of being chosen as the assumptions of the model.

In my opinion, the *test of political relevance*, rather than personal pessimism (as suggested by many critics, e.g. Skinner), provides a far more convincing explanation than for Hobbes's insistence on the non-cooperative and indeed aggressive characteristics of man and for his neglect of the more positive and endearing traits of humanity.[3]

I claim that the main reason why Hobbes excludes from his description of man qualities such as generosity, sympathy, adaptability, good humour, etc., is his belief that a political geometer must be parsimonious with assumptions and mention only those that are relevant to derive his theorems.

In conclusion, Hobbes the geometer offers a definition of man that captures not only those characteristics that are (i) permanent, and (ii) common to all (as discussed in chapter 1), but also (iii) easily confirmed by individuals' self-analysis and observation of others, and (iv) politically relevant to explain civil war and human conflict.

Thus, although both Hobbes and Euclid start their deductions from a set of definitions, the hand of a political geometer is far less free than his mathematical counterpart. Whereas the reader of Euclid's *Elements* plays no part in the theorems and thus is content with clear and unambiguous definitions, the reader of Hobbes's political geometry is both the observer of and the main ingredient of the theorem and must be convinced of the suitability of the assumptions chosen by the political geometer.

11.2 Definitions and Theorem

In *De Cive* Hobbes claims that his political theorem is derived from two axioms or 'maximes of humane Nature':

> one arising from the *concupiscible* part, which desires to appropriate to it selfe the use of those things in which all others have a joynt interest, the other proceeding from the *rationall*, which teaches every man to fly a contre-naturall Dissolution, as the greatest mischiefe that can arrive to Nature (*De Cive*, 27).

Hobbes's Impossibility Theorem

Both Hobbes's own correspondents and all his later readers have agreed that the above list of assumptions is incomplete. In other words, to demonstrate that the state of nature is a state of war (the first step of his argument), Hobbes resorts to a larger set of assumptions about men than the two maxims described above.

In addition to fear and self-interest, Leibniz mentions among Hobbes's assumptions the equality to kill of Hobbesian men, their right to all things, and the limited amount of resources in the state of nature (see *Correspondence II*, letter 195).

Similarly (see previous chapter) most game theorists agree that in his discussion of the state of nature Hobbes gives the status of assumptions to the following ideas: instrumental rationality (R), concern for self-preservation (S), equality to kill (E) unrestricted liberty (UL), the desire for glory of some individuals (G), the limited resources of the earth (LR).

It is worth noticing that these assumptions are present in all three Hobbes's political works. Hence, in spite of the changes on a number of topics between *De Cive* and *Leviathan* highlighted by writers such as McNeilly, Skinner, and even by myself, one must not lose sight of the fact that the foundations of political geometry are the same in all Hobbes's works.

Only one qualification is in order. Whereas in *Elements of Law* and *De Cive* Hobbes maintains that *virtually all* people are glory-seekers, in *Leviathan* he remarks that *only some* are so. This difference, although very significant from a philosophical point of view (as I argued in Chapters 7 and 9), has no relevant consequences for the message of Hobbes's political argument, since the state of war and the necessity of a social contract materialise even if only a limited number of individuals are glory-seekers. Indeed it is not impossible that one of the reasons why Hobbes chose to discard the original stronger assumption in *De Cive* (that all are glory-seekers) and to replace it with a milder assumptions in *Leviathan* (that only some are glory-seekers) is because the latter is more likely to be acceptable to all people.

From the above set of assumptions Hobbes derives his demonstration of the state of nature as a state of war. The story goes like this: in the state of nature, although resources are very limited (LR) because of the lack of industry, commerce, and human labour, nevertheless there would be enough for everyone to survive if people were like bees and ants and cared only about self-preservation. Unfortunately, there are some glory-seekers (G), namely people that try to become superior to others. As there are no common standards of good and evil, no shared values that restrict individual liberty (UL), the rational way for a glory-seeker to become superior to others and to be acknowledged as such by them is to try to have more of the only thing that everybody values, namely, the means of survival (S) (wells, fertile land etc.). As resources are limited, when a glory-seeker appropriates more than he needs, in doing so he deprives others of the means of subsistence. The non-glory-seekers are aware of the existence of glory-seekers and also of their drive to dispossess others. Hence it is rational (R) of them to be diffident of everybody (the fact that your neighbour has never attacked you so far does not mean that he will not attack you in the future) and to anticipate their attack by striking first. The result is war of everybody against everybody. This is the first step of Hobbes's demonstration. He writes:

> I demonstrate in the first place, that the state of men without civill society ... is nothing else but a meere warre of all against all (*De Cive*, 34)

Leibniz accepts that the first result of Hobbes's assumptions is the war of all against all. He remarks:

> it was easy for you to conclude that in that state of affairs a just war would be waged by all against all (*Correspondence II*, letter 195, 734).

All game theorists support Hobbes's claim that the state of nature is a state of war. In particular, Kavka's game-theoretical model shows that *an actual war* takes place among Hobbesian men. My own model, instead, suggests (see previous chapter) that the Hobbesian state of nature is a state of war *of minds*. One of Hobbes's correspondents, the young and brilliant Peleau, seems to interpret the war described by Hobbes in the very sense supported by my model rather than by Kavka's. He writes:

> I found that, in my opinion, there is now and has always been *a war of minds*, so far as opinions and feelings are concerned, and that this war is exactly like the state of nature (*Correspondence I*, letter 110, 424; emphasis added).

The interpretation of the state of nature as a war of minds rather than as an actual war is supported by the remark by Hobbes that the war in the state of nature is *perpetual* ('war ... is perpetuall in its own nature', *De Cive*, 49). Obviously an actual war would not be perpetual because it would be soon in a general slaughter, since 'equal powers opposed, destroy one another' (*Elements of Law*, 34). Moreover, Hobbes declares explicitly in *Leviathan* that war is an attitude of mind rather than actual battle ('the nature of war, consisteth not in actual fighting; but in the known disposition thereto', *Leviathan*, 113).

It is easy to see that up to this stage of the demonstration there is no difference between the findings of the geometer's and the finding of the rational actor's approach. They both deduce from the original assumptions the following theorem:

> *Hobbes's Theorem: In a state of unrestricted liberty (UL), for men who regard death as the greatest evil that might occur to them (S) and know that other people, too, are concerned about their survival but might be glory-seeking (G), it is rational (R) to decide to kill, which decision, because of the equal dangerousness and vulnerability of men, is against reason (nonR).*

The geometer notices the paradoxical nature of the theorem. Indeed, we can refer to it as an *Impossibility Theorem*, in the sense that the assumptions bring about the result that it is both rational and not rational to decide to kill.[4]

Hobbes was not unfamiliar with the notion of establishing a result by means of an impossibility theorem, as shown, for example, by his (indirect) exchange of correspondence with the mathematician René-François de Sluse who quite neatly describes

> a demonstration proving an impossibility ... [which] having made [some] suppositions, shows that something else must follow from them which is incompatible with their existence (18\28 Jan 1664, enclosed with a letter by Samuel Sorbière to Hobbes, *Correspondence II*, letter 165, 617).

Leibniz, too, saw the paradox in Hobbes's argument and wrote

> I, who am neither put off by paradoxes, nor carried away by the charms of novelty ... I am not in the habit of rejecting an author's conclusions without looking at the demonstration which he uses to support them (*Correspondence II*, letter 195, 733).

Having created a paradox (where people who care above all about survival end up endangering it), Hobbes's next step is to claim that:

he therefore that desireth to live in such an estate, as is the state of liberty and right of all to all, *contradicteth himself* (*Elements of Law* 73; emphasis added).

Whosoever therefore holds, that it had been best to have continued in that state in which all things were lawfull for all men, *he contradicts himself* (*De Cive*, 49; emphasis added).

Leibniz, again, accepts this second step of Hobbes's demonstration; he writes:

since that war would involve general slaughter, because of the equality of people's forces (given that the strongest man can be killed by the weakest), the argument for peace began to be raised at the point. Thus far I have no complaints (*Correspondence II*, letter 195, 734).

It is at this stage of Hobbes's argument that the geometer's and the rational agent's approaches part company, in so far as the latter can merely suggest that peace is desirable, but is utterly unable to propose any rational strategy to attain it.

Faced with the inability of the rational-actor perspective to account for the establishment of the Hobbesian social contract, we can subscribe to either of two mutually exclusive interpretations: (i): if the rational-agent approach is assumed to provide the best analytical framework to formalise Hobbes's theory, then we have to infer that Hobbes must have failed in his demonstration of the social contract, or (ii) if the failure of explaining the social contract is due to the rational-actor perspective itself, then Hobbes's theoretical enterprise may be rescued. The latter is the point of view taken in this book. Below I shall see how, *by taking the geometer's point of view*, a consistent account can be provided of the final steps of Hobbes's argument.

11.3 Escape from the Impossibility Result

Hobbes, the political geometer, has an option unavailable to the rational agent in the state of nature: dissatisfied with the result obtained (an irrational state of war), the geometer can work out how the paradox can be avoided and a different result (a state of peace) be attained. Obviously, the only way to obtain a different outcome, is to alter one or more of the original assumptions.

But of the six original assumptions (R, S, G, LR, E, UL), five cannot be changed because, according to Hobbes, they describe eternal characteristics of human nature. Only one assumption can be relaxed, namely, the unrestricted liberty of individuals (UL). In Hobbes's own words:

> I demonstrate ... that all men ... doe desire to be freed from this misery. But that this cannot be done except by compact, they *all quit that right which they have unto all things* (*De Cive*, 34; emphasis added).

As assumption UL states that in natural conditions there exists no power superior to individuals capable of restricting their liberty, it follows that any relaxation of UL must entail the existence of some such power.

Hobbes calls this power 'Leviathan' and explains that it can reside in the hands of a single man, or a few men, or an assembly. The Leviathan is from now on in charge of the unconditional protection of everybody's self-preservation. Hobbes argues that for the Leviathan to be able to perform his task, it must have the same unrestricted liberty enjoyed by individuals before its creation. To give the Leviathan less than unrestricted liberty would mean to impose limits onto his ability to protect the lives of his subjects. Hobbes claims that to entrust our lives to some power that has less liberty of action than we ourselves had before its creation is against reason. He writes:

> the Obligation, and Liberty of the Subject, is to be derived ... from the End of the Institution of Soveraignty, namely the Peace of the Subjects within themselves, and their Defence against a common Enemy (*Leviathan*, 150).

> When therefore our refusall to obey, frustrates the End for which the Soveraignty was ordained; then there is no Liberty to refuse: otherwise there is (*Leviathan*, 151).

Only if the Leviathan endangers our safety (whether rightly or wrongly) we have the right to resist:

> since therefore no man is tyed to *impossibilities*, they who are threatned with *death* ... or wounds ... are not obliged to endure them (*De Cive*, 58-9).

Whereas therefore for the rational actor there is no escape from Hobbes's state of nature, the geometer can replace one of the original assumptions (people's natural right to all things, UL) with the creation *ex machina* of an artificial power to whom everybody owes *Uni-conditional Obedience* (UO, i.e., obedience in all cases except when one's life is endangered). The result of the new set of assumptions (R, S, G, E, LR, and Uni-conditional Obedience to the Leviathan) is a state of peace. From now on the Leviathan will introduce rules of *meum* and *tuum* (private property), of good and evil (common values), and other laws with the aim of controlling the competition between glory-seekers and of forbidding life-endangering activities.

I can find no better way to sum up the whole of Hobbes's argument than to quote *verbatim* Leibniz's *Caesarinus Fürstenerius* (1677),[5] where he examines the theory of 'the sharp-witted Englishman Thomas Hobbes':

> He says that by nature men have the right to do whatever seems to them to be useful; that from this their rights extend over all things. But from this, he goes on, arise internecine wars, causing the destruction of individuals, and therefore peace is necessary and this right of all men over all things must be taken away, as must be the individual judgement from which it flows. Each man must transfer his will to the state, i.e. to a monarchy or some assembly of the magnates or the people, or to some natural or civil person, so that each man is understood to will whatever the government or person which represents him wills. Furthermore, this civil person, the government, cannot be anything but unitary, and it is fruitless to divide the rights of supreme power among several persons or *collegia*. For if, for example, one should be given the right to propose laws, another that of imposing tributes, the state would be dissolved in the event of an angry disagreement. For without the power of managing affairs, which is money, nothing can be accomplished, and so it is clear that he who can deny the other the tributes can also deprive him of his remaining rights – which, Hobbes says, is absurd.[6]

11.4 Geometer, Agent, and Reader

Hobbes is aware that the ability to calculate the logical implications of a set of assumptions belongs only to a few; he claims that it is neither innate nor learnt by experience, but requires the sort of education and application that are available only in civil associations:

[the] skill of proceeding upon generall, and infallible rules, called Science; which very few have ... not being a native faculty, born with us; nor attained, (as Prudence,) while we look after somewhat els (*Leviathan*, 87).

Geometers, in other words, can exist only within political associations. Although Hobbes believes that only few can be 'geometers' and *construct* theorems, he is convinced that the ability to *understand* his theory is open to all. In *Leviathan* he claims that his theorem '

> though this may seem too subtle a deduction ... to be taken notice of by all men ... yet ... [it is] intelligible ... even to the meanest capacity (*Leviathan*, 82).

In *Behemoth,* too, Hobbes declares that

> the rule of *just* and *unjust*, sufficiently demonstrated, and from principles evident to the meanest capacity, have not been wanting; and not withstanding the obscurity of their author, have shined, not only in this, but also in foreign countries, to men of good education (*Behemoth*, 39).

For Hobbes the only requirement for a person to follow his demonstration and to understand its conclusion is to be in a calm, or 'quiet', state of mind:

> it's true, That *hope, fear, ambition* ... and other perturbations of the mind, doe hinder a man so, as he cannot attaine to the knowledge of these Lawes, whilst those passions prevail in him: But there is no man who is not sometimes in a quiet mind (*De Cive*, 72).

As geometers can exist only in peaceful political associations, so readers of geometry need a similar environment. The impossibility of detachment and of calm for the individual in the state of nature is the main reason why he cannot see what a detached reader or observer can see. The reader of Hobbes's theory who enjoys the comfort of peace can comprehend Hobbes's theorem and the folly to let the political state fall into a state of anarchy.

The Hobbesian reader, following the steps of the geometer, can acknowledge the logical necessity of the proposed solution without having to work it out himself. Whereas the rational actor cannot reach an actual agreement with other agents, the reader can appreciate the need for a 'virtual contract'.[7] This is in line with Hobbes's belief that historically the social contract is never the source of governments; in *Leviathan* we read:

> there is scarce a Common-wealth in the world, whose beginnings can in conscience be justified (*Leviathan*, 486).

11.5 Correspondents' Responses to the Theorem

Most of Hobbes's correspondents were completely convinced by the logic of his political geometry. Here are a few examples:

Sorbière: You are indeed the father of politics and its leading expert, the person who, like Galileo in physics, put an end to empty quibbling on that subject ... No seeker after truth ... will be able to doubt that what you have asserted about the state of nature and the state of dominion is absolutely certain and proven (*Correspondence II*, letter 141, 517).

du Verdus: you ... have written more cogently than anyone else [on the power of the state], so cogently that all the parts of your book's argument, based on two principles which could not be doubted, are linked together in the same way that geometrical propositions should be (*Correspondence I*, letter 68, 197).

> you are the only person to have demonstrated, from the nature of civil society, that the authority of the state is absolute and indivisible. That is something that it is absolutely necessary for subjects to be well convinced of, and which they cannot truly understand without hating civil war and without being content to live in peace among themselves under the power of the state (*Correspondence I*, letter 74, 228).

Leibniz, too, was fascinated by the logic of Hobbes's argument, as he admitted openly:

> I am not in the habit of flattering, but everyone who has been able to understand your writings on political theory agrees with me that nothing can possibly be added to the clarity of their argument, which is so admirable when they are expressed so concisely. Nothing could be more well-turned or more consistent with ordinary usage than your definitions. As for the theorems which are deduced from

them, some people hold fast to them and other misuse them for bad purposes ... through ignorance of how they should be applied (*Correspondence II*, letter 189, 716-7).

There were also criticisms on some of the assumptions on which Hobbes's political geometry was resting. I have already addressed Peleau's doubts about Hobbesian equality in chapter 2 (see section 2.4) and Sorbière's reservations about Hobbes's assumption on glory in Chapter 7 (see section 7.4). Leibniz, too, levelled some typically pertinent criticisms to Hobbes's geometrical construction. To one such, about the assumption of self-preservation, I turn now, deferring to the next chapter the discussion of a second, more general, criticism on method.

In letter 195 Leibniz, after having praised the geometrical nature of Hobbes's demonstrations, makes two related points that show the depth of his understanding of Hobbes's theory and reveal clearly the utterly *secular* nature of Hobbes's construct:

> I can see clearly enough the your demonstrations, like those of geometry, are universal and abstracted from the matter which they deal with; so that even though you give each person the right to do anything for the sake of his own preservation, *you do not deny that if there were some omnipotent being, and if there is some future life* in which rewards and punishments will be issued, the consequences would be not so much that your theories had ceased to be true, as that particular application of them had ceased to be valid .... in short, it is not that the defence of this life would be ruled out by divine law, but merely *it would cease to be the thing of ultimate importance* (*Correspondence II*, 734; emphasis added).

It is clear from this quotation that Leibniz: (i) recognised that Hobbes's specific definition of 'violent death at the hands of others' as being the greatest evil (what I called assumption S^∞ in section 10.5) is of paramount importance to the coherence of Hobbes's argument; and (ii) indirectly highlighted the uncompromisingly secular nature of Hobbes's theory. In fact, what the italicised sentence in the above quotation states quite unambiguously is that Hobbes's theory, in his own formulation, holds only if there exist no God and no afterlife, i.e., only if two of the fundamental tenets of most religions (and certainly of Christianity) are rejected.

In this perspective, Hobbes's claim that man cares above all about his own survival and that he has the natural right to defend his life by all available means (including killing), can be seen as a truly momentous statement against the religious interpretations of man. In other words, Hobbes insisted on the right to self-preservation because he wanted to create a theory for the secular man, with secular desires and secular needs. The more Hobbes defends the right to self-preservation as a natural right recognised by reason, the more he distances himself from theologians and increases the gap between reason and nature on the one hand, and religious belief on the other. Unlike Locke, Hobbes says that we should defend our life not because it is entrusted to us by God, but simply because it is natural and rational to do so.

Chapter 12

The Ideology of Political Geometry

Introduction

> For he alone [the head of state] is not a member of the commonwealth, but its creator or preserver, and he alone is authorised to coerce others without being subject to any coercive law himself ... For if he too could be coerced, he would not be the head of state, and the hierarchy of subordination would ascend infinitely. But if there were two persons exempt from coercion, neither would be subject to coercive laws, and neither could do to the other anything contrary to right, which is impossible.

An innocent undergraduate asked to guess the paternity of this quotation could be forgiven for ascribing it to Hobbes (often described in textbooks as the 'apologist of Absolutism'), whereas, of course, it is a remark by Kant to be found in a section of *Theory and Practice* interestingly entitled 'Against Hobbes'.[1]

Although Absolutism is the political ideology to which Hobbes is most commonly associated, different interpreters have seen in Hobbes the origin of the most diverse ideological positions. He has been portrayed as a spokesman of the rising bourgeoisie of the 17th century (Macpherson), as a moralist (Warrender), as a Christian moralist (Martinich), as a socialist who believed that inequality and private property are social constructs (Tönnies), as an ideologist of law and order (Preston King), as a proto-liberal and one of the founders of the idea of the welfare state (Kavka), as a conservative (Bobbio), as a theorist of the sexual contract and of the political subjugation of women (Pateman), to name but a few.

Indeed, throughout Hobbes's works one can find statements that might seem to support all of the above definitions, as well as other remarks that would seem to refute them all conclusively.

The aim of this final chapter is twofold: on the one hand, I wish to show that the attempt to pigeon-hole Hobbes's thought in a single ideological box is an almost impossible exercise; on the other hand, I suggest that if we want to single out *the prevailing ideological*

155

conviction in Hobbes's thought, this has to be his faith in the method of political geometry. Let us consider the following remark by Leibniz:

> if we listen to Hobbes, there will be nothing in our land but out-and-out anarchy ... Hobbes' fallacy lies in this, that he thinks things that can entail inconvenience should not be borne at all – which is foreign to the nature of human affairs. I would not deny that, when the supreme power is divided, many dissensions can arise; even wars, if everyone holds stubbornly to his own opinion. But experience has shown that men usually hold to some middle road, so as not to commit everything to hazard by their obstinacy. Prominent examples are Poland and the Netherlands.[2]

Experience shows, Leibniz argues, that internal dissensions always exist in political states and yet they rarely bring about civil war. He gives historical examples of his own times and suggests that since Hobbes's prediction that disagreements cause inevitably sedition and civil war is historically inaccurate, this shows that political reality is more complex than allowed for in Hobbes's model.

I would argue that Leibniz's pertinent critique, by pointing to Hobbes's unqualified belief in political geometry, raises doubts in the possibility of ever being able to capture the dynamics of politics by a limited number of assumptions. Ultimately it suggests that the limitations of Hobbes's thought are in fact the limitations of the very ideology of political geometry.

Finally I shall compare two novels of our times (Camus' *The Plague* and Orwell's *Nineteen Eighty Four*) with Hobbes's description of the state of nature with the aim to highlight the modernity of his thought on man, the passions, and rationality.

12.1 Hobbes, Ideologies and Ideas

Here is a small selection of ideologies and ideas with which Hobbes has been associated. The point of the exercise is to show the inherent futility of any attempt to constrain Hobbes's complex thought in any one ideological straightjacket.

12.1.1 Conservatism, pessimism, and custom

It is sometimes said that Hobbes shares with Conservatism a pessimistic view of human nature and an enthusiastic endorsement of the ideology of law and order. Indeed, Hobbes would have agreed with the claim that if we were angels, we would not need politics.

In Chapter 11, I argued that Hobbes's tendency in his political works to overlook the more endearing among human characteristics (e.g., love, pity, compassion, sympathy, etc.) is due less to his pessimism than to his commitment to the principle of political relevance, in so far as these traits are politically inconsequential in that they do not explain why we need political authority, law and punishment. For a political theorist such as Hobbes, who wants to account for the occurrence of conflictual behaviour and civil war, only negative human traits (e.g., greed, glory, envy) are of interest.

In Chapter 6 I have argued that Hobbes is, for example, far less pessimistic than Thucydides, to the extent to which he believes that understanding politics can help us to influence it. Thus, whereas it is beyond doubt that Hobbes's view of human nature is not optimistic (someone who believes that the state of nature is a state of war can hardly be described as an optimist), it may appear more pessimistic than it actually is.

Unlike Burke, Hobbes does not see in custom and tradition the distillation of the wisdom of past generations. Again unlike Burke, he rejects the Aristotelian interpretation of the state as a natural development of the family where inequality and hierarchy are natural. For Hobbes, the origin of inequality lies not in nature, but in society, through the introduction of private property and other artificial rules.

12.1.2 Fascism, Peace, and the State

It is easy to see why some critics have seen parallels between Hobbes's theory and Fascism, as both attach paramount importance to the state, attribute to it absolute unlimited and indivisible power and condemn political factions.

The anti-Fascist elements in Hobbes's theory, however, are equally easy to identify: denial that in nature there are heroes, or supermen; his opposition to political activism; his commitment to rationality; his belief in the absolute value of peace. It is difficult to imagine anyone who could have opposed the following statement by Mussolini more vehemently than Hobbes:

> Above all, Fascism, ... believes neither in the possibility nor in the utility of perpetual peace. It thus repudiates the doctrine of Pacifism – born of a renunciation of the struggle and an act of cowardice in the face of sacrifice.

> War alone brings about to its highest tension all human energy and puts the stamp of nobility upon the peoples who have the courage to meet it ... a doctrine which is founded upon the harmful postulate of peace is hostile to Fascism ... This anti-Pacifist feeling is carried by Fascism even into the life of the individual.[3]

Indeed Hobbes acknowledges absolute power to the Leviathan and favours the government by one man, but not out of idealisation of the state, nor of the authority. To Lord Acton's aphorism that 'absolute power corrupts absolutely', Hobbes probably would have replied that the power of one man is dangerous indeed, but the power of one hundred men is one hundred times more dangerous.

In one of the very few places where Leibniz's reading of Hobbes is not as acute as usual, he writes:

> Therefore Hobbesian empires, I think, exist neither among civilized peoples nor among barbarians, and I consider them neither possible nor desirable, *unless those who must have supreme power are gifted with angelic virtues*. For men will choose to follow their own will, and will consult their own welfare as seems best to them, as long as they are not persuaded of the supreme wisdom and capability of their rulers, which things are necessary for perfect resignation of the will. *So that Hobbes' demonstrations have a place only in that state whose king is God, whom alone one can trust in all things.*[4]

Nowhere does Hobbes suggest that he assumes the supreme power to be 'gifted with angelic virtues'. Quite the opposite, in fact. Hobbes simply believes that the Leviathan, in pursuing *his own* self-interest pursues also the self-interest of the commonwealth, since the wealth and the safety of the state is advantageous to both rulers and ruled.

12.1.3 *Christian morality, the beggar, and the apple tree*

As is often the case in the history of political thought, the biased reading of a classic text by critics keen to buttress their ideology with the support of a past master produces a contrary and equally biased response by others. The Warrender-Taylor thesis, according to which Hobbes is a moralist, has been viewed as an attempt to break the association, frequently asserted in the 1930s, between Hobbes and

Fascist ideology. While one can sympathise with its laudable aim, the Warrender-Taylor thesis is now regarded by many interpreters as lacking textual support. If any morality at all is to be found in Hobbes's theory, it is likely to be either prudential or formal (as argued, respectively, by Gauthier and Oakeshott).

In all his works Hobbes claims consistently that all actions of all men are motivated in the last analysis by self-interest: '

> the only reason why something appeals to, or is craved by, a person is that it benefits him, self-advantage being the proper and sufficient object of the will (*Anti-White*, 487).
>
> no desire exists except that of reaching a goal, or self-benefit (*Anti-White*, 400).

In *Anti-White* Hobbes remarks that even pity for our fellow men is motivated by self-interest. He explains that our helping the poor can be ascribed to one of the three following self-regarding motivations: (i) we help the unfortunate to avoid sorrow; or (ii) to be praised by others as 'merciful or generous'; or (iii) 'so to merit Divine Mercy'. Not without irony, Hobbes remarks that although the last is 'the best motive', it is 'nonetheless a useful one' (*Anti-White*, 402-3). Interestingly, an anecdote from Hobbes's life related by Aubrey confirms the above view.

> One time, I remember, going into the Strand, a poor and infirm old man craved his alms. He beholding him with eyes of pity and compassion, put his hands in his pocket, and gave him 6d. Said a divine (that is Dr Jasper Mayne) that stood by –'Would you have done this, if it had not been Christ's command?' 'Yes,' said he. 'Why?' said the other. 'Because,' said he, 'I was in pain to consider the miserable condition of the old man; and now my alms, giving him some relief, doth also ease me' (*Brief Lives*, 158-9).

Hobbes regards the pursuit of self-interest, as a natural unalterable characteristic of man.[5]

Unlike Augustine or any Christian moralist, when Hobbes lists the pleasures of the human mind he pointedly fails to mention the pleasure of grace, the solace of faith, the belief in divine providence, the consolation of the after-life. Unlike Locke, Hobbes never makes the point that we should defend our lives because they have been entrusted to us by God, nor does Hobbes require parents to look after their children in the state of nature. On the contrary, he explicitly states that women would be justified if they decided to abandon their offspring for the sake of their own self-preservation. Although Hobbes never denies nor puts in question the existence of god, his god is a peculiarly unobtrusive one, with no interest in political theory nor, indeed, in human affairs altogether.

Hobbes suggests that, as Adam challenged God out of pride and dared to eat from the tree of knowledge of good and evil, in the state of nature his heirs are condemned to eat from that same tree. This gives rise to complete moral chaos and finally war. Salvation is provided by the Leviathan who plays the part of an artificial god. Like his heavenly counterpart, he imposes a crucial restriction to individual liberty, in so far as citizens can no longer eat from the political tree of good and evil: they cannot question the laws of the commonwealth, their liberty being defined by the boundaries of the law or where the law is silent. The result is earthly peace and concord.

In his works Hobbes rejects the moralistic view, endorsed for example by Thomas White, that there are 'bad pleasures' (such as desire of money and honour) and 'good pleasures', such as the 'pleasure of conferring benefits on others'. For Hobbes

> to shield the needy, to raise the afflicted and the like presuppose the setting aside for this purpose of riches and power ... [but] riches ... cannot be provided unless they are both strongly desired and diligently sought after (*Anti-White*, 476).

Therefore, Hobbes suggests, anyone who wants to become good and virtuous in Thomas White's sense has to become bad first (in Thomas White's sense), i.e., he must attain riches and power, which in turn cannot be obtained without much effort and industry. For Hobbes it does not make sense to speak of bad and good pleasures independently from the laws of the commonwealth. He puts the difference between a good and a bad man down to the fact the former strives for things that are lawful, the latter for unlawful goals:

> those must be considered good that the state says are good and bad who it says are bad, for every private citizen has vested his individual opinion in the state (*Anti-White*, 462).

Hobbes devotes large sections of *Leviathan* to show that the recommendations of Christian morality are compatible with prudential morality. He reassures his Christian readership that the state is likely to incorporate Christian morality within its own rules. However, and this is the crucial test as far as the alleged Christian morality entertained by Hobbes is concerned, should any conflict occur between Christian morality and state's laws, Hobbes warns us that our *only* duty as Christians is to believe that God exists and that Christ is His Son: a morally undemanding request from a most unobtrusive Supreme Being.

12.1.4 The Utilitarian, the Happy, and the Poor

As I argued in Chapter 3, for Hobbes the principles of human actions are pain and pleasure and happiness consists 'in the gratifying thought of advancing from the enjoyment of one good thing to that of another' (*Anti-White*, 468). Happiness is not identified with 'the pleasure of possessing' but with 'the pleasure of expectation' (*Anti-White*, 467), defined as

> the joy noticed in a prolonged and serene progress of searching ... not rest or inactivity or the deprivation of desire, but a gentle motion from a good that has been acquired to one that must be acquired (*Anti-White*, 465).

In his works, Hobbes reminds us indirectly but consistently that man's happiness lies in the attainment of neither virtue nor truth. The indirect challenge to the Stoics' and Lucretius' conviction that true happiness is 'to view, from a temple raised high upon the placid teachings of the wise, the wanderings of those who seek in vain the happy life', comes from Hobbes's observation that most people believe themselves 'to be looking down from temples of no less height upon the wanderings of others' (*Anti-White*, 477). For Hobbes, while it is true that wisdom and virtue give rise to happiness, it is also true that every man believes himself to possess more wisdom, more prudence, and more virtue than the rest. According to Hobbes, the opinion of being wise, rather than wisdom itself is for Hobbes a source of happiness for man.

An indirect criticism to the Platonic idea that happiness consists in the attainment of the truth can be found in Hobbes's observation that

> whether someone has known truth or has only thought he has, happiness is the same and pleases him as much as the

happiness of true philosophy would please him. Hence this pleasure belongs no more to ... philosophers than to those who are losing their reason (*Anti-White*, 478).

It is not surprising that, as argued by Richard Tuck,[6] the Classical Utilitarians felt that Hobbes anticipated some of their views. The similarities between Hobbes's theory and Utilitarianism include the explanation of human actions in terms of pain and pleasure; secularism, consequentialism, the acceptance of the individual definition of the good, the belief in a strong legislator in charge of pursuing the good of the commonwealth, the commitment to instrumental rationality and to prudential morality, the view that at a collective level the State can pursue the individuals' objectives much more than individuals themselves could without any state intervention.

On the other hand, Hobbes imposes much more severe limits onto individual liberty than is the case in Classical Utilitarianism. The main reason, I would suggest, is that in Hobbes's theory conflict is endemic. For Mill, for example, human conflict can always be solved. For Hobbes, instead, because of the human desire of glory and superiority, the maximisation of the welfare of society is a formidable, indeed unattainable, task. As Hobbes points out, glory and power cannot be distributed equally because if everybody has them, nobody does. Glory, honour, prestige are intrinsically scarce resources, as Bentham himself did not fail to notice.

Unlike Bentham, Hobbes does not assign the state the task to either maximise or increase the happiness of people, but only to ensure the minimal conditions (i.e., peace and prosperity) under which citizens can pursue *their own* definition of happy life. The main task of the State is to protect citizens from the greatest of pains, the state of anarchy that condemns them to a miserable, solitary, brutish, and short life. Any individual preference that can compromise internal peace is seen as illegitimate by Hobbes; here the set of forbidden pleasures includes freedom of expression and of association, political participation, and resistance.

Not surprisingly, Hobbes is far less aware than the Utilitarians of the 18th century of the relevance of social and economic issues. In *Anti-White* Hobbes does notice that there can be social 'causes impairing happiness':

> some persons are born to riches and great place ... others are of poor parentage and obscure origins ... the latter must toil for the greatest part of their life to acquire possessions; and

in the remainder of it, oppressed by the inconveniences of old age, they cannot use what they have secured (*Anti-White*, 481-2).

Here Hobbes describes the stark contrast between the predicament of the poor, engaged in a hopeless attempt to improve his lot, and the circumstances of the rich, who have by custom all the advantages and get no pleasure out of them because they take them for granted:

> those born to riches or to civil power or to honour derive no more pleasure from these things than they derive from their being men or from possessing arms and feet (*Anti-White*, 468).

He is also aware of the tension between the poor and the rising classes:

> Least of all is it the wealth and the titles of those born rich and honoured that wounds the poor; rather it is the riches and titles of those who ... have *become* rich or worthy of honour (*Anti-White*, 468).

Interestingly, in the triad of the *Elements of Law*, *De Cive*, and *Leviathan* the suffering of the poor disappears altogether from the political stage. The poor, sympathetically described in *Anti-White*, becomes the 'ignorant' in *De Cive and Leviathan*, the man easily deceived by demagogues and manipulated by priests. The 'men of obscure parentage', whose economic struggle is recorded in *Anti-White*, in the *Elements of Law*, *De Cive*, and *Leviathan* become merely 'arms' used by seditious people to overturn governments This suggests that, although Hobbes was aware to some extent of social and economic tensions in his society, he thought that they were not crucial for the understanding of politics. For Hobbes it is the opinions and ideology of people, motivated by their passions and largely independent of their economic and social circumstances, that are the engine of politics and, as such, ought to be the main object of enquiry.

12.1.5 Hobbes, the Oppressive Liberal?

In the twentieth century a number of interpreters have been inclined to offer a liberal reading of Hobbes. *Prima facie*, the very suggestion of any resemblance between Liberalism and Hobbes seems quite absurd, in view of the undisputed and virulently anti-liberal elements that characterise his political theory. Here one could mention Hobbes's rejection of freedom of expression and of association, his endorsement of censorship, his opposition to political dialogue and political participation, his deep distrust in democracy, the idea that state power ought to be absolute, indivisible and unlimited, the denial of any civil rights except self-preservation, the view that property in political associations is not an inalienable right but a concession that can be revoked by the state, and so illiberally on.

However, there are other and equally important features of Hobbes's theory shared by many liberal thinkers. I could refer here to Hobbes's strong belief in methodology, his deep trust in instrumental rationality, his agnosticism regarding the definition of the 'good life', his view of the state as a rational and artificial construction, his belief in natural equality and natural freedom; his commitment to the individual. Hobbes rejects the idea that the ultimate end of man is to live according to reason: 'to live by right reason is not the ultimate good which we seek after; it is a means to achieving' other goals, which in the case of a religious person is 'the enjoyment of the Kingdom of Heaven', for others is the 'triumph of this world' (*Anti-White*, 403). Not without irony Hobbes remarks that

> anyone you care to point to ... believes that the world is run rationally when everything in it is most advantageously directed to the happiness of good men, i.e. to one's own (*Anti-White*, 460).

I hope to have shown in this section that the attempt to squeeze Hobbes's wealth of ideas into a single ideological box is an impossible, indeed a futile, exercise. In the next section, I shall argue that Hobbes's main ideological trait resides in his belief in Political Geometry (thus, in so far as the latter is shared by at least some variants of political liberalism, accounting for the alleged 'liberal' aspects of his theory).

12.2 The Ideology of Political Geometry

Although the term 'political geometry', as used in this work, is my own, there are many good studies which consider Hobbes's theory as proceeding from a set of assumptions about human nature to its logical conclusions. Here I do not intend to add to Watkins' interesting examination of the compositive-resolutive method of Hobbes nor qualify Lukes'[7] critique of Hobbes's abstract individualism.

The Ideology of Political Geometry

My aim in this section is less ambitious: I shall deploy two twentieth-century works of literature as catalysts to reveal some of the beliefs about agent, observer, and rationality that I have attributed to Hobbes in this book. I have tried to argue that a fuller understanding of Hobbes's political philosophy can be gained by considering his philosophy of the individual in its entirety, i.e., by analysing not only the *rational agents* who act out the drama of the state of nature, but also the *reader-observer* who can derive and appreciate the political implications of Hobbes's theorem of reason. Whereas Hobbesian scholarship is rich with penetrating analyses of the Hobbesian agent, the reader-observer has attracted little attention, and only from writers interested in the rhetorical techniques used by Hobbes in *Leviathan*.

Some of the critiques levelled against Hobbes's conception of man are unduly harsh because they consider exclusively the Hobbesian man in the state of nature and not the Hobbesian reader-observer. For example, when MacIntyre claims that

> The criticism of our desires and their rational remoulding have no place in the Hobbesian system. It follows that, inevitably, our desires are for one individual object after another; and thus desires cannot include the desire for a certain kind of life, the desire that our desires should be of a certain kind.[8]

He, too, like most interpreters, identifies Hobbes's man entirely with the agent in natural conditions, immersed in the present and absorbed by the overwhelming preoccupation of securing his life. However, as I have argued in this work, Hobbes describes not only the agent in the state of nature, but also another individual, who in his moments of peace and calm can detach himself from the present and can take the point of view of the philosopher, of Hobbes himself. Whereas the agent has desires only of a first order, the observer-reader-philosopher can afford second-order desires, namely he can have desires about desires.

In Chapter 9 I tried to qualify and hence rectify one common contention in the literature, namely that the Hobbesian agent is self-contained, like an island, and that his desires are given and unalterable. Whereas for Hobbes our passions are indeed unalterable, the *content* of our passions, namely the specific desires and preferences that we have are far from being eternal and immutable. They change with the varying circumstances; above all, they change in the transition from the natural to the political state. This is the reason why education is effective, according to Hobbes, and why he attributes to his *Leviathan* a didactical function.

Hobbes believes that society, by means of education, books, habits, etc., can change substantially our desires. By desiring to live in society, the Hobbesian man wants these changes. By creating the state, he chooses to develop the individuality and richness of motivation that only the political state can bring about. Thus, while we cannot change ourselves as long as we inhabit the state of nature, by choosing to live in political associations, we choose to give new contents to our passions.

The rational agent is absorbed in his miserable predicament, but the observer, the geometer, can choose a different destiny for all men through social structures. Man is a project, not a given. For Hobbes, state and society, and not nature, are ultimately responsible for bad citizens.

12.2.1 Hobbes, Orwell, and Room 101

There is no escape from the fact that Hobbes's description of the human condition is not appealing. His Leviathan is as frightening as Big Brother in Orwell's *Nineteen Eighty Four*.

Some interpreters[9] have drawn a parallel between Orwell's Newspeak and in particular his request of 'an efficient, stripped down language which economises on redundant expressions'[10] and Hobbes's theory. Minogue highlights the similarity between Hobbes's view in *Leviathan* that words are power and must be subject, like all other forms of power, to the rules of the sovereign and Orwell's totalitarian view that the purpose of Newspeak is 'to remove many terms of living English ... to make the things they name inaccessible to thought'.[11]

I would argue that Orwell's novel offers another insight in Hobbes's theory, in so far as his description of room 101 (the torture chamber) can help us realise why Hobbes was so convinced that 'violent death at the hand of others' is the greatest evil imaginable for man.

When Winston Smith enters room 101, where he is compelled to face the worst of his nightmares, a face-mask teeming with rats, he cannot help trying to shift the unendurable torture to the one love of his life ('Do it to Julia! Not me!'). In so doing, Winston betrays not only Julia, but also ultimately himself. The experience of room 101 shows to Winston that his animal instinct for survival is stronger that his disinterested and noble loyalty to Julia, which in turn was the one thought that allowed him to entertain a good opinion of himself and to fight the system. After his betrayal of Julia, Winston will never recover from his loss of self-respect and dignity.

Similarly, the experience of the state of nature proves to the Hobbesian man that when he is faced by violent death he reacts as a distressed animal dominated by only one motive – self-preservation – and thus loses those characteristics (curiosity, desire of excellence, and knowledge) that make him human. The Hobbesian man realises that when survival is at stake he cannot behave differently from any other member of the human mass, or indeed from any animal. In the state of nature, where the concern for physical integrity is dominating everybody's life, the Hobbesian man's desire and ability to develop a unique identity remain unfulfilled. The state of nature, by turning men into undifferentiated animals, robs them of the potential to become - and the dignity to be- unique individuals.

Hobbesian men are not afraid of death, when their allotted time on earth has expired. From Aubrey's account we know that Hobbes himself in his old age was not afraid of dying. However, just as Hobbes himself went into exile during the Civil War and repeatedly postponed planned journeys to Venice because he was afraid for his personal safety, so Hobbesian men in the state of nature are said to fear 'sudden death', 'violent death at the hand of others', 'pain', 'torture', and premature demise.

Hobbes suggests that man wants to enter political associations with the understanding that if the state condemns him (whether rightly or wrongly) to visit room 101, then he retains the right to rebel and resist. This is his right to self-respect and dignity.

In the Hobbesian state of nature agents are condemned to utter anonymity. If someone transgresses the laws of nature, Hobbes argues, all people indiscriminately pay the consequences. Nature, one could say, does not take the separateness of Hobbesian individuals seriously. In the political state, instead, the separateness of citizens is acknowledged, as each is punished or rewarded for what he and he alone has done. Citizenship gives the Hobbesian man an identity. Property and laws give him a history, different from everybody else's.

12.2.2 Hobbes, Camus, and The Plague

In my view the novel that offers the most stimulating insight in

Hobbes's argument is Camus's *The Plague*.[12] First, I shall highlight the extraordinary similarities between Camus's dramatic description of a fictional plague and Hobbes's philosophical account of the state of nature, thereby indirectly showing how close Hobbes is to contemporary sensitivity.[13] Secondly and perhaps more importantly, I shall focus on the major difference that distances Camus from Hobbes. This difference is a crucial element of Hobbes's political geometry.

According to Camus, the plague is endemic, always dormant inside each of us, ready to burst at any time. And so, for Hobbes, is the state of nature. When the plague/state of nature erupts, what we take for granted disappears, and we discover ourselves in exile from our own habits, friends, family, and certainties. Just as personal relationships in the Hobbesian state of nature are informed and deformed by diffidence, so Camus shows that in times of plague 'mistrust ... keeps [people] apart. For it's common knowledge that you can't trust your neighbour'.[14]

Camus's individuals experience the 'agony of uncertainty that never leaves them'; they learn to live 'in a state of constant fear'[15] and this teaches them 'prudence'. For Camus the plague induces fear, 'and with fear serious reflection began'. This observation mirrors accurately Hobbes's account of the state of nature where fear, generated by uncertainty, engenders prudence and motivates people to find ways to escape.

As in the Hobbesian state of nature the overriding passion is fear of death, so Camus tells us that 'at the height of the epidemic we saw only one case in which natural emotions overcome the fear of death ... That was an exception'.[16]

As the Hobbesian state of nature entails no industry, no commerce, no trade, so in Camus's town 'commerce, too, had died of plague', the plague having brought about the complete 'disorganization of the town's economic life'.[17] Some of Camus's most poignant prose is reserved to express lyrically Hobbes's implication that in the state of nature/plague, the only time is the present:

> [the plague] rules out any future, cancels journeys, silences the exchange of views (Camus, *The Plague*, 34).
> Thus each of us had to be content to live only for the day, alone under the vast indifference of the sky (Camus, *The Plague*, 63).
> Without memories, without hope, they lived for the moment only. Indeed the Here and Now had come to mean

everything for them ... nothing was left us but a series of present moments (Camus, *The Plague*, 150).

I argued in Chapter 1 that without past and future, the personal differences between Hobbesian men disappear. Similarly for Camus, during the plague, without future, the personal life of people loses its meaning:

> the plague had gradually killed off in all of us the faculty not of love only but even of friendship. Naturally enough, since love asks something of the future ... this meant giving up what was most personal in their lives (Camus, *The Plague*, 150).

Like Hobbes's so Camus's individuals are condemned to solitude:

> in this extremity of solitude none could count on any help from his neighbour; each had to bear the load of his troubles alone ... the attempt to communicate had to be given up (Camus, *The Plague*, 64).

For Hobbesian men as for Camus's townsfolk, 'personal interest ... continued to occupy the foreground of their thoughts'. But hope never dies for the Hobbesian man and for Camus's characters:

> [after each set-back] our townspeople would begin to hope again (72) ... there was no room in any heart but for a very old, grey hope, that hope which keeps men from letting themselves drift into death and is nothing but a dogged will to live (Camus, *The Plague*, 213).

As the Hobbesian state of nature is essentially a mental construct, yet one which can have disastrous consequences, likewise Camus's plague can be construed as an abstraction:

> an element of abstraction, of a divorce of reality, entered in such calamities. Still when abstraction sets to killing you, you have got to get busy with it ... but where some saw abstraction, others saw the truth (Camus, *The Plague*, 75, 78).

Even more relevant is the similarity regarding the immanence of the state of nature/plague: neither is just a story, just a myth invented by others. It is a potential destruction that the Hobbesian man always carries within his self, just as the man of Camus has always the plague in his heart:

each of us has the plague within him; no one, no one on earth, is free from it. And I know, too, that we must keep endless watch on ourselves lest in a careless moment we breathe in somebody's face and fasten the infection on him. What's natural is the microbe. All the rest – health, integrity, purity (if you like) – is a product of the human will, of a vigilance that must never falter (Camus, *The Plague*, 207).

As the Hobbesian state of nature can be interpreted as a consequence of the Pride and Fall of Adam, so one of Camus's characters sees in the plague the hand of God that punishes the proud of heart:

from the dawn of recorded history the scourge of God has humbled the proud of heart ... Calamity has come on you, my brethren, and, my brethren, you deserve it (Camus, *The Plague*, 80).

Camus also agrees with Hobbes that evils such as civil wars and the plague are due to ignorance and not to cruelty:

the evil that is in the world always comes of ignorance, and good intentions may do as much harm as malevolence, if they lack understanding (Camus, *The Plague*, 110).

Hobbes's views on the illusory freedom and equality in the state of nature find a close counterpart in Camus:

week by week the prisoners of plague put up what fight they could. Some ... even contrived to fancy they were still behaving as free men and had the power of choice ... No longer were there individual destinies; only a collective destiny, made of plague and the emotions shared by all. Strongest of these emotions was the sense of exile and of deprivation, with all the cross-currents of revolt and fear set up by these (Camus, *The Plague*, 138).

The equality of Hobbesian men in the state of nature is like the equality of Camus's townsfolk: an equal chance to die and thus an equality that nobody wants:

the plague was not respecter of persons and under its despotic rule everyone ... was under sentence ... plague had levelled out discrimination ...they were assured of the inerrable equality of death – but nobody wanted that kind of equality (Camus, *The Plague*, 140, 151, 194).

As in the Hobbesian state of nature there is no living community, but only the wandering of groups of desperate individuals, so for Camus the plague disrupts long-established communities and compels people to live in relative isolation.

Both Camus and Hobbes stress the instructive effects of catastrophic events such as the plague or civil wars. In *Behemoth*, Hobbes remarks that times of civil war give a deeper insight in human affairs than peaceful times.[18] Similarly in *The Plague* we read the following dialogue: "'you think ... that the plague has its good side; it opens men's eyes and forces them to take thought?'... "what's true of all the evils in the world is true of plague as well. It helps men to rise above themselves'" (106).

Both Camus and Hobbes are pessimistic about man's ability to learn from past experiences and believe in the permanently looming danger of the plague/civil war:

[the townsfolk] disbelieved in pestilences. A pestilence isn't a thing made to man's measure; therefore we tell ourselves that pestilence is a mere bogey of the mind, a bad dream that will pass away. ...Our townsfolk ...forgot to be modest - that was all -and thought that everything still was possible for them; which presupposed that pestilences were impossible (34).

This is similar to Hobbes's lamentation in *Behemoth* that the reason why people fall into a state of civil war is that they forget the past, become arrogant and thus create the conditions for falling victims again of the state of war.

All these similarities show how modern is the soul of the man described by Hobbes. Like in Camus's novel, in the Hobbesian state of nature, man is isolated, he speaks a language that nobody understands, he experiences an equality with others (equal chance to die) that he does not want, he is the victim of a destiny (war) that he has not chosen and that he is unable to avoid. For both Camus and Hobbes individual rationality during the plague/state of nature offers no salvation.

In Camus's novel, Dr Bernard Rieux, the protagonist-narrator who always tries to be an 'impartial observer' (246) and aims at 'objectivity' (148), finds no protection from the danger of the plague in his rationality. Camus suggests that when the plague strikes a rational frame of mind is as useless as an abandon to passions and irrationality. Similarly for Hobbes, the agent in the state of nature is not delivered from his suffering by his rationality. As argued in Chapter 10, for the rational actor there is no escape from the horror of the state of nature.

However, there is an important difference between Camus and Hobbes's accounts which is worthy of attention and highlights a belief by Hobbes which is a pillar of his ideology.

Camus suggests at the very end of his novel that the bacillus of the plague may and will come back again, of its own volition, and hit another happy city:

> [Dr Rieux has learnt] ... that the plague bacillus never dies or disappears for good; that it can lie dormant for years and years in furniture and linen-chests; that it bides its time in bedroom, cellars, trunks, and bookshelves; and that perhaps the day would come when, for the bane and the enlightening of men, it roused up its rats again and sent them forth to die in a happy city (Camus, *The Plague*, 252).

A different and much more optimistic message emerges from all Hobbes's writings. Hobbes places the responsibility for the collapse back into the state of nature squarely and entirely on the shoulders of men. For Hobbes, without the active help of seditious men, the 'bacillus' of the state of nature is powerless and cannot disrupt human life. He suggests that, although individual rationality does not rescue the agent from the state of nature, the collective rationality of citizens enlightened by his 'political geometry' can either save mankind forever from the occurrence of civil war (*De Cive*, 25-6), or at least can postpone it indefinitely (*Leviathan*, 221).

In Chapter XXXI of *Leviathan* Hobbes confesses that sometimes he is afraid that his own 'labour' is 'as useless, as the Common-wealth of Plato'. He reminds us that for Plato

> it is impossible for the disorders of State, and change of Governments by Civill Warre, ever to be taken away, till Sovereigns be Philosophers (*Leviathan*, 254).

But Hobbes soon recovers hope and confidence, because

> neither Plato, nor any other Philosopher hitherto, hath put into order, and sufficiently, or probably proved all the Theorems of Morall doctrine, that men may learn thereby, both how to govern, and how to obey; I recover some hope, that one time or another, this writing of mine, may fall into the hands of a Sovereign, who will consider it himself (for it is short, and I think clear) without the help of any interested, or envious Interpreter; and by exercise of entire Soveraignty,

in protecting the Publique teaching of it, convert this Truth of Speculation, into Utility of Practice (*Leviathan*, 254)

Whereas Camus does not offer any recipe for the deliverance of man from despair and isolation, Hobbes recommends the education of citizens in his own science of politics and promises salvation.

As argued in Chapter 9, at the time of writing *Elements of Law* and *De Cive* Hobbes was vague and ambiguous about the effectiveness of education. I have pointed out however that in *De Homine* he has no hesitation in claiming that only one of the six sources of human behaviour is natural, whereas the others are socially determined. Hence the didactic element, present in *Leviathan* and absent in *De Cive*, has been explained in this work as the result of the growing conviction by Hobbes (implied strongly in *De Homine* and *Behemoth*) that society, and not nature, is responsible for bad citizens and can rescue man through education. I have argued that increased malleability is the novelty of the later Hobbesian man. No new pessimism, as claimed by Skinner, but a new hope shines in Hobbes's later works, because 'Few are those who cannot be taught' (*De Homine*, 52).

Notes

Introduction. The Political Geometry of Glory (pp. 1-8)

[1] Quentin Skinner, *Reason and Rhetoric in the Philosophy of Hobbes*, Cambridge: Cambridge University Press, 1996.
[2] *Elements of Law*, 68.
[3] *Correspondence II*, letter 197, from Hobbes to Wood (1674), 747.
[4] Quentin Skinner, *Reason and Rhetoric in the Philosophy of Hobbes*, 426.
[5] Quentin Skinner, *Reason and Rhetoric in the Philosophy of Hobbes*, 351.
[6] Michael Oakeshott, 'Introduction to *Leviathan*', in *Rationalism in politics and other essays*. (Indianapolis: Liberty Press, 1991), 245-6.
[7] Preston King, personal correspondence.
[8] F. S. McNeilly, *The Anatomy of Leviathan*. (London: Macmillan, 1968), see especially Chapter 6.

Chapter 1. The Co-ordinates of Man: Time and Space (pp. 11-21)

[1] On this, see John Watkins, *Hobbes's System of Ideas: A Study in the Political Significance of Philosophical Theories*, 2nd ed. (London: Hutchinson, 1973), pp. 34-42.
[2] It may be recalled that Harvey had been taught by Galileo in Padua.
[3] For a survey of the reactions of Hobbes's contemporaries to his theories, see, for example, Samuel I. Mintz, *The Hunting of Leviathan*, (Cambridge: Cambridge University Press, 1962).
[4] In 1936 Leo Strauss, for example, in the preface to *The Political Philosophy of Hobbes. Its basis and its genesis*. (Chicago and London: University of Chicago Press, 1963; first published in 1936), makes clear that the 'particular object' of his study is to show 'that the real basis of Hobbes's political philosophy is not modern science' (p. ix). In 'The Ethical Doctrine of Hobbes', *Philosophy*, 13 (1938) 406-24, A. E. Taylor, too, contends that Hobbes's ethical theory is 'disengaged' from the rest of his philosophy 'with which it has no logically necessary connection', 408. In a similar vein, Howard Warrender in *The Political Philosophy of Hobbes. His theory of Obligation*. (Oxford: Clarendon Press, 1970, first published 1957), argues that if in fact Hobbes wanted to derive his moral theory from an empirical theory 'he must be held to have failed in his main enterprise' (p. 6), because, despite Hobbes's claims to the contrary, his political theory is completely unrelated to his natural science.
[5] The scholarship on motion has shown little interest in Chapter XI of *De Corpore* (vol. I of *The English Works of Thomas Hobbes*, Molesworth edition, London: John Bohn, 1839). A typical sentiment is expressed by Brandt who, referring to this chapter, writes: 'Here Hobbes defines the

concepts of identity and difference ... Hobbes adds nothing worth mentioning to the definitions given already by Aristotle', Frithiof Brandt, *Thomas Hobbes' Mechanical Conception of Nature*. (Copenhagen: Levin and Munksgaard, 1927), pp. 290-91. Among the exceptions, see William Sacksteder, 'Hobbes' Geometrical Objects', *Philosophy of Science*, 48 (1981) 573-90, and Martin Bertman, *Body and Cause in Hobbes: Natural and Political*. (Wakefield, NH: Longwood Academic, 1991).

Chapter 2. Fatal Equality (pp. 22-30)

[1] On this topic, see Martin A. Bertman, 'Equality in Hobbes, with reference to Aristotle', *Review of Politics*, XXVIII (1976) 534-44.
[2] Motion is also defined as 'actual power' and power as 'future motion', *De Corpore*, 131.
[3] Gary B. Herbert, 'Thomas Hobbes's counterfeit equality', *Southern Journal of Philosophy*, 14 (1976) 269-82, 271.
[4] Joel Kidder, 'Acknowledgements of equals: Hobbes's ninth law of nature', *Philosophical Quarterly*, 33 (1983) 133-46, 141.
[5] For a typical example, see David P. Gauthier, *The Logic of Leviathan. The moral and political theory of Thomas Hobbes*. (Oxford: Clarendon Press, 1969), 15.
[6] It seems to me that Hobbes is one of the few writers in the history of political thought that establish the equality of people by taking what Bernard Williams, in his inspirational essay on equality ('The idea of Equality' in Peter Laslett and W.G. Runciman (eds), *Philosophy, Politics, and Society*. (Oxford: Blackwell, 1962), pp. 110-131) defines as *the technical point of view*, contrasted with the *human point of view*, adopted, for example, by Kant.
[7] Hobbes's reply must have convinced du Verdus because he remarks in the same letter (p. 328): 'For it is still very natural to say that all men are naturally equal among themselves, that is, both equally independent of one another by nature, and capable of doing equal things'.

Chapter 3. The Axiom of Glory (pp. 31-44)

[1] A. MacIntyre, *A Short History of Ethics*, (London: Routledge, 1967), 138.
[2] On this, see Chapter 11.
[3] *Elements of Law*, 'Introduction' by Maurice M. Goldsmith, p. *xxi*.
[4] '*Joy*, arising from imagination of a mans own power and ability, is that exultation of the mind which is called glorying', *Leviathan*, 42.
[5] For example, Bernard Gert in his 'Introduction' to *De Homine*, 3.
[6] See, for example, Iain Hampsher-Monk, *A History of Modern Political Thought*, (Oxford: Blackwell, 1992), 23-4.

[7] In *Leviathan* Hobbes resorts once again to an example taken from mechanics: 'For the nature of Power, is in this point, like to Fame, increasing as it proceeds; or like the motion of heavy bodies, which the further they go, make still the more hast' (*Leviathan*, 62).

[8] 'Competition of Riches, Honour, Command, or other Power, enclineth to Contention, Enmity, and War' (*Leviathan*, 70); 'Desire of Praise, disposeth to laudable actions, such as please them whose judgement they value ... Desire of Fame after death does the same' (*Leviathan*, 71).

Chapter 4. Glory: Parallels and Intersections (pp. 45-57)

[1] See especially *The Political Philosophy of Hobbes*, 35-43.

[2] See, for example, *Reason and Rhetoric in Hobbes*, 37-39.

[3] Thomas Hobbes, *The Collected Works of Thomas Hobbes*, edited by William Molesworth, Vol. VI, (London: John Bohn, 1840), *The Art of Rhetoric*, pp. 419-510.

[1] Michael Oakeshott, *Hobbes on Civil Association*. (Oxford: Blackwell, 1937), 59-60.

[4] Tom Sorell, *Hobbes*. (London: Routledge, 1986), 34-7.

[5] *The Political Philosophy of Hobbes*, 44-9.

[6] Arrigo Pacchi, 'Hobbes and the Passions', *Topoi*, 6 (1987) 111-119, p. 115.

[7] Baldassare Castiglione, *The Book of the Courtier*. (London: Dent, 1994).

[8] C.B. Macpherson, *The Political Theory of Possessive Individualism. Hobbes to Locke*. (London: Oxford University Press, 1962), 105.

[9] Francis Bacon, *The Essays*. (Harmondsworth: Penguin, 1985), 217; Hobbes, *Elements of Law*, 37.

[10] Francis Bacon, *The Essays*, ibid.

[11] Francis Bacon, *The Essays*, 218.

[12] Francis Bacon, *The Essays*, 102.

[13] Francis Bacon, *The Essays*, 217.

[14] Leo Strauss, *The Political Philosophy of Hobbes. Its Basis and Its Genesis*. (Chicago: University of Chicago Press, 1952), 35.

[15] Strauss himself did not fail to stress the relevance of Thucydides for a full understanding of Hobbes. In the literature more and more interpreters have pointed out that Hobbes's translation of Thucydides influenced his own ideas on an extremely wide range of topics. Among many others it is worth mentioning the contribution by Richard Schlatter ('Thomas Hobbes and Thucydides', *Journal of the History of Ideas*, 6 (1945) 350-362), C.W. Brown ('Thucydides, Hobbes, and the Derivation of Anarchy', *History of Political Thought*, 8 (1987) 33-62), G. Klosko and D. Rice ('Thucydides' and Hobbes's State of Nature', *History of Political Thought*, 6 (1985) 405-409), Miriam Reik (*The Golden Lands of Thomas Hobbes*. (Detroit: Wayne State University Press, 1977)), Clifford Orwin ('Stasis and Plague: Thucydides on the Dissolution of Society', *Journal of Politics*, 50 (1988)

Notes 177

831-847), Peter R. Pouncey (*The Necessities of War. A Study of Thucydidean Pessimism.* (New York: Columbia University Press, 1980)), Arnold A. Rogow (*Thomas Hobbes. Radical in the Service of Reaction.* (New York: Norton, 1986)), and more recently Quentin Skinner (*Reason and Rhetoric in the Philosophy of Hobbes.* (Cambridge: Cambridge University Press, 1996)).

[16] As my main concern is to examine Hobbes's understanding of Thucydides, rather than an assessment of the *History* in its own terms, I shall quote from Hobbes's own translation rather than from more accurate recent translations.

[17] On the historical circumstances surrounding Hobbes's translation of Thucydides' *History*, see Arnold A. Rogow, *Thomas Hobbes. Radical in the Service of Reaction*, Chapter 4.

[18] The meaning attached by Hobbes to these three terms has been examined in Chapter 2. In Thucydides' *History*, of course, we do not find exact counterparts of Hobbes's concepts. However, as a rule, Thucydides' φιλοτιμία and τιμή are usually translated by Hobbes as ambition and honour; φρόνημα and δόξα are rendered as pride and glory.

[19] For a comparative analysis of Sparta and Athens, see Leo Strauss, *The City and Man.* (Chicago: Chicago University Press, 1964).

[20] On this, see Richard Schlatter, 'Introduction', in R. Schlatter (ed.), *Hobbes's Thucydides*, (New Brunswick, N.J.: Rutgers University Press, 1975), pp. xi-xxviii.

Chapter 5. Ambition: Paradoxes and Puzzles (pp. 58-73)

[1] On the accuracy of Hobbes's translation, see C. Orwin, 'Stasis and Plague: Thucydides on the Dissolution of Society', *Journal of Politics,* 50 (1988) 831-847, 834, footnote 6.

[2] See, for example, Geoffrey Brennan and James Buchanan, *The Power to Tax,* (Cambridge: Cambridge University Press, 1980).

[3] For a critique of Brennan and Buchanan's interpretation of Hobbes, see M. La Manna and G. Slomp, 'Leviathan: Revenue-Maximizer or Glory-Seeker?', *Constitutional Political Economy,* 5 (1994) 159-172.

[4] The only non-glory-related passion in Hobbes's list in the *Elements of Law* is the reference to 'private wealth'.

[5] The present discussion of the relationship between Thucydides' *History* and Hobbes's political theory draws on my 'Hobbes, Thucydides and the Three Greatest Things' *History of Political Thought,* IX (1990) 565-586. See also Richard Schlatter, 'Thomas Hobbes and Thucydides', *Journal of the History of Ideas,* 6 (1945) 350-362, and his 'Introduction' *Hobbes's Thucydides.* (New Brunswick: Rutgers University Press, 1975); C.W. Brown, 'Thucydides, Hobbes, and the Derivation of Anarchy', *History of Political Thought,* 8 (1987) 33-62; G. Klosko and D. Rice, 'Thucydides

and Hobbes's State of Nature', *History of Political Thought*, 6 (1985) 405-409.

[6] ὠφελία is a very broad term that can indicate, among other things, whatever is to one's advantage or interest. Some interpreters have suggested that the third part of the triad mentioned by the Athenians is 'self-interest'. See, for example, Pouncey, *The Necessities of War*, p. 21; Peter T. Manicas, 'War, Stasis, and Greek Political Thought', *Comparative Studies in Society and History*, 24 (1982) 673-688, 684; Leo Strauss, *The City and Man*, 172. Personally I do not subscribe this view. I believe that ὠφελία in the above quotation, translated by Hobbes with the equally ambiguous term 'profit', is to be understood in the narrow sense of economic advantage or interest.

[7] In the Correspondence we learn that Hobbes referred sometimes to himself jokingly as Thucydides (see letter 28).

Chapter 6. The Dilemma of Fear and Hope (pp. 74-83)

[1] 'Of all the Greek historians, Thucydides was his source of particular delight', (*Prose Life*, 246).

[2] Klosko and Rice, 'Thucydides' and Hobbes's State of Nature', 406-7.

[3] John H. Finley, *Three Essays on Thucydides*, (Cambridge, Mass.: Harvard University Press, 1967), 152.

[4] In *Leviathan* Hobbes notices that 'though nothing can be immortal, which mortals make; yet, if men had the use of reason they pretend to, their commonwealths might be secured, at least from perishing from internal disease', 308.

[5] On this see Richard Schlatter, 'Introduction', in R. Schlatter (Ed), *Hobbes's Thucydides*, (New Brunswick, N.J.: Rutgers University Press, 1975), pp. xi-xxviii.

Chapter 7. The Trajectory of Glory (pp. 84-96)

[1] For a different view on the relation between glory and sensual pleasure, see Strauss, *Natural Right and History*, 189.

[2] In *De Corpore* instead Hobbes seems to put down the difference in interests to a difference in education (Epistle to the Reader, p. xiv), Thomas Hobbes, *Elements of Philosophy*, vol. I of *The English Works of Thomas Hobbes*, edited by Sir William Molesworth (London: John Bohn, 1839).

[3] See David Heyed, 'The Place of Laughter in Hobbes's Theory of Emotions', *Journal of History of Ideas*, 43 (1982) 285-95. A recent discussion of laughter in Hobbes can be found in Skinner, *Reason and Rhetoric*.

[4] Maurice M. Goldsmith, *Hobbes's Science of Politics*, 79.

[5] See, for example, *Correspondence I*, letter 28, 52-3.

[6] Arthur Conan Doyle, *The Penguin Complete Sherlock Holmes*, (Harmondsworth: Penguin, 1981), 'The Adventure of the Empty House', pp. 483-496, 495.
[7] Arrigo Pacchi, 'Hobbes and the Passions', *Topoi*, 6 (1987) 111-19, 116.
[8] *Ibid.*
[9] René Descartes, *The Passions of the Soul* [1649], (Indianapolis and Cambridge: Hackett, 1989), pp. 102-103.
[10] René Descartes, *The Passions of the Soul*, especially pp. 105, 129.

Chapter 8. Glory and the Excellent Sex (pp. 97-107)

[1] The original text (in Italian) is even more passionate.
[2] Preston King, *The Ideology of Order*, (London: Allen & Unwin, 1974), especially Ch. 15 on 'Mother and Infant'.
[3] Carole Pateman, 'God Hath Ordained to Man a Helper: Hobbes, Patriarchy and Conjugal Right', in Mary Lyndon Shanley and Carole Pateman (eds), *Feminist Interpretations and Political Theory*, (London, Polity Press, 1991), pp. 53-73, 54. See also Carole Pateman, *The Sexual Contract* (London, Polity Press, 1988).
[4] On the 'is-ought' problem in Hobbes, see Preston King, *The Ideology of Order*, Ch. 12; Martin A. Bertman, *Hobbes: The Natural and the Artifacted Good*, (Bern: Peter Lang, 1981), Ch. 3, especially pp. 48 ff.
[5] Preston King, *The Ideology of Order*, 191.
[6] Bernard Williams, 'The Idea of Equality', in Peter Laslett and W.G. Runciman (eds), *Philosophy, Politics and Society* (Oxford: Blackwell, 1962), 110-131.
[7] For example, Hobbesian women are more inclined than men to 'weeping' which is the physical reaction to 'sudden dejection' (*Leviathan*, 46).
[8] According to Hobbes, it is the desire of real power that drives some women to pretend to possess magic powers and to resort to witchcraft.

Chapter 9. The Determinants of the Citizen: Nature and Nurture (pp. 108-117)

[1] Preston King, *The Ideology of Order*. (London: Allen & Unwin, 1974), 190.
[2] Arrigo Pacchi, 'Hobbes and the Passions', *Topoi*, 6 (1987) 111-119, 118
[3] A. P. Martinich, *A Hobbes Dictionary*. (Oxford: Blackwell, 1995), 95.

Chapter 10. The Rational Actor at Play (pp. 120-138)

[1] Patrick Neal, 'Hobbes and Rational Choice Theory', *Western Political Quarterly*, 41 (1988) 635-52.
[2] Gabriella Slomp and Manfredi La Manna, 'Hobbes, Harsanyi and the Edge of the Abyss', *Canadian Journal of Political Science*, XXIX (1996) 47-70;

see also the comment by Alexander Coram ('To infinity and beyond: Hobbes and Harsanyi still nowhere near the abyss', *Canadian Journal of Political Science*, XXX (1977) 555-59) and our rejoinder ('To Infinity and No Farther: A Reply to Coram', *Canadian Journal of Political Science*, XXX (1977) 560-63).

[3] J.G.A. Pocock, 'Interregnum and Restoration', in *The varieties of British political thought, 1500*-1800, edited by J.G.A. Pocock, (Cambridge: Cambridge University Press, 1993), pp. 146-179, 161-162.

[4] Assumptions IR and CK are part of what Neal, 'Hobbes and Rational Choice Theory', calls 'E-rationality'.

[5] According to Hobbes, the content of the right of nature and of the natural laws can be understood by everybody, and everybody can be assumed to understand it; see *Leviathan*, chap. XV, especially 144.

[6] A selected sample includes John Watkins, 'Imperfect Rationality,' in R. Borger and F. Cioffi, eds., *Explanation in the Behavioural Sciences* (Cambridge: Cambridge University Press, 1970), David Gauthier, *The Logic of Leviathan* (Oxford: Clarendon Press, 1969), Michael Taylor, *The Possibility of Cooperation*. (Cambridge: Cambridge University Press, 1987).

[7] Gauthier, *The Logic of Leviathan*, 17.

[8] Gauthier, *The Logic of Leviathan*, 15.

[9] Gauthier, *The Logic of Leviathan*, 83.

[10] Gauthier, *The Logic of Leviathan*, 18. According to Gauthier 'given that a man, in order to survive, may *need* some object which is also *needed* by his fellows, then competition necessarily follows' (*ibid.*, italics added). As explained below, the relevance of this statement to Hobbes's state of nature is either dubious (if 'need' is interpreted as 'indispensable for survival') or highly questionable (if 'need' means 'desire').

[11] Gauthier points at contempt (p. 1 6) as a further source of the Hobbesian conflict.

[12] Gauthier, *The Logic of Leviathan*, 97-8.

[13] Gauthier, *The Logic of Leviathan*, 97.

[14] Especially in *Hobbesian Moral and Political Theory*, (Princeton University Press: Princeton, N.J., 1986).

[15] Kavka, *Hobbesian Moral and Political Theory*, 191.

[16] Hampton, *Hobbes and the Social Contract Tradition*, 85.

[17] Hampton, *Hobbes and the Social Contract Tradition*, 80.

[18] Hampton, *Hobbes and the Social Contract Tradition*, 81.

[19] Kavka, *Hobbesian Moral and Political Theory*, especially 182-188.

[20] Hampton, *Hobbes and the Social Contract Tradition*, 150-160.

[21] Michael Taylor, *The Possibility of Cooperation*, Chapters 2 and 3.

[22] Kavka, *Hobbesian Moral and Political Theory*, 188.

[23] Hampton, *Hobbes and the Social Contract Tradition*, 150-60.

[24] Hampton, *Hobbes and the Social Contract Tradition*, 186.

Notes

[25] Patrick Neal, 'Hobbes and Rational Choice Theory', *Western Political Quarterly*, 41 (1988) 635-52.

[26] Neal, 'Hobbes and Rational Choice Theory', 637-8.

[27] Neal, 'Hobbes and Rational Choice Theory', 642.

[28] *Ibid*.

[29] Robert Sugden, 'Rational Choice: A Survey of Contributions from Economics and Philosophy', *Economic Journal*, 101 (1991) 751-785.

[30] Like Hampton, Kavka, too, highlights 'the problems of identifying violators' (Kavka, *Hobbesian Moral and Political Theory*, 125) in the Hobbesian state of nature.

[31] For a formal proof, see Slomp and La Manna, 'Hobbes, Harsanyi, and the edge of the abyss'.

[32] Notice that this assumption, explicitly made in Neal's model, is stronger than the one made by Gauthier where violent death is simply the worst *ranked* outcome.

[33] Kavka, *Hobbesian Moral and Political Theory*, 123-4.

[34] Iain Hampsher-Monk, *A History of Modern Political Thought*, (Oxford: Blackwell, 1992).

Chapter 11. Hobbes's Impossibility Theorem (pp. 139-154)

[1] In letter 34 to Mersenne, Hobbes wryly comments that 'nor does he [Descartes] need any foundations, when he can build whatever he likes, by the power of his imagination, in the very air' (*Correspondence I*, 108).

[2] 'Two great antitheses dominate the political thought of all times: oppression-freedom, and anarchy-unity. Hobbes definitely belongs to the company of those whose political thought has been inspired by the latter antithesis; the ideal which he defends is not liberty against oppression, but unity against anarchy', Norberto Bobbio, *Thomas Hobbes and the Natural Law Tradition*. (Chicago: University of Chicago Press, 1993), 29.

[3] Indeed by reading his correspondence we get the impression that Hobbes was not the pessimist that many generations of interpreters have maintained. He comes across as a very cheerful and warm man, stubborn but self-ironic, surrounded by a circle of affectionate friends that could not be more different from the characterisation of the natural man given by Hobbes in his political writings. For example, in his last moving letter to Hobbes, Sorbière assesses his own life in a way which is in complete contrast with the Hobbesian glory-seeker whose existence is a search for power after power. He writes: I shall withdraw from this life like a guest who has feasted well, and shall not struggle against the will of God (*Correspondence II*, letter 185, 707). Whereas the Hobbesian glory-seeker is capable only of scornful laughter, Hobbes's own friends seemed to be capable of a healthier sort of laughter. Thus Sorbière: 'good laughter is

conducive to good health, both in body and in mind' (*Correspondence II*, letter 114, 435).
[4] The reference to the most celebrated impossibility theorem of this century is not coincidental. In a joint paper with M. La Manna I argue that there exists a surprisingly strict correspondence between Arrow's Impossibility Theorem and Hobbes's claim of the logical necessity of an absolute sovereign.
[5] Gottfried W. Leibniz, *Political Writings*, 2nd ed., edited by Patrick Riley, (Cambridge: Cambridge University Press, 1988), Chapter 8, pp. 111-120.
[6] Leibniz, *Political Writings*, 118.
[7] Russell Hardin, 'Hobbesian Political Order', *Political Theory*, 19 (1991) 156-180.

Chapter 12. The Ideology of Political Geometry (pp. 155-173)

[1] Immanuel Kant, 'On the Common Saying: "This May be True in Theory, but it does not Apply in Practice"', Part II ('On the Relationship of Theory to Practice in Political Right'), in *Political Writings* 2nd ed., edited by Hans Reiss, (Cambridge: Cambridge University Press, 1991), 75.
[2] Leibniz, 'Caesarinus Fürstenerius' (1677), in *Political Writings*, edited by Patrick Riley, 2nd ed., (Cambridge: Cambridge University Press), 1988, 118-19.
[3] Benito Mussolini, *The political and social doctrine of Fascism*, (authorized translation by Jane Soames), (London: Hogarth Press, 1933), 11-12.
[4] Leibniz, 'Caesarinus Fürstenerius', p. 120 (emphasis added).
[5] Only in a passage of *The Three Dialogues* recently attributed to Hobbes by Reynolds and Saxonhouse one can find a different view: '[in Roman History] you shall scarce read of any, that was not either a man of action or direction ... and ability to give counsel, is at least, not inferior to the former ... To prepare a man fit for both, nothing so much prevails, as a hard and weary life, such an agitation as will not permit idleness, nor the mind to settle too much upon private ends, which being so, could never be aptly applied for Public [ends] ... For if a man give over himself to an easeful life, the sharpness of his senses will be dulled, and grow retired, applying himself to his own contents, and then, can never have sufficiency, nor will to prevail for the public, once being confined to his own particular interest, and looking no further. Many men are naturally given to such a life, and some by accident fall into it, but certainly their memory dies with them: for *no man is born only for himself*. This is so well known, that I will not seek farther to illustrate it', *The Three Discourses*, 74.
The whole passage is in my view so out of character, so unlike any other comment on human nature made by Hobbes, that in my eyes the very attribution of *The Three Discourses* to Hobbes's pen is put into question. Nowhere else in his writings Hobbes claims that 'no man is born only for himself'. Moreover, although in many of his writings Hobbes condemns

idleness and claims that 'work is good; it is truly a motive for life ... Idleness is torture' (*De Homine,* 51), he usually condemns it precisely for the opposite reason explained in the above quotation, namely because it induces young men to try to become politically involved, to give public counselling and to innovate the laws of the commonwealth. In my view, the statistical wordprint analysis carried by Reynolds and Saxonhouse to attribute *The Three Discourses* to Hobbes is no substitute for philosophical analysis of the text. As the passage cited above should make clear, there are strong philosophical grounds for doubting the Hobbesian paternity of *The Three Discourses.* In fact, in this book I have consciously treated the *Discourses* as not belonging to Hobbes's *opus.* I acknowledge that a historian of Quentin Skinner's stature does not contest the attribution of *The Three Discourses* to Hobbes. However, his own discussion of the issue raises at least the possibility that the discourses could have been written by William Cavendish, educated and therefore greatly influenced by Hobbes, rather than by Hobbes himself.

[6] Richard Tuck, *Hobbes,* in Quentin Skinner *et al., Great Political Thinkers.* (Oxford: Oxford University Press, 1992), 211-12.

[7] Steven Lukes, *Individualism.* (Oxford: Blackwell, 1973).

[8] Alasdair MacIntyre, *A Short History of Ethics.* (London: Routledge, 1967 and 1995), 139.

[9] For example, Kenneth Minogue, 'Hobbes and Political Language', paper presented at the APSA meeting, Atlanta, 31 August-3 September 1989.

[10] Minogue, 'Hobbes and Political Language', 13.

[11] Minogue, 'Hobbes and Political Language', 13-14.

[12] All reference are to Albert Camus, *The Plague,* translated by Stuart Gilbert, (Harmondsworth: Penguin Books, 1960).

[13] It is not the case that any description of a natural calamity with political repercussions like the plague (e.g., Thucydides', Camus') inevitably finds resonance in Hobbes's state of nature. Consider, for example, Alessandro Manzoni's account of the plague in 17th-century Milan in *The Betrothed,* where there are no echoes of Hobbes's bleak state of nature. The reason being, I surmise, that Manzoni is as deeply Catholic as Hobbes is irredeemably secular.

[14] Camus, *The Plague,* 160.

[15] Camus, *The Plague,* 161.

[16] Camus, *The Plague,* 59.

[17] Camus, *The Plague,* 66, 145.

[18] See *supra* Section 4.2.3.

Selected Bibliography

Bacon, Francis, *The Essays*. (Harmondsworth: Penguin, 1985).
Baumgold, Deborah, *Hobbes's Political Theory*. (Cambridge: Cambridge University Press, 1988).
Bertman, Martin A., 'Equality in Hobbes, with reference to Aristotle', *Review of Politics*, XXVIII (1976) 534-44.
Bertman, Martin A., *Hobbes: The Natural and the Artifacted Good*, (Bern: Peter Lang, 1981).
Bertman, Martin A., *Body and Cause in Hobbes: Natural and Political*. (Wakefield, NH: Longwood Academic, 1991).
Blits, Jan H., 'Hobbesian Fear', *Political Theory* 17 (1989), 417-31.
Bobbio, Norberto, *Thomas Hobbes and the Natural Law Tradition*. (Chicago: University of Chicago Press, 1993).
Brandt, Frithiof, *Thomas Hobbes' Mechanical Conception of Nature*. (Copenhagen: Levin and Munksgaard, 1927).
Brennan, Geoffrey and James Buchanan, *The Power to Tax*, (Cambridge: Cambridge University Press, 1980).
Brown C.W., 'Thucydides, Hobbes, and the Derivation of Anarchy', *History of Political Thought*, 8 (1987) 33-62.
Brown, C.W., 'Thucydides, Hobbes and the Linear Causal Perspective', *History of Political Thought* X (1989) 215-56.
Brown, Keith (ed.), *Hobbes Studies* (Oxford: Blackwell, 1965).
Camus, Albert, *The Plague,* translated by Stuart Gilbert, (Harmondsworth: Penguin Books, 1960).
Castiglione, Baldassare, *The Book of the Courtier*. (London: Dent, 1994).
Catlin, G., *Thomas Hobbes, as Philosopher, Publicist and Man of Letters*. (Oxford: Blackwell, 1922).
Coady, C. A. J., 'Hobbes and "the Beautiful Axiom"', *Philosophy* 65 (1990) 5-17.
Coram. Alexander, 'To infinity and beyond: Hobbes and Harsanyi still nowhere near the abyss', *Canadian Journal of Political Science,* XXX (1977) 555-59.
Cranston, Maurice and Richard Peters (eds), *Hobbes and Rousseau*. (New York: Doubleday, 1965).
Den Uyl, Douglas J. and Stuart D. Warner, 'Liberalism and Hobbes and Spinoza' *Studia Spinoziana* 3 (1987) 261-318.
Descartes, René, *The Passions of the Soul* [1649]. (Indianapolis and

Cambridge: Hackett, 1989).
Dunn, John, *The History of Political Theory and other essays.* (Cambridge: Cambridge University Press, 1996).
Edmunds, Lowell, *Chance and Intelligence in Thucydides.* (Cambridge, Mass.: Harvard University Press, 1975).
Finley, John H., *Three Essays on Thucydides.* (Cambridge, Mass.: Harvard University Press, 1967).
Frohnen, Bruce P. 'Oakeshott's Hobbesian Myth: Pride, Character and the Limits of Reason', *Western Political Quarterly* 43 (1990) 789-809.
Gauthier, David P. *The Logic of Leviathan. The moral and political theory of Thomas Hobbes.* (Oxford, Clarendon Press, 1969).
Gauthier, David P., 'The Social Contract as Ideology', *Philosophy and Public Affairs* 6 (1977) 130-164.
Gert, Bernard, 'Hobbes and Psychological Egoism', *Journal of the History of Ideas* 28 (1967) 503-20.
Gert, Bernard, 'Introduction', *Thomas Hobbes. Man and Citizen.* (New York: Doubleday, 1972).
Goldsmith, Maurice M., *Hobbes's Science of Politics.* (New York: Columbia University Press, 1966).
Goldsmith, Maurice M., 'Introduction', in Thomas Hobbes, *Behemoth or the Long Parliament* 2nd ed., edited by Ferdinand Tönnies (London: Frank Cass: 1969), v-xiv.
Goldsmith, Maurice M., 'Hobbes's Mortall God: Is There a Fallacy in Hobbes's Theory of Sovereignty?', *History of Political Thought* 1 (1980) 33-50.
Gough, J., *The Social Contract: A critical study of its development* 2nd ed., (Westport, Conn.: Greenwood, 1978).
Hampsher-Monk, Iain, *A History of Modern Political Thought.* (Oxford: Blackwell, 1992).
Hampton, Jean, *Hobbes and the Social Contract Tradition.* (Cambridge: Cambridge University Press, 1986).
Hardin, Russell, 'Hobbesian Political Order', *Political Theory,* 19 (1991) 156-180.
Herbert, Gary B., 'Thomas Hobbes's counterfeit equality', *Southern Journal of Philosophy,* 14 (1976) 269-82.
Herbert, Gary B., *Thomas Hobbes. The Unity of Scientific and moral Wisdom.* (Vancouver: University of British Columbia Press, 1989).
Heyed, David, 'The Place of Laughter in Hobbes's Theory of

Emotions', *Journal of History of Ideas*, 43 (1982) 285-95.
Hill, Christopher, *Puritanism and Revolution*. (London: Seckert & Warburg, 1958).
Hood, F., *The Divine Politics of Thomas Hobbes*. (Oxford: Clarendon Press, 1964).
Hungerland, Isabel C. and George R. Vick, 'Hobbes's theory of signification', *Journal of the History of Philosophy* 11 (1973) 459-82.
James, D. G., *The Life of Reason: Hobbes, Locke, Bolingbroke.* (London: Longmans, 1949).
Johnston, David, *The Rhetoric of Leviathan*. (Princeton: Princeton University Press, 1986).
Kant, Immanuel, 'On the Common Saying: "This May be True in Theory, but it does not Apply in Practice"', Part II ('On the Relationship of Theory to Practice in Political Right'), in *Political Writings* 2nd ed., edited by Hans Reiss, (Cambridge: Cambridge University Press, 1991).
Kavka, Gregory, 'Hobbes's War of All Against All', *Ethics* 93 (1983) 291-310.
Kavka, Gregory, *Hobbesian Moral and Political Theory,* (Princeton University Press: Princeton, N.J., 1986).
Kidder, Joel, 'Acknowledgements of equals: Hobbes's ninth law of nature', *Philosophical Quarterly*, 33 (1983) 133-46.
King, Preston, *The Ideology of Order*. (London: Allen & Unwin, 1974).
Klosko G. and D. Rice, 'Thucydides' and Hobbes's State of Nature', *History of Political Thought*, 6 (1985) 405-409.
Kraynak, Robert P., *History and Modernity in the Thought of Thomas Hobbes*. (Ithaca: Cornell University Press, 1990).
Laird, J., *Hobbes*. (London: Benn, 1934).
La Manna, Manfredi and Gabriella Slomp, 'Leviathan: Revenue-Maximizer or Glory-Seeker?', *Constitutional Political Economy*, 5 (1994) 159-172.
Leibniz, Gottfried W., *Political Writings*, 2nd ed., edited by Patrick Riley, (Cambridge: Cambridge University Press, 1988).
von Leyden, Wolfgang, *Hobbes and Locke: The Politics of Freedom and Obligation*. (London: Macmillan, 1981).
Lukes, Steven, *Individualism*. (Oxford: Blackwell, 1973).
Lund, William R., 'Hobbes on opinion, private judgment and civil war', *History of Political Thought* XIII (1992) 51-72.

Selected Bibliography

MacIntyre, Alasdair, *A Short History of Ethics*. (London: Routledge, 1967 and 1995).

Macpherson, C.B., *The Political Theory of Possessive Individualism. Hobbes to Locke*. (London: Oxford University Press, 1962).

Mandeville, Bernard, *The Fable of the Bees* [1714]. (Harmondsworth: Penguin,1989).

Manicas, Peter T., 'War, Stasis, and Greek Political Thought', *Comparative Studies in Society and History*, 24 (1982) 673-688.

Martinich, A.P., *The Two Gods of Leviathan: Thomas Hobbes on Religion and Politics* (Cambridge: Cambridge University Press, 1992).

Martinich, A.P., *A Hobbes Dictionary*. (Oxford: Blackwell, 1995).

McLean, Iain, 'The Social Contract in Leviathan and the Prisoner's Dilemma Supergame', *Political Studies* 29 (1981) 339-51.

McNeilly, F.S., *The Anatomy of Leviathan*. (London: Macmillan, 1968).

Minogue, Kenneth, 'Introduction', Thomas Hobbes, *Leviathan*. (London: Dent, 1973).

Minogue, Kenneth, 'Hobbes and Political Language', paper presented at the American Political Science Association Meeting, Atlanta, Ge., 31 August - 3 September 1989.

Mintz, Samuel I., *The Hunting of Leviathan*, (Cambridge: Cambridge University Press, 1962).

Neal, Patrick, 'Hobbes and Rational Choice Theory', *Western Political Quarterly*, 41 (1988) 635-52.

Oakeshott, Michael, *Hobbes on Civil Association*. (Oxford: Blackwell, 1937.

Oakeshott, Michael, *Rationalism in politics and other essays*. (Indianapolis: Liberty Press, 1991).

Orr, Robert, 'Hobbes on the Regulation of Voluntary Motion', in G. Feaver and F. Rosen (eds), *Lives, Liberty and the Public Good*. (London: Macmillan, 1987), pp. 45-60.

Orwin Clifford, 'Stasis and Plague: Thucydides on the Dissolution of Society', *Journal of Politics*, 50 (1988) 831-847.

Orwin Clifford, 'The Just and the Advantageous in Thucydides: The Case of the Mytelenaian Debate', *American Political Science Review* 78 (1984) 485-94.

Pacchi, Arrigo, 'Hobbes and the Passions', *Topoi*, 6 (1987) 111-119.

Pacchi, Arrigo, 'Some Guidelines into Hobbes's Theology', *Hobbes Studies* 2 (1989) 87-103.

Pateman, Carole, 'God Hath Ordained to Man a Helper: Hobbes, Patriarchy and Conjugal Right', in Mary Lyndon Shanley and Carole Pateman (eds), *Feminist Interpretations and Political Theory*. (London: Polity Press, 1991), pp. 53-73.
Pateman, Carole, *The Sexual Contract.* (London: Polity Press, 1988).
Peters, Richard, *Hobbes.* (Harmondsworth: Penguin, 1956).
Plamenatz, John, *Man and Society.* Vol. I: *Political and Social Theory: Machiavelli through Rousseau.* (New York: McGraw-Hill, 1963).
Pocock, J.G.A., 'Interregnum and Restoration', in *The varieties of British political thought, 1500*-1800, edited by J.G.A. Pocock, (Cambridge: Cambridge University Press, 1993), pp. 146-179.
Pouncey Peter R., *The Necessities of War. A Study of Thucydidean Pessimism.* (New York: Columbia University Press, 1980).
Prokhovnik, Raia, *Rhetoric and Philosophy in Hobbes' Leviathan* (London: Garland, 1991).
Raphael, D. D., *Hobbes: Morals and Politics.* (London: Allen & Unwin, 1977).
Reik Miriam, *The Golden Lands of Thomas Hobbes.* (Detroit: Wayne State University Press, 1977).
Robertson, G. C., *Hobbes.* (Edinburgh: Blackwood, 1886).
Ryan, Alan, 'Hobbes and Individualism', in Rogers, G. A. J. and Ryan Alan (eds), *Perspectives on Thomas Hobbes.* (Oxford: Clarendon Press, 1988).
Rogow, Arnold A., *Thomas Hobbes. Radical in the Service of Reaction.* (New York: Norton, 1986).
Sacksteder, William, 'Hobbes' Geometrical Objects', *Philosophy of Science,* 48 (1981) 573-90.
Sacksteder, William, *Hobbes Studies* (1879-1979): *a Bibliography* (Bowling Green, Oh.: Ohio State University Press, 1982).
Sarasohn, L. T., 'Motion and morality: Pierre Gassendi, Thomas Hobbes and the mechanical world-view', *Journal of the History of Ideas* 46 (1985) 363-79.
Schlatter, Richard, 'Thomas Hobbes and Thucydides', *Journal of the History of Ideas*, 6 (1945) 350-362.
Schlatter, Richard, 'Introduction', in R. Schlatter (ed), *Hobbes's Thucydides.* (New Brunswick, N.J.: Rutgers University Press, 1975), pp. xi-xxviii.
Schrock, Thomas S., 'The rights to punish and resist. Punishment in Hobbes's *Leviathan*', *Western Political Quarterly* 44 (1991)

853-890.
Skinner, Quentin, 'Hobbes's *Leviathan*', *The Historical Journal* 7 (1964) 321-333.
Skinner, Quentin, 'The ideological context of Hobbes's political thought', *The Historical Journal* 9 (1966) 286-317.
Skinner, Quentin, *The Foundations of Modern Political Thought*, vol. II: The *Age of Reformation*. (Cambridge: Cambridge University Press, 1978).
Skinner, Quentin, *Reason and Rhetoric in the Philosophy of Hobbes*. (Cambridge: Cambridge University Press, 1996).
Slomp, Gabriella, 'Hobbes, Thucydides and the Three Greatest Things' *History of Political Thought*, IX(4) (1990) 565-586.
Slomp, Gabriella, 'Hobbes and the Equality of Women', *Political Studies* 42 (1994) 441-452.
Slomp, Gabriella, 'From *Genus* to *Species*: The Unravelling of Hobbesian Glory', *History of Political Thought* XIX (1998), 1-18.
Slomp, Gabriella and Manfredi La Manna, 'Hobbes, Harsanyi and the Edge of the Abyss', *Canadian Journal of Political Science*, XXIX (1996) 47-70.
Slomp Gabriella and Manfredi La Manna, 'To Infinity and No Farther: A Reply to Coram', *Canadian Journal of Political Science*, XXX (1977) 560-63.
Sorell, Tom, *Hobbes*. (London: Routledge, 1986).
Sorell, Tom, 'Hobbes's Persuasive Civil Science', *Philosophical Quarterly* 40 (1990) 342-351.
Sorell, Tom (ed.), *The Cambridge Companion to Hobbes* (Cambridge: Cambridge University Press, 1996).
Spragens, Thomas, *The Politics of Motion. The World of Thomas Hobbes*. (London: Croom Helm, 1973).
State, S.A. *Thomas Hobbes and the Debate over Natural Law and Religion* (London: Garland, 1991).
Stephen, Leslie, *Hobbes*. (London: Macmillan, 1904).
Strauss, Leo, *Natural Right and History*. (Chicago: University of Chicago Press, 1953).
Strauss, Leo, *The City and Man*, (Chicago: Chicago University Press, 1964).
Strauss, Leo, *The Political Philosophy of Hobbes. Its basis and its genesis*. (Chicago and London: University of Chicago Press, 1963; first published in 1936).

Sugden, Robert, 'Rational Choice: A Survey of Contributions from Economics and Philosophy', *Economic Journal* 101 (1991) 751-785.

Taylor, A. E., 'The Ethical Doctrine of Hobbes', *Philosophy*, 13 (1938) 406-24.

Taylor, Michael, *The Possibility of Cooperation.* (Cambridge: Cambridge University Press, 1987).

Tuck, Richard, *Natural Rights Theories: Their Origin and Development.* (Cambridge: Cambridge University Press, 1979).

Tuck, Richard, *Hobbes*, in Quentin Skinner *et al., Great Political Thinkers.* (Oxford: Oxford University Press, 1992).

Verdon, Michel, 'On thge laws of physical and human nature: Hobbes's physical and social cosmologies', *Journal of the History of Ideas* 43 (1982) 653-663.

Warrender, Howard *The Political Philosophy of Hobbes. His theory of Obligation.* (Oxford: Clarendon Press, 1970, first published 1957).

Watkins, John, 'Philosophy and politics in Hobbes', *The Philosophical Quarterly* 5 (1955) 125-46.

Watkins, John, 'Imperfect Rationality,' in R. Borger and F. Cioffi, eds., *Explanation in the Behavioural Sciences* (Cambridge: Cambridge University Press, 1970).

Watkins, John, *Hobbes's System of Ideas: A Study in the Political Significance of Philosophical Theories*, 2nd ed. (London: Hutchinson, 1973).

Williams, Bernard, 'The idea of Equality' in Peter Laslett and W.G. Runciman (eds), *Philosophy, Politics, and Society.* (Oxford: Blackwell, 1962), pp. 110-131.

Wolin, Sheldon, *Politics and Vision.* (Boston: Little, Brown, 1960).

Name Index

A

Acton, Lord 158
Adam 47, 160, 170
Aesop 50
Alcibiades 54, 62, 76
Alexander, the Great 44
America 122
Archidamus 66, 77
Aristophanes 58
Aristotle xi, 45-6, 51, 62, 98, 175fn
Athens 55, 76, 78-9, 81-83, 177fn
Aubrey, John xii, 11, 22, 31, 45-6, 49, 90, 93, 97, 108, 141, 159, 167
Augustine, Saint 45, 47, 159
Augustus, Emperor 44

B

Bacon, Francis 45-6, 49-51, 176fn
Barber, Richard xii
Barry, Brian 140
Bentham, Jeremy 111, 162
Bertman, Martin 175fn, 179fn
Bobbio, Norberto 155, 181fn
Borger, R. 180fn
Brandt, Frithiof 174-5fn
Brennan, Geoffrey 68, 177fn
Brown, C. W. 176-7fn
Buchanan, James 68, 177fn
Burke, Edmund 157

C

Camus, Albert 7-8, 167-73, 183fn
Castiglione, Baldassare 45, 176fn
Cavendish, the Hon. Charles (2nd son of the 2nd Earl of Devonshire) 38, 48
Cavendish, William, 2nd Earl of Devonshire 183fn
Cicero 45, 50
Cioffi, F. 180fn
Commodus 44
Conan Doyle, Arthur 179fn
Coram, Alexander 180
Corcyra 56, 59-60, 63-6, 83
Creon 64-5
Cromwell, Oliver 61
Cupid 97

D

de' Medici, Cosimo, see Medici
de Sluse, René-François, see Sluse
Descartes, René 32-3, 38, 89, 91, 94-5, 143, 179fn, 181fn
Devonshire, see Cavendish
Diodotus 65, 80-1
du Prat, François, see Prat
du Verdus, François, see Verdus

191

E

Elisabeth I of England 22
England 52, 74, 94, 97, 113
Euclid 4, 7, 141-2, 144
Euripides 58

F

Fell, John 38
Finley, John H. 78, 178fn
Florence 11

G

Galilei, Galileo 11, 174fn
Galileo, see Galilei
Gaskin, J.C.A. xii
Gauthier, David 6, 29, 121, 126-8, 135-6, 140, 159, 175fn, 180-81fn
Gert, Bernard xii, 5, 114, 175fn
Gilbert, Stuart 183fn
Godolphin, Sidney 114
Goldsmith, Maurice M. 3, 33, 48, 89, 175fn, 178fn
Greece 64, 75, 81
Guisony, Pierre 94

H

Hampsher-Monk, Iain 5, 139, 175fn, 181fn
Hampton, Jean 6-7, 121-2, 128, 131-3, 135-6, 138, 140, 180-1fn
Hardin, Russell 182fn
Harvey, William 11, 174fn
Heliogatus 44
Herbert, Gary B. 175fn
Hermocrates 63, 65, 77
Heyed, David 178fn
Holmes, Sherlock 92-3, 179fn
Homer 58
Horace 58
Hume, David 7

K

Kant, Immanuel 155, 175fn, 182fn
Kavka, Gregory 6, 29, 121, 128-32, 135, 138, 146, 155, 180-1fn
Kidder, Joel 175fn
King, Preston 3, 98-99, 102, 105, 109, 155, 174fn, 179fn
Klosko, G. 76, 176-8fn

L

La Manna, Manfredi 122, 177fn, 179fn, 181-2fn
Laslett, Peter 175fn, 179fn
Leibniz, Gottlieb Wilhelm 1, 12, 29, 74, 141-2, 145-8, 150, 152-3, 156, 158, 182fn
Locke, John 8, 26, 144, 154, 159, 176fn
London 1, 11
Lucretius 161
Lukes, Steven 164, 183fn
Lyndon Shanley, Mary 179fn

M

Machiavelli, Niccolò 8, 45, 50
MacIntyre, Alasdair 8, 33, 165, 175fn, 183fn
Macpherson, C. B. 4, 46, 49, 52, 54, 62, 68, 111, 155, 176fn
Malcolm, Noel xii, 98, 141
Manicas, Peter T. 178fn
Manzoni, Alessandro 183fn
Marsennus, see Mersenne
Martinich, A. P. 114, 155,

Name Index

179fn
Mayne, Jasper 159
McLean, Iain 121, 140
McNeilly, F. S. 2-5, 33-4, 40, 73, 93, 112, 145, 174fn
Medici, Cosimo de' 94
Mersenne, Marin 12 39, 94, 181fn
Milan 183fn
Mill, John Stuart 162
Minogue, Kenneth 166, 183fn
Mintz, Samuel I. 174fn
Molesworth, William *xi, xii*, 174fn, 176fn, 178fn
Mussolini, Benito 157, 182fn

N

Neal, Patrick 6, 29, 121, 133-5, 179-81fn
Nero 44
Netherlands 156

O

Oakeshott, Michael 3, 5, 47-8, 89, 121, 159, 174fn, 176fn
Orwell, George 8, 156, 166
Orwin, Clifford 176-7fn
Oxford 22, 38

P

Pacchi, Arrigo 94-5, 114, 176fn, 179fn
Padua 174fn
Pateman, Carole 98-101, 104-5, 155, 179fn
Peleau, François 1, 28, 93, 101-2, 146, 153
Pericles 3-4, 65, 79-80
Plato 45, 172
Plautus 58
Pocock, J. G. A. 123, 180fn

Poland 156
Pouncey, Peter R. 177-8fn

R

Reik, Miriam 176fn
Reiss, Hans 182fn
Reynolds, N. B. *xii*, 182-3fn
Rice, D. 76, 176-8fn
Rieux, Bernard 171-2
Riley, Patrick 182fn
Rogow, Arnold A. 1, 177fn
Rousseau, Jean-Jacques 116
Runciman, W. G. 75fn, 179fn
Ryan, Alan 3

S

Sacksteder, William 175fn
Saxonhouse, Arlene W. *xii*, 182-3fn
Schlatter, Richard 176-8fn
Scotland 48
Sicily 55
Skinner, Quentin 1-3, 8, 45-6, 95, 145, 173, 174fn, 177-8fn, 183fn
Slomp, Gabriella 177fn, 179fn, 181fn
Sluse, René-François, de 147
Smith, Winston 166
Soames, Jane 182fn
Socrates 14-5, 20
Sophocles 58
Sorbière, Samuel 1, 32, 84, 93-4, 141, 147, 152-3, 181fn
Sorell, Tom 2, 47, 176fn
Sourdis, Marquis de 84
Sparta 52, 59, 177fn
Spragens, Thomas 3
Strauss, Leo 3-4, 22, 46, 48-9, 51, 54, 174fn, 176-8fn

Sugden, Robert 6, 134-5, 181fn

T

Tacitus 45
Taylor, A. E. 158-9, 174fn
Taylor, Michael 121, 131, 140, 180fn
Thucydides *xi*, 45-6, 51-66, 71-3, 75-83, 121, 157, 176-8fn, 183fn
Tönnies, Ferdinand *xi*, 155
Tuck, Richard *xi*, 5, 162, 183fn

V

Venice 167
Verdus, François du 1, 12, 19, 28, 32, 50, 72, 97, 141, 152, 175fn
Virgil 58

W

Warrender, Howard *xi*, 155, 158-9, 174fn
Watkins, John W. 3, 121, 140, 164, 174fn, 170fn
Watson, Dr John H. 92
White, Thomas 14-5, 114, 160
Whitmore Jones, Harold *xii*
Williams, Bernard 103-4, 175fn, 179fn
Wood, Anthony 38, 174fn